Financial Institutions and Markets

Financial Institutions and Markets

Current Issues in Financial Markets

Edited by Robert R. Bliss and
George G. Kaufman

palgrave
macmillan

FINANCIAL INSTITUTIONS AND MARKETS
Copyright © Robert R. Bliss and George G. Kaufman, 2008.

First published in 2008 by PALGRAVE MACMILLAN® in the United States –
a division of St. Martin's Press LLC, 175 Fifth Avenue, New York, NY 10010.

Where this book is distributed in the UK, Europe and the rest of the world,
this is by Palgrave Macmillan, a division of Macmillan Publishers Limited,
registered in England, company number 785998, of Houndmills,
Basingstoke, Hampshire RG21 6XS.

Palgrave Macmillan is the global academic imprint of the above companies
and has companies and representatives throughout the world.

Palgrave® and Macmillan® are registered trademarks in the United States,
the United Kingdom, Europe and other countries.

ISBN-13: 978-0-230-60906-8
ISBN-10: 0-230-60906-6

Library of Congress Cataloging-in-Publication Data

Financial institutions and markets : current issues in financial markets /
edited by Robert R. Bliss and George G. Kaufman.
      p. cm.
   ISBN 0-230-60906-6
   1. Financial institutions—United States.   2. Financial institutions.
   I. Bliss, Robert R.   II. Kaufman, George G.

   HG181.F632   2008
   332.10973—dc22   2008013986

A catalogue record of the book is available from the British Library.

Design by Macmillan Publishing Solutions

First edition: December 2008

10   9   8   7   6   5   4   3   2   1

Printed in the United States of America.

Contents

List of Figures

List of Tables

About the Contributors

Christine E. Blair is a senior financial economist in the FDIC's Division of Insurance and Research. Christine has worked on a wide range of economic and banking issues for the FDIC, including banking and commerce, deposit insurance reform, deposit insurance pricing, and financial modernization. She is a contributing author to *Mandate for Change: Restructuring the Banking System* (1987), *Guidance for Developing Effective Deposit Insurance Systems* (2001), and *Deposit Insurance* (2007). Before joining the FDIC she was an assistant professor of economics at Southern Connecticut State University. She holds a Ph.D. in economics from Fordham University.

Nicole Y. Cote is a graduate from the University of New Hampshire with a degree in public policy economics. She began her career at the Boston Fed as an intern and then went on to work as an economic analyst at the Dallas Fed, where she contributed to this book. Currently, Nicole is employed as a finance manager for TracyLocke in Dallas.

Robert (Bob) DeYoung is the Capitol Federal Professor in Financial Institutions and Markets at the University of Kansas School of Business. In addition to his university duties, Bob is a research program coordinator at the FDIC's Center for Financial Research, a regular visiting scholar at the Federal Reserve Bank of Kansas City, and coeditor of the *Journal of Financial Services Research*.

Gillian G.H. Garcia is an independent economic consultant specializing in financial institutions. She has taught at the University of California, Berkeley, and worked at the Federal Reserve Bank of Chicago, the International Monetary Fund, the Senate Banking Committee, and the U.S. Government Accountability Office.

Benton E. Gup holds the Robert Hunt Cochrane/Alabama Bankers Association Chair of Banking at the University of Alabama, Tuscaloosa, Alabama. He has published widely on banking and financial markets and authored and edited numerous books including *The Valuation Handbook: Valuation Techniques from Today's Top Practitioners* (forthcoming); *Handbook for Directors of Financial Institutions* (forthcoming); *Corporate*

Governance in Banking: A Global Perspective (2007); *Money Laundering, Financing Terrorism, and Suspicious Activity* (2007); *Capital Market, Globalization, and Economic Development* (2005); *Commercial Banking: The Management of Risk,* 3rd ed. (2005); *The New Basel Capital Accord* (2004); and *Too-Big-To-Fail: Policies and Practices in Government Bailouts* (2004).

Marc D. Hayford is professor and department chair of economics at Loyola University of Chicago. He has authored and coauthored numerous articles in professional journals. He is the former president of the Illinois Economics Association and is an associate editor of *The Journal of Economic Asymmetries.* He also coedited *The Global Economy: Financial, Technological and Legal Asymmetries* (2003). Professor Hayford specializes in monetary and fiscal policy and received his Ph.D. from Brown University.

Eva H.G. Hüpkes is head of regulation at the Swiss Federal Banking Commission (SFBC [as of January 2009 the Swiss Financial Market Authority (FINMA)]) and currently cochair of the Basel Committee Working Group on Cross-Border Bank Resolution. Eva is a lecturer at the University of Zurich and also serves as consulting counsel to the IMF, advising national authorities on the implementation of international standards relating to banking regulation and supervision. She is a member of the New York Bar and holds degrees from the University of Geneva, the Graduate Institute of International Studies, Geneva, and Georgetown University, and a Ph.D. in law from the University of Berne. She is the author of *The Legal Aspects of Bank Insolvency* (Kluwer 2000) and *Resolving Insolvent Banks—an International Legal Perspective* (translated, in Chinese, China Press 2006).

Christian Johnson is a law professor at the University of Utah College of Law where he teaches banking and finance. Christian is the author of *A Guide to Using and Negotiating OTC Derivatives Documentation* and the coauthor of *Accounting for Mortgages and Mortgage Backed Securities, Accounting and Disclosure for Derivative Transactions,* and *A Practical Guide to Repo Agreements and Mastering Collateral Management.* Christian has also written over three dozen articles on banking and finance issues.

George G. Kaufman is the John F. Smith Professor of Economics and Finance at Loyola University, Chicago, and consultant to the Federal Reserve Bank of Chicago. He has published widely on financial markets and institutions and authored and edited numerous books in the field, including *Global Financial Crises* (Kluwer 2000), *Asset Price Bubbles* (MIT Press 2003), *Systemic Financial Crises* (World Scientific 2005), and the annual *Research in Financial Services* (JAI/Elsevier Press 1989–2003). Dr. Kaufman is coeditor of the *Journal of Financial Stability* and a founding editor of the *Journal of Financial Services Research*. He is former president of the Western Finance Association, the Midwest Finance Association, and the North American Economic and Finance Association. He serves as cochair of the Shadow Financial Regulatory Committee. He holds a Ph.D. in economics from the University of Iowa.

A.G. Malliaris is professor of economics and finance and holds the Walter F. Mullady Sr. Chair in Business Administration at Loyola University, Chicago. Professor Malliaris has published widely in financial economics. He has authored and coauthored numerous books, including *Stochastic Methods in Economics and Finance* (1982); *Differential Equations, Stability and Chaos in Dynamic Economics* (1989); *Foundations of Futures Markets* (1999); and *Economic Uncertainty, Instabilities and Asset Bubbles* (2005). He has also edited and coedited several books, including *Futures Markets, Options Markets* (2001); *Global Financial Asymmetries* (2002); and *The Global Economy: Financial, Monetary, Trade and Knowledge Asymmetries* (2003).

Tareque Nasser is currently a finance Ph.D. candidate at the University of Alabama, Tuscaloosa. He received his undergraduate degree in finance from the Assumption University of Thailand and graduate degree in economics from the University of Wollongong, Australia. He worked at the Assumption University of Thailand as a lecturer prior to his pursuance of doctoral degree at the University of Alabama. While at the University of Alabama he worked with Dr. Benton E. Gup as a graduate research assistant.

Ronnie J. Phillips received his BA in Urban Studies from the University of Oklahoma in 1973 and his Ph.D. in economics from The University of Texas at Austin in 1980. He is a senior fellow at Networks Financial Institute in Indianapolis, Indiana, and professor of economics at Colorado State University, where he has taught since 1983. He is the author of *The Chicago Plan and New Banking Reform* (Sharpe 1995). He has published widely on banking issues, entrepreneurship, and public policy in books, academic journals, newspapers, magazines, and public policy briefs. His current research interests are payday lending and entrepreneurship in the music industry.

Harvey Rosenblum is executive vice president and director of research at the Federal Reserve Bank of Dallas. He is currently the executive director of the International Banking, Economics, and Finance Association (IBEFA); a member of the board of directors of the National Bureau of Economic Research (NBER); a member of the editorial board of the *North*

American Journal of Economics and Finance; and past president of the National Association for Business Economics (NABE). Dr. Rosenblum serves as a member of the Texas Product Development and Small Business Incubator Board. In addition, he is a visiting professor of finance at Southern Methodist University. He received his Ph.D. in economics from the University of California, Santa Barbara.

1

When a Bank Is Not a Bank: The Case of Industrial Loan Companies

*Christian Johnson and George G. Kaufman**

Introduction

What is a "bank"? There are commercial banks and savings banks as well as river banks, snow banks, telephone banks, blood banks, and many more. Dictionaries list a large number of alternative definitions. The definition matters not only for purposes of semantics, so that we understand each other, but also because some types of banks—commercial and savings banks, for example—are perceived to be sufficiently vital to the economy that they are regulated by the government to promote their safe and efficient operation. But, for effective regulation, it is necessary to carefully define the entity to be regulated. The issue of what constitutes a bank for regulatory purposes metamorphosed in 2005 from being an arcane subject of interest primarily to a small number of regulatory attorneys to being of interest to a much larger and broader group. This interest was sparked when the large retailer Wal-Mart applied to the Federal Deposit Insurance Corporation (FDIC) to obtain federal deposit insurance for a newly chartered "bank" in Utah that was not subject to the ownership restrictions applicable to most other "banks." This chapter examines the definition of "bank" for financial regulatory purposes, traces and explains the evolution of the definition, and explores the controversy surrounding the attempt by Wal-Mart in 2005 to establish its own bank. Wal-Mart has since withdrawn its application.

All depository institutions, including commercial and savings banks, need to obtain a special charter from either the federal government or their home-state government rather than a general corporate charter. The charter identifies the activities in which the institutions are permitted to engage. Each chartering and regulatory agency specifies a definition of "bank" to which its authority applies. Restrictions on permissible activities may be imposed by the FDIC on insured banks and by the board of governors of the Federal Reserve System on holding companies that own bank subsidiaries.

The definition of bank need not be the same across agencies or be constant for any one agency. Differences and changes in definition may occur for a number of reasons, including differences in regulatory objectives among agencies, changes in legislation, changes in the demand for different types of financial services, changes in the supply of particular financial services, innovations in financial products and institutions, and changes in the operations of financial institutions.

In recent months, controversy over the definition of a bank has been ignited by an attempt, since abandoned, by Wal-Mart to obtain FDIC insurance for an industrial loan company (ILC) to be chartered in Utah.[1] An ILC is a "bank" chartered in a limited number of states that is granted the same or slightly fewer product powers than are commercial banks chartered in those states. Importantly, ILCs are currently explicitly exempted from the definition of "bank" in the Bank Holding Company Act (BHCA) if, among other characteristics, they do not accept demand deposits when their assets exceed $100 million. As long as the proposed ILC had satisfied these conditions, the parent holding company, Wal-Mart, would not have been legally classified as a bank holding company (BHC)— a holding company that owns one or more institutions legally defined as a "bank"—and would have been subject neither to Federal Reserve regulations nor to BHCA restrictions. If it had not satisfied these conditions, the nonfinancial activities of the parent company, Wal-Mart, would have prohibited its ownership of a bank subsidiary.

This "loophole" in the legal definition of a bank appears to permit the piercing of the separation of banking (financial) and commerce (nonfinancial) that the BHCA was designed to maintain and provides holding companies owning ILCs an unfair advantage over holding companies that own legally defined banks, such as commercial banks. This generated opposition to Wal-Mart's application for FDIC insurance, which was necessary for it to be an ILC that is exempt from BHCA restrictions. In response to this opposition, the FDIC imposed a six-month moratorium in July 2006 on this and all other pending applications for federal insurance either for a new ILC or for an existing ILC undergoing a change in control through January 31, 2007. The FDIC then extended the moratorium on new and pending applications from commercial (nonfinancial) firms for the operation of federally insured ILCs to January 31, 2008.[2] In March 2007, however, Wal-Mart withdrew its application.

Evolution of the Definition of "Bank" and "Bank Holding Company"

A bank is a type of financial institution. A financial institution is an entity that deals primarily in financial instruments and derives most of its revenues from interest and fees charged on its loans, investments, and deposits or from trading in these securities. A popular dictionary of banking terms defines a bank as "usually a corporation, that accepts deposits, makes loans, pays checks, and performs related services for the public."[3]

What differentiates a bank from most other financial institutions is that a bank can accept deposits of funds that it may re-lend but that need to be repaid to the depositor at full value at a future specified or unspecified date. As such, banks belong to the broader class of depository institutions, which includes other institutions that are chartered to accept deposits and make loans but have traditionally provided a narrower and more specialized range of services, such as savings and loan associations and credit unions.

As noted, unlike most other business corporations, banks require a special corporate bank charter from a government entity; in the United States this is either from the federal government (national bank) or from the home-state government (state bank).[4] Banks' powers are defined in their charters. For example, national banks chartered by the comptroller of the currency may

> exercise . . . all such incidental powers as shall be necessary to carry on the business of banking by discounting and negotiating promissory notes, drafts, bills of exchange, and other evidences of debt; by receiving deposits; by buying and selling exchange, coin and bullion; by loaning money on personal security.[5]

The National Bank Act, as currently amended, specifies individually the permissible powers in addition to deposit taking and loan making.

The charter imposes both advantages and disadvantages on a bank. The institution can offer various types of deposits such as demand, time, and savings. These deposits are currently insured up to a maximum amount of $100,000 per eligible account by the FDIC, which is an agency of the federal government. The bank is also provided direct access to the national payments system through the Federal Reserve's check and electronic clearing facilities. To the extent that bank charters are not granted freely, the chartering agencies may restrict entry and reduce competition.

In return for these advantages, the charter subjects the bank to a number of disadvantages in the form of costly regulation and supervision for reasons of safety, fairness, efficiency, and monetary policy. In the words of former Federal Reserve chairman Paul Volcker,

> Handling other people's money, which is what banking is all about, connotes a fiduciary responsibility. . . . To that end, banking systems in virtually all countries are regulated.[6]

Types of regulation and supervision that have been frequently imposed on chartered banks include

- restriction on types of products and services that may be offered,
- restriction on the number and location of offices,
- application of minimum capital requirements,
- restriction on ownership by holding companies,
- restriction on mergers with other banks,
- restriction on interest paid on deposits and charged on loans,
- examination by bank regulatory agencies for financial soundness and compliance with other regulations,
- frequent reporting of financial condition to the regulatory agencies, and
- special nondiscrimination lending and reporting requirements.

Until relatively recently, the term "bank" was often defined only loosely in federal legislation.[7] For example, the Federal Reserve Act of 1913 defines bank to include state bank, banking association, and trust company, except cases in which national banks or Federal Reserve banks are specifically referred to.[8]

The important Banking Act of 1933 (Glass-Steagall) refers to the definition used in the Federal Reserve Act. However, the term "bank" came to be more precisely defined with the BHCA of 1956. The definition reflects the primary purpose of the act, which was to prevent both excessive economic concentration in banking and conflicts of interest that could arise if banks and nonbanks were under common ownership, enabling banks to provide preferential treatment to customers of their affiliates.[9] (The major changes in the legislated definitions of "bank" and "bank holding company" since 1956 are summarized in tables 1.1 and 1.2.)

Thus, the act restricted the nonfinancial activities of BHCs, prohibited BHCs from owning subsidiaries that engaged in nonfinancial activities or in financial activities that were defined by the Federal Reserve as not being so closely related to banking as to be incidental to it, and restricted the ability of BHCs to acquire banks in other states.[10] The Fed developed

Table 1.1   Changes in definition of bank in Bank Holding Company Act

1956	Any national or state-chartered commercial, savings, or trust bank
1966	Any institution that accepts demand deposits
1970	Any institution that both accepts demand deposits and makes business loans
1987	All banks insured by the FDIC, except thrifts, credit card banks, and industrial loan companies and banks

Table 1.2   Changes in the definition of bank (savings and loan) holding company for purposes of Holding Company Act

1956	Bank Holding Company Act (BHCA) applied to holding companies (HC) owning two or more chartered banks
1967	Saving and Loan Holding Company Act (SLHCA) applies provisions similar to BHCA to S&Ls owning two or more institutions
1970	BHCA expands definition of covered HC to owning only one bank or more
1987	BHCA expands covered HCs to any owning one or more FDIC-insured banks but lists specific exemptions
1999	Gramm-Leach-Bliley Act expands the scope of SLHCA to include S&Ls owning one or more institutions

a "laundry list" of financial activities that it considered sufficiently incidental to banking to be offered by nonbank subsidiaries of BHCs. Although commercial banks' charters generally prohibited them from engaging in nonfinancial (commerce) activities, there were no previous restrictions on the activities of subsidiaries of holding companies that also owned one or more chartered banks or on the nonfinancial activities of such companies.

To achieve its objective, the BHCA needed to define "bank holding company." Because the major concern with both excessive economic concentration and conflicts of interest related to banking firms, the act defined bank holding company with respect to the type of bank that it owned or controlled. The 1956 act defined bank to include "any national banking association or any State bank, savings bank, or trust company"[11] and bank holding company as "any corporate firm that owned two or more banks so defined."[12] In addition, BHCs had to register with the Federal Reserve and receive permission from the Fed for further acquisitions.

In time, the BHCA's definition of a bank was viewed as broader than necessary to achieve its objectives, as the definition included many types of financial institutions that were unlikely to produce excessive economic concentration or meaningful conflicts of interest if owned by a holding company that also owned nonbank subsidiaries. Thus, in 1966, the BHCA was amended to define a bank more narrowly as "any institution that accepts deposits that the depositor has a legal right to withdraw on demand."[13]

This amendment changed the definition of bank from a chartering test to an activities test. Because deposits subject to withdrawal on demand (demand deposits) were at the time generally restricted to commercial banks, this definition effectively defined a BHC only as a company that owned two or more commercial banks.

The Senate report that accompanied this and other amendments at the time to the BHCA explained the reason for the change as follows:

> Section 2(c) of the [1956 BHCA] defines "bank" to include savings banks and trust companies, as well as commercial banks. The purpose of the [BHCA] was to restrain undue concentration of control of commercial bank credit, and to prevent abuse by a holding company of its control over this type of credit for the benefit of its nonbanking subsidiaries. This objective can be achieved without applying the [BHCA] to savings banks, and there are at least a few instances in which the reference to "savings bank" in the present definition may result in covering companies that control two or more industrial banks. To avoid this result, the bill redefines "bank" as an institution that accepts deposits payable on demand (checking accounts), the commonly accepted test of whether an institution is a commercial bank so as to exclude industrial banks and nondeposit trust companies.[14]

Note the express exclusion of industrial banks in the legislative history from the definition of "bank" for purposes of the act.

In 1970, the definition of "bank" for purposes of the act was narrowed further to

> any institution organized under the laws of the United States, any State of the United States . . . which (1) accepts deposits that the depositor has a legal right to withdraw on demand, and (2) engages in the business of making commercial loans.[15]

This definition excluded a few institutions that accepted demand deposits but did not make business loans. Lending for noncommercial purposes was considered less likely to cause the problems that the act was designed to prevent. In addition, in response to a sharp increase in the number of holding companies owning only one bank and engaging in activities not permitted for holding companies owning two or more banks, the 1970 amendments also broadened the definition of a BHC to cover ownership of only one bank so defined.

In the early 1980s, however, an increasing number of BHCs organized or purchased banks that either accepted demand deposits but did not make commercial (business) loans or made commercial loans but did not accept demand deposits. Thus, they were not defined as "banks" for purposes of the act at that time. These institutions became known as "nonbank banks." Holding companies that owned such nonbank banks were not subject to the restrictions of the act that were imposed on holding companies that owned banks that met the definition of the act, particularly the prohibition against banks being owned by companies that were nonfinancial firms or owned such firms. Indeed, most but not all of the newly chartered nonbank banks were owned by holding companies that also owned nonfinancial firms.

To restrict this type of holding company going forward, the act was amended in 1987 by the Competitive Equality Banking Act (CEBA) to broaden the definition of bank from institutions that both accept demand deposits and make business loans to all banks insured by the FDIC.[16] (Existing nonbank banks were grandfathered, but subject to asset growth restrictions.) However, this definition captured some banks and other financial institutions that were generally considered unlikely to cause either excessive economic concentration or conflicts of interest if they were owned by a nonfinancial holding company or by a holding company that owned financial companies that were not on the Federal Reserve's permissible list.

To address this problem, the CEBA amendments for the first time specifically excluded from the definition of "bank" foreign banks, federally insured savings and loan associations, credit unions, credit card banks, and most federally insured ILCs. However, as seen earlier, ILCs were already noted as not being a target of the BHCA in the Senate report accompanying the 1966 amendments. What most of these exempted institutions had in common is that, at the time, while they generally accepted deposits and made loans, they did not offer demand deposits and did little, if any, commercial lending. Companies that owned such excluded institutions were not subject to the act's restrictions. In explaining his support for the new definition, Volcker, chairman of the Federal Reserve at the time, testified before the Senate Banking Committee:

> Essentially, the nonbank bank has become a device for tearing down the separation of commerce and banking by permitting a commercial firm to enter traditional banking business without abiding by the provisions of the Bank Holding Company Act. . . . Fundamentally at stake is not a few in-house consumer banking offices of some retail chains. . . . We want to protect against instability, excessive concentration of power, and undue conflicts of interest, while preserving the institutional framework for monetary policy. In seeking these goals, the separation of banking and commerce has been a basic part of the American tradition for what seems to me sound reasons.[17]

The specific exemption for ILCs and industrial banks in CEBA was introduced in the final drafting of the act by then senators Alan Cranston of California and Jake Garn of Utah, who served on the Senate Banking Committee and represented the two states with the largest number of such institutions.[18]

In 1999, Congress effectively reaffirmed the ILC exemption from the definition of "bank" and thereby also the restrictions of the BHCA when it included a provision in the Gramm-Leach-Bliley Act (GLBA) that slightly expanded the permissible activities of eligible ILCs but did not otherwise change the exemption.

It is evident from this chronology of the evolution of the definition of both "bank" and "bank holding company" for regulatory purposes that the legal definition at any moment in time reflects the pressing public concerns of the time. As the concerns changed, so frequently did the definitions.

ILCs

Partially as a result of the broadening of the definition of bank in the BHCA through time, both nonfinancial firms that wished to own a bank and were prohibited from doing so by the BHCA and nonbank financial companies that wished to own banks but did not wish to be legally classified as a BHC, and therefore be subject to Federal Reserve regulation, became more restricted in their options. ILCs were a remaining available option.[19] CEBA explicitly exempted ILCs from the definition of bank in the BHCA if

1. in 1987, the state in which they were chartered required them to be insured by the FDIC, and either
2. they have less than $100 million in assets or, if more, they do not offer demand deposits,[20] or
3. there has been no change in control since 1987.

In addition, in 1999, some firms that could have owned a single (unitary) thrift institution were brought under the restrictions of the Savings and Loan Holding Company Act (SLHCA) by the GLBA. However, such firms may have preferred an ILC because, unlike a thrift institution, an ILC is not subject to the qualified lender provision, which effectively requires thrifts to hold a minimum percentage of mortgage loans in their portfolios.[21]

Seven states that charter ILCs satisfy the federal deposit insurance requirement of CEBA. They are California, Colorado, Hawaii, Indiana, Minnesota, Nevada, and Utah. A number of companies that wanted to escape the restrictions of the BHCA or the SLHCA chose to purchase or organize ILCs in these states, primarily in Utah, California, and Nevada, or to grow existing ILCs faster than they would have otherwise.

ILCs originated in the early 1900s as small depository institutions aimed primarily at the financial needs of low- and moderate-income households that were not being well served by existing larger financial institutions. They differed little either in mission or in operation from other consumer-oriented smaller financial institutions of the day, such as Morris Plan banks and credit unions.[22] They were chartered only at the state level, but could generally branch across state lines. ILCs remained relatively small until the end of the 1990s when their aggregate asset size jumped dramatically, even though they declined in number. Although the FDIC has insured Morris Plan banks since the FDIC's establishment in 1934, ILCs became eligible for FDIC insurance only in 1982, after the enactment of the Garn-St. Germain Act.

Since the enactment of CEBA in 1987, when the ability of firms to avoid the BHCA restrictions by owning banks that either did not take demand deposits or did not make business loans was terminated, aggregate assets at federally insured ILCs increased from less than $5 billion to more than $150 billion by year-end 2006. All but $15 billion of this increase occurred since 1998, when the ability of additional firms to avoid the restrictions of the SLHCA by owning only one thrift institution (unitary thrift holding companies) was terminated by the GLBA. Despite their rapid growth, in 2006 ILCs accounted for less than 2 percent of total assets at FDIC-insured institutions.[23]

At the same time, the number of federally insured ILCs declined sharply from 105 to 59.[24] Only three of the largest fifteen ILCs in 1987 remained active in 2006. By far, the largest increase in ILC assets in this period occurred in Utah, which increased its market share of national ILC assets from 11 percent to 82 percent by 2004.[25] Both the rapid growth of ILCs in total and the particularly rapid growth in Utah can be explained in part by changes in Utah's legislation and the state's supportive regulatory environment for ILCs.[26] In 1986, Utah put a moratorium on new ILC charters after a number of ILCs had experienced significant financial difficulties that required some $45 million of state assistance to meet their depositor claims. The moratorium was lifted in 1997 after the industry regained its financial health, and the number of charters grew from 18 to 33 by June 30, 2006. Total assets also grew from $18 billion in 1997 to $133.8 billion in 2006.[27] Over the same period, the size of the individual institutions also changed greatly. In 1987, the largest Utah-chartered ILC had $290 million in assets.[28] At year-end 2006, the largest ILC in Utah reported assets of $67 billion.[29]

While most ILCs are relatively small, seven had assets in excess of $10 billion at year-end 2006 and ranked among the largest 125 FDIC-insured depository institutions of the nearly 9,000 such institutions in the country. (A listing of the largest 15 ILCs by asset size at year-end 2006 is shown in table 1.3.)

Table 1.3   Fifteen largest industrial loan companies, by asset size, 2006

Rank	ILC	Parent holding company	State chartered	Chartered	Federally insured	Total assets 2006 ($ billion)
1.	Merrill Lynch Bank USA	Merrill Lynch	Utah	1988	1988	67.2
2.	UBS Bank USA	UBS	Utah	2003	2003	22.0
3.	American Express Centurion Bank	American Express	Utah	1989	1989	21.1
4.	Morgan Stanley Bank	Morgan Stanley	Utah	1990	1990	21.0
5.	GMAC Automotive Bank	Cerberus Capital Management Consortium	Utah	2004	2004	19.9
6.	Fremont Investment and Loan	Fremont General Corp.	California	1937[a]	1984	12.9
7.	Goldman Sachs Bank	Goldman Sachs	Utah	2004	2004	12.6
8.	USAA Saving Bank	USAA Life Co.	Nevada	1996	1996	5.8
9.	Capmark Bank (formerly GMAC Commercial Mortgage Bank)	KKR	Utah	2003	2003	3.8
10.	Lehman Brothers Commercial Bank	Lehman Brothers	Utah	2005	2005	3.2
11.	CIT Bank	CITGroup	Utah	2000	2000	2.8
12.	BMW Bank of North America	BMW Group	Utah	1999	1999	2.2
13.	GE Capital Financial Inc.	General Electric	Utah	1993	1993	2.0
14.	Advanta Bank Corp.	Advanta	Utah	1991	1991	2.0
15.	Beal Saving Bank	Beal Financial Group	Nevada	2004	2004	1.9

[a]Originally chartered ILC was purchased by Fremont General in 1990.
Sources: iBanknet and Federal Deposit Insurance Corporation.

All but three of these were chartered in Utah. The industry is also highly concentrated. In mid-2006, the largest ILC accounted for 40 percent of all assets in the industry and the five largest accounted for about 75 percent of the industry's total assets.[30]

Contrary to their earlier days, few of today's larger ILCs are independent community-oriented institutions. Although large ILCs are prohibited from taking demand deposits, the current powers of ILCs are not greatly different in most states from those of commercial banks; many ILCs operate as limited service or specialized lending institutions.

ILC parent holding companies represent a wide range of financial and nonfinancial firms, and the activities of their subsidiary ILCs are directed at an equally broad range of economic sectors that may or may not be associated with the primary activities of the parent. The largest four ILCs are owned by major financial firms, including one of the largest commercial banks in the world. The largest ILC, Merrill Lynch Bank USA, is owned by the investment banking firm of Merrill Lynch. It focuses on securities-based consumer loan products as well as on consumer and business loans. The bank also makes first and second mortgage loans, as well as community development loans and investments to satisfy its Community Reinvestment Act (CRA) responsibilities.[31] The next largest ILC focuses on loans to high-wealth households, and the third on loans generated through general credit cards originated by its parent firm.

Some ILCs are owned by financial firms or by firms that are not otherwise generally prohibited from owning a bank. Other ILCs are owned by nonfinancial firms that use their ILCs to finance the sales of goods they either manufacture or sell or to finance unrelated activities. These firms could not own commercial banks under the current provisions of the BHCA. According to their websites and CRA reports, Volkswagen owns an ILC that primarily finances indirect automotive, home-equity, and credit card loans. Until recently General Motors (GM) owned General Motors Acceptance Corporation (GMAC), which in turn owned two Utah ILCs; one of which focuses on commercial mortgage loans and the other on automotive loans. The GMAC Automotive Bank was the fifth largest ILC in 2006. In November 2006, in an exception to its moratorium, the FDIC permitted a change in ownership of the larger of the two ILCs owned by GM, which was undergoing major restructuring, to a consortium of four financial institutions. BMW uses its Utah ILC to finance sales of BMW automobiles and motorcycles, and the large retailer Target uses its Utah ILC to finance its in-house credit card sales for small business customers.

The wide variety of both ownership and business lines of ILCs is reflected in the eight types of business models into which the two principal ILC trade groups divide the industry: (1) ILCs owned by securities

Table 1.4   ILC business models

Business model	Description	ILC example
Banks owned by securities companies	Provide commercial and consumer credit to customers of securities companies	Merrill Lynch Bank USA
Banks owned by commercial finance companies	Provide commercial loans to customers who are not customers of an affiliate	Advanta Bank
Banks owned by consumer finance companies	Provide credit cards and other forms of consumer credit and services to customers who are not customers of affiliates	American Express Centurion Bank
Banks owned by a commercial company conducting an independent core financial services business	Provide traditional banking services to customers that are not customers of affiliates	GE Capital Financial
Commercially owned banks offering financial services to customers of the corporate group that are not affiliate transactions	Provide credit and financial services to customers of owner	BMW Bank of North America
Banks owned by a commercial company that finances transactions with affiliates subject to the restrictions in Sections 23A and 23B of the Federal Reserve Act and the antitying provisions of the Bank Holding Company Act	Provide credit to customers of affiliates (credit and services are subject to the covered transaction rules)	Target Bank
Banks owned by title insurance holding companies	Provide financial services	First Security Thrift
Independently owned banks	Provide financial services (owners not engaging in commercial activities prohibited by bank holding company rules)	Celtic Bank

Source: Utah Association of Financial Services and California Association of Industrial Banks (2006).

companies, (2) ILCs owned by commercial finance companies, (3) ILCs owned by consumer finance companies, (4) ILCs owned by a commercial company conducting an independent core financial services business, (5) ILCs owned by commercial firms offering financial services to customers of the corporate group that are not affiliate transactions, (6) ILCs owned by a commercial company that finance transactions with affiliates subject to the restrictions in Sections 23A and 23B of the Federal Reserve Act and to the antitying provisions of the BHCA, (7) ILCs owned by title insurance holding companies, and (8) independently owned ILCs.[32] A brief description of each business model and an ILC example are given in table 1.4.

Primarily because of the rapid growth of ILCs in recent years and the ongoing controversy surrounding Wal-Mart itself, its application for mandatory FDIC insurance for its proposed ILC in Utah attracted immediate attention and widespread opposition from many bankers, retailers, and policymakers, including members of Congress. The opposition arose despite Wal-Mart's stated intentions in the application of not engaging in full-service banking, but only in credit and debit card and fund transfer (payments system) operations. At its filing, the application raised at least two important public policy issues:

1. Should a decision to increase the mix between banking and commerce be made administratively by a regulatory agency within the authority Congress granted it, or should it be made legislatively by Congress in the light of the changed circumstances described earlier?
2. Are the current regulatory prudential powers of the FDIC sufficient for consolidated supervision of ILC holding companies relative to the prudential powers of the Federal Reserve for BHCs under the BHCA?

Because Wal-Mart was not the first large nonbank firm to have received or applied for FDIC insurance for an ILC or even the first large commercial firm—only the most controversial—these two issues were not necessarily muted by the withdrawal of its application. As discussed earlier, large firms such as Merrill Lynch, GM (until recently), BMW, and Target all own ILCs. Home Depot has an insurance application pending, but the moratorium has delayed action on it.

Public Policy Issues

The mixing of banking and commerce

The mixing of banking and commerce in "universal" banks, as exists in many countries, has long been controversial in U.S. banking history. Most state charters for banks and the federal charter for national banks limit the activities of banks to accepting deposits and making loans, but permit other services viewed as incidental to banking. This was generally interpreted by regulators as prohibiting the banks from engaging in some financial activities, such as insurance underwriting and real estate brokerage, and all nonfinancial activities. Until the enactment of the BHCA in 1956, these limitations were not generally applied to BHCs, so that commercial firms could own banks. Thus, Ford Motors and Sears, among other large nonfinancial firms, operated banks. But, as discussed earlier, growing fears in the 1950s that such combinations could lead to both excessive economic and social power and potential conflicts of interest favoring sellers resulted in the enactment of the BHCA in 1956 and its expansion in 1970. Since then, the thrust of legislation, which often is preceded by changes in the marketplace, has reversed. The financial powers of BHCs have been expanded significantly, most recently in the GLBA (or the Bank Modernization Act), and the nonfinancial powers moderately. However, unlike ILCs, commercial banks may still not be owned by commercial firms.

Going forward, two questions appear to arise. First, the ILC industry has changed dramatically since 1987, when ILCs were first specifically exempted from the restrictions of the BHCA primarily because they were small and insignificant on a national scale. Thus, it may be reasonably asked whether this issue has now become sufficiently important that further piercing of the separation of banking and commerce is too important to leave to the regulatory agencies by default.[33] Rather, does it now deserve congressional review?[34] Indeed, in her explanation for the one-year extension of the moratorium on granting insurance to additional ILCs owned by commercial firms in January 2007, FDIC chairman Sheila Bair noted, "The moratorium will provide Congress with an opportunity to address the issue legislatively."[35,36] Moreover, the extension of the moratorium applies only to ILCs to be owned by commercial firms and not by nonbank financial firms, which do not involve a mixing of banking and commerce.

In particular, would Congress have specifically exempted ILCs from the BHCA in earlier years had some of the institutions been as large then as they are today? For example, the largest ILC in 1987 had total assets worth some $400 million. Indeed, only one of the current largest 15 ILCs was chartered and federally insured before 1987. It is effectively a new industry. In testimony, in 2006, at the FDIC's open hearing on the Wal-Mart application, former senator Garn, who sponsored the exemption in 1987, stated that he had not intended for ILCs to move into the retail banking business and now opposes such expansion.[37] Moreover, if after review, Congress determined that increased mixing of banking and commerce is desirable, should this be limited to ILCs or should this be extended to all bank and financial holding companies to level the playing field?[38]

Since the FDIC's initial adoption in July 2006 of its moratorium on new and pending applications for federal deposit insurance for both the new ILCs and existing ILCs undergoing a proposed change in control, assets at ILCs as a whole have increased sharply. In the six months before the moratorium, assets at the 25 largest ILCs at year-end 2006 increased by some $12 billion—from $145 billion at year-end 2005 to $157 billion at midyear 2006—or 8 percent. In the next six months following the moratorium, assets at these ILCs jumped by $51 billion, or fully 32 percent.

Most of this unusual spurt in asset size can be attributed to three ILCs: two of these are owned by nonbank financial firms and the third had received special permission from the FDIC for a change in control from GMAC to a consortium of four financial firms in anticipation of a major restructuring of GM. The asset jump at these ILCs may have been precautionary in case Congress limited the ILC exemption to the ownership restrictions of the BHCA. If so, these ILCs may have anticipated that, as frequently is the case, existing ILCs would be grandfathered but their future growth may be restricted.

Second, by 1999, when Congress last retained the ILC exemption by broadening it slightly, the ILC industry had already begun a rapid expansion. The largest ILC, owned by American Express, had assets in excess of $15 billion, and four other ILCs had assets in excess of $2 billion each; a commercial firm owned one of them. Thus, if Congress was not sufficiently concerned at the time, and has taken no action since, one may question whether it is appropriate for a regulatory agency to delay approval of applications that are not in conflict with existing law until Congress acts. Indeed, some have suggested that, in this instance, the issue goes beyond appropriateness of the mixing of banking and commerce and appears as an issue with Wal-Mart per se.[39] Wal-Mart is the world's largest retailer with an extensive distribution network and a perception as utilizing aggressive marketing and labor practices that has antagonized a significant part of the U.S. population.[40]

Indeed, an application for an Utah-chartered ILC by Target in 2004 was viewed as sufficiently routine by the FDIC to be approved at the staff level rather than by its board of directors.[41] Nor did the approval of the application ignite much public opposition. In contrast, Wal-Mart's application to the FDIC attracted nearly 14,000 letters, including 150 from members of Congress, almost all opposed to the application, and caused the FDIC to schedule three days of open hearings that drew some 70 witnesses, again almost all opposed.[42]

Although Wal-Mart has withdrawn its application, concern exists over the possibility of reapplication after the expiration of the moratorium and

Table 1.5   Comparison of explicit supervisory powers of the FDIC, Federal Reserve Board, and OTS

Description of explicit supervisory authority	FDIC[a]	Board	OTS
Examine the relationships, including specific transactions, if any, between the insured institution and its parent or affiliates.	●[b]	●[b]	●[b]
Examine beyond specific transactions when necessary to disclose the nature and effect of relationship between the insured institution and the parent or affiliate.	●[b]	●[b]	●[b]
Examine the parent or any affiliate of an insured institution, including a parent or affiliate that does not have any relationships with the insured institution or concerning matters that go beyond the scope of any such relationships and their effect on the depository institution.	○	●[b]	●[b]
Take enforcement actions against the parent of an insured institution.	⊙[b,c]	●[b]	●[b]
Take enforcement actions against affiliates of the insured institution that participate in the conduct of affairs of, or act as agents for, the insured institution.	⊙[b]	●[b]	●[b]
Take enforcement actions against any affiliate of the insured institution, even if the affiliate does not act as agent for, or participate in the conduct of, the affairs of the insured institution.	○	●[b]	●[b]
Compel the parent and affiliates to provide various reports such as reports of operations, financial condition, and systems for monitoring risk.	⊙[b,d]	●[b]	●[b]
Impose consolidated or parent-only capital requirements on the parent and require that it serve as source of strength to the insured depository institution.	⊙[d]	●[b]	●
Compel the parent to divest off an affiliate posing a serious risk to the safety and soundness of the insured institution.	⊙[e]	●[b]	●[b]

●Explicit authority.
⊙Less extensive authority.
○No authority.

[a]FDIC may examine an insured institution for interaffiliate transactions at any time and can examine the affiliate when necessary to disclose the transaction and its effect on the insured institution.

[b]The authority that each agency may have regarding functionally regulated affiliates of an insured depository institution is limited in some respects. For example, each agency, to the extent it has the authority to examine or obtain from a functionally regulated affiliate, is generally required to accept examinations and reports by the affiliates' primary supervisors unless the affiliate poses a material risk to the depository institution or the examination or report is necessary to assess the affiliate's compliance with a law the agency has specific jurisdiction for enforcing with respect to the affiliate (e.g., the Bank Holding Company Act in the case of the Board). These limits do not apply to the Board with respect to a company that is itself a bank holding company. These restrictions also do not limit the FDIC's authority to examine the relationships between an institution and an affiliate if the FDIC determines that the examination is necessary to determine the condition of the insured institution for insurance purposes.

in the absence of congressional action. Wal-Mart has recently established a full-service bank in Mexico and has announced its intentions to offer a wide range of nonbank financial services at its U.S. stores.

The FDIC's prudential authority over ILCs

Because ILCs are state-chartered, FDIC-insured institutions and none have chosen to be members of the Federal Reserve System, their primary federal regulator is the FDIC. In addition, they are regulated by the banking agency in the state in which they are chartered. All three federal regulators of commercial banks—the comptroller of the currency, the Federal Reserve, and the FDIC—effectively have the same statutory prudential authority for the banks they supervise. But this is not necessarily true of their authority over parent holding companies of these banks. The Federal Reserve has clear authority under the BHCA to supervise and examine BHCs, as defined in the act, on a consolidated basis.[43] This would include the operation of the parent holding company, subsidiary banks, and any subsidiary nonbank firms. The underlying justification for such consolidated supervision is that these entities are usually managed in terms of risk exposures on a centralized or consolidated basis, so that full understanding of the risk exposure of any one component of the entity requires knowledge of all components combined.

Consolidated top-down supervision is widely viewed as necessary despite the fact that Federal Reserve regulations 23A and 23B limit the

---

Table 1.5   (*Continued*)

[c]FDIC may take enforcement actions against institution-affiliated parties of an ILC. A typical ILC holding company qualifies as an institution-affiliated party. FDIC's ability to require an ILC holding company to provide a capital infusion to the ILC is limited. In addition FDIC may take enforcement action against the holding company of an ILC to address unsafe or unsound practices only if the holding company engages in an unsafe and unsound practice in conducting the affairs of the depository institution.

[d]FDIC maintains that it can achieve this result by imposing an obligation on an ILC holding company as a condition of insuring the ILC. FDIC also maintains it can achieve this result as an alternative to terminating insurance. In addition, FDIC officials stated that the prospect of terminating insurance may compel the holding company to take affirmative action to correct violations in order to protect the insured institution. According to FDIC officials, there are no examples where FDIC has imposed this condition on a holding company as a condition of insurance.

[e]In addition to an enforcement action against the holding company of an ILC in certain circumstances (see note b), as part of prompt corrective action the FDIC may require any company having control over the ILC to (1) divest itself of the ILC if divestiture would improve the institution's financial condition and future prospects or (2) divest a nonbank affiliate if the affiliate is in danger of becoming insolvent and poses a significant risk to the institution or is likely to cause a significant dissipation of the institution's assets or earnings. However, the FDIC generally may take such actions only if the ILC is already significantly undercapitalized.

Note: FDIC is the Federal Deposit Insurance Corporation. OTS is the Office of Thrift Supervision.

Source: Hillman (2006), pp. 15–16.

amount of transactions between the bank and the other affiliates of the holding company and require that permissible transactions be priced on an "arm's-length" basis. These regulations attempt to isolate the bank subsidiary from the other components of the holding company, so that the bank more closely resembles an independent, free-standing institution. A recent study (table 1.5) by the Congress's Government Accountability Office (GAO) compared the current statutory consolidated supervision powers of the FDIC and the Federal Reserve (as well as the Office of Thrift Supervision for parent holding companies of savings and loan associations) and found the FDIC's weaker.[44]

For example, with limited exceptions, the FDIC focuses on the ILC itself rather than the parent on a consolidated basis—a bottom-up approach. The FDIC generally examines or imposes sanctions and enforcement actions on the parent company or its non-ILC affiliates only if it is concerned about the financial condition of the insured ILC. Thus, for example, the FDIC recently issued a cease-and-desist order against Fremont Investment and Loan (an ILC) in California and its parent holding companies for problems at the ILC related to its underwriting of subprime mortgage loans without either noting the large losses simultaneously experienced for the same reason by the parents or requiring similar changes to be made by them as at the subsidiary ILC.[45] Major differences in the explicit supervisory powers of the federal agencies over parent holding companies of insured depository institutions according to the GAO are shown in table 1.5.

It may be argued that the more limiting powers over parent holding companies may hamper the FDIC's ability to evaluate and protect the safety and soundness of ILCs. Partially in recognition of this concern, the FDIC announced in its extension of the moratorium that it had proposed a regulation that would provide for enhanced supervision of ILC parent holding companies that engage only in financial activities to ensure their ability to provide financial support to their institutions and require them to maintain the capital of the ILC at a specified minimum level.[46] This proposal is still pending. The proposal did not include parent holding companies that engage in nonfinancial activities, pending additional study by both the FDIC and Congress.

Recent Developments

In May 2007, in order to resolve the above issues before the expiration of the FDIC moratorium on January 31, 2008, the House of Representatives passed the Industrial Bank Holding Company Act of 2007. The act would prohibit any firm that receives more than 15 percent of its annual gross revenues on a consolidated basis from nonfinancial activities from owning or controlling an ILC. In October 2007, the Senate Banking Committee held hearings on identical Senate Bill 1356. Firms that owned an ILC before January 28, 2007, were generally grandfathered. But, an ILC subsidiary of a commercial firm that did not own the subsidiary before 2003 cannot engage in activities in which it did not engage on January 28, 2007, or operate branches in states in which it did not operate branches on that date. The act would also broaden the FDIC's authority to examine and require reports from the ILC parent holding company and affiliates and to enforce sanctions and capital standards on these entities. This change would bring the regulatory environment for ILC holding companies into greater conformity with that for BHCs and give the FDIC powers over ILC holding companies more similar to those the Federal Reserve has over BHCs.

Wal-Mart withdrew its application to operate an ILC, but apparently not its intention to engage in a wide range of bank-like activities for which a bank charter is not required. It has announced its intention to open "money centers" in its stores that will offer, among other financial products, low-cost, prepaid, stored-value cards as well as check cashing and money transfer (remittance) services. In addition, it will offer a Wal-Mart branded Visa debit card through a third-party bank vendor. Payroll and social security checks could be directly transmitted by customers to Wal-Mart to be added to the stored-value card or to support the debit card. This is intended to increase both safety and convenience over currency transfers. Through time, Wal-Mart has expressed intentions toward additional financial services directed largely at low-income, "unbanked" customers, who represent an important core of their retail base.[47]

Postscript

The FDIC moratorium expired on schedule on January 31, 2008 and was not renewed. Nor had Congress enacted any legislation by that date. Through the end of June 2008, the Senate had not taken final action on pending Bill 1356. It appears that the combination of Wal-Mart's withdrawal of its application and the intensification of the turmoil in the financial markets through the first half of 2008 has drawn Congress' attention away from the ILC controversy and reduced the urgency for federal legislation. Applications for FDIC insurance for new ILC's have slowed and the FDIC has not approved insurance for any additional commercially owned ILCs, with the exception of affirming its earlier temporary approval of Cerberus Capital Management's acquisition of GMAC bank. Cerberus holds investments in non-financial firms. Nevertheless, the issue is unlikely to be settled once and for all and may arise once again when another large retail commercial firm attempts to acquire an ILC.

Notes

*The authors are, respectively, professor of law and John Smith Professor of Finance and Economics at Loyola University, Chicago. The authors are indebted to Christine Blair and Donald Hamm of the FDIC, Tara Rice of the Federal Reserve Bank of Chicago, the participants at presentations at the Western Economic Association and the Federal Reserve Bank of Chicago for their valuable assistance and suggestions, and the staff of the Knowledge Center of the Federal Reserve Bank of Chicago for collecting much of the underlying documentation. An earlier version of this chapter was published as "A Bank by Any Other Name . . ." in *Economic Perspectives* (Federal Reserve Bank of Chicago), Fourth Quarter, 2007.

1. In some states, Utah, for example, ILCs are referred to as industrial banks. The Wal-Mart application was initially filed in Utah for a charter in July 2005 and simultaneously with the FDIC for insurance. The FDIC application was withdrawn in March 2007. See Wal-Mart Stores, Inc. (2005).
2. FDIC (2007b).
3. Fitch (2000), p. 40.
4. Depository institutions are one of the few types of corporations that may be chartered by either the federal government or the home state.
5. National Bank Act, Chapter 106, Section 8, June 3, 1864, 13 Stat. 99, codified at 12 USC § 24.
6. Volcker (1987), p. 200.
7. This section draws on Di Clemente (1983).
8. Federal Reserve Act, 63rd Congress, Chapter 6, Section 1, December 23, 1913, 38 Stat. 251.
9. Bank Holding Company Act of 1956, Senate report, no. 84–1095, July 25, 1955, pp. 1–4.
10. The separation of banking and commerce was not complete. BHCs were permitted limited investment in nonfinancial firms. A review of the permissible nonfinancial activities of banks appears in Haubrich and Santos (2003).
11. Bank Holding Company Act of 1956, Chapter 240, Section 2(c), May 9, 1956, 70 Stat. 133.
12. Ibid. Companies that owned or controlled savings and loan associations and other thrift institutions insured first by the Federal Savings and Loan Insurance Corporation (FSLIC) (and then by the FDIC) were not defined as BHCs and were initially not subject to any restrictions. After the enactment of the SLHCA in 1967, those companies, for a time, were subject to fewer restrictions until 1999, when the BHCA and SLHCA became more comparable.
13. Public Law 89–485, Section 3(c), July 1, 1966, 80 Stat. 236.
14. S. Rep. no. 1179, 89th Congress, 2nd Session. 2391 (1966).
15. Bank Holding Company Act of 1970 (Public Law 91–607), Section 2(c), December 31, 1970, 84 Stat. 1760.
16. Competitive Equality Banking Act of 1987 (Public Law 100–86), Section 101, August 10, 1987, 101 Stat. 552.
17. Volcker (1987), p. 200.

18. Comment submitted by Wal-Mart to the FDIC, October 10, 2006, Appendix 1, p. 40, available at www.fdic.gov. Wilmarth (2007, p. 1572), however, argues that Senator Garn's cosponsor was Senator William Proxmire of Wisconsin rather than Senator Cranston.

19. If the parent holding company also owns a thrift institution, the company is subject to regulation by the Office of Thrift Supervision (OTS) as a savings and loan holding company.

20. This may not be overly restrictive since large ILCs may offer consumer NOW accounts, which resemble demand deposits.

21. 12 USC § 1467(a)(m)(1).

22. For additional information about and for the history of Morris Plan banks, see http://eh.net/encyclopedia/article/philips.banking.morris_plan.

23. Hillman (2006), pp. 5–7. Jones (2006).

24. There are apparently many more small ILCs that are not federally insured, not included in the federal statistics, and not exempt from the restrictions of the BHCA. Weiss (2007).

25. Government Accountability Office (2005), p. 20.

26. Sutton (2002).

27. State of Utah, Commissioner of Financial Institutions (2006).

28. Ibid. State of Utah, Commissioner of Financial Institutions (1987).

29. See www.ibanknet.com (financial reports of industrial loan companies).

30. Hillman (2006).

31. Public Disclosure, January 10, 2006, Community Reinvestment Act Performance Evaluation, Merrill Lynch Bank USA, available at www.FDIC2. gov/crapes.

32. Utah Association of Financial Services and the California Association of Industrial Banks (2006), pp. 11–13. See also Weiss (2007).

33. For a summary of the public policy issues in mixing banking and commerce, see Haubrich and Santos (2003); Blair (2004, 2007); and Ergungor and Thomson (2006).

34. An analogous situation may be the demise of the controversial restrictions on underwriting and trading in private securities by banks and BHCs introduced in the Banking (Glass-Steagall) Act of 1933. In response to changing economic conditions and in the absence of congressional action, the board of governors and the other bank regulatory agencies slowly started to permit BHCs into these activities in 1982 through administratively liberalizing the interpretation of the restrictive language in the act for subsidiaries authorized in Section 20 of the Federal Reserve Act. Congress ultimately enacted liberalizing legislation in the GLBA. For a history of these issues see Kaufman and Mote (1989, 1990).

35. FDIC (2007c).

36. The FDIC has approved a number of applications for insurance since the adoption of the moratorium from firms that it considers as financial or that propose activities by ILCs that are complementary to financial activities and thus are not covered by the moratorium. The extension of the moratorium applies only to ILCs to be owned by commercial firms and not by nonbank financial firms, which do not involve a mixing of banking and commerce.

37. Wilmarth (2007), p. 1572.
38. Since the initial adoption by the FDIC in July 2006 of the moratorium on new and pending applications for federal deposit insurance both for new and for existing ILCs undergoing a proposed change in control, assets at ILCs as a whole have increased sharply. In the six months before the moratorium, assets at the 25 largest ILCs at year-end 2006 increased by some $12 billion—from $145 billion at year-end 2005 to $157 billion at midyear 2006—or 8 percent. In the six months following the moratorium, assets at these ILCs jumped by $51 billion, or fully 32 percent. The asset jump at these ILCs may have been precautionary, in case Congress limited the ILC exemption to the ownership restrictions of the BHCA. If so, these ILCs may have anticipated that, as frequently is the case, existing ILCs would be grandfathered but their future growth would be restricted.
39. Featherstone (2005).
40. Jorde (2003, 2006). This was not Wal-Mart's first attempt to establish and operate a bank or thrift institution. It had previously attempted to obtain a thrift institution in Oklahoma in 1998 and an ILC charter in California in 2002, but was denied first by the enactment of the GLBA in 1999, which ended the unitary thrift exemption, and then by enactment of restrictions on commercial firm ownership of California-chartered ILCs by the California state legislature. It currently leases space to branch offices of some 300 independent banks in more than 1,000 of its stores. But an earlier attempt in 2001 to have its own employees man such branch offices and share in the proceeds with a chartered thrift institution was denied by the OTS (Nolan, 2006).
41. Adler (2007a).
42. Wilmarth (2007), pp. 1545–46. In addition, as of January 2007, five states had enacted legislation since the Wal-Mart application in Utah to prevent Utah-chartered ILCs from branching further into their states, and another five were considering such legislation. (Adler, 2007b).
43. The OTS has similar consolidated supervisory authority for savings and loan holding companies. As of year-end 2006, eight of the 15 largest ILCs holding 71 percent of the assets of these ILCs were owned by parent companies that also owned a thrift institution and thus were classified as savings and loan holding companies and subject to OTS's consolidated supervision (Reich, 2007).
44. Hillman (2006). This has also been argued by Federal Reserve officials (Kohn, 2007).
45. FDIC (2007a).
46. FDIC (2007c). However, this still leaves them with weaker consolidated supervisory powers relative to the Federal Reserve. Equating the two would require congressional action.
47. McWilliams (2007). Barbaro and Dash (2007).

References

Adler, Joe. 2007a. FDIC board sends staff a policy reminder. *American Banker*, July 5, 1–3.

────── 2007b. More states put ILC curbs on agenda. *American Banker,* January 18, 1.

Alvarez, Scott. 2006. Testimony before the U.S. House, Committee on Financial Services, Washington, D.C.: Federal Reserve Board.

Barbaro, Michael, and Eric Dash. 2007. At Wal-Mart, a back door into banking. *Wall Street Journal* C1, June 21.

Blair, Christine. 2007. Banking and commerce: What difference does Wal-Mart make? Paper presented at the 2007 Western Economic Association Meeting, June 30, in Seattle, WA.

────── 2004. The mixing of banking and commerce: Current policy issues. *FDIC Banking Review* 16: 97–120.

Di Clemente, John. 1983. The meeting of passion and intellect: A history of the term "bank" in the Bank Holding Company Act, Federal Reserve Bank of Chicago, Staff memoranda, no. 83, 1.

Ergungor, O. Emre, and James Thomson. 2006. Industrial loan companies. *Economic Commentary,* Federal Reserve Bank of Cleveland.

Featherstone, Liza. 2005. The bank of Wal-Mart? *The Nation,* September 12.

Federal Deposit Insurance Corporation. 2007a. FDIC issues cease and desist order against Fremont investment and loan, Brea, California, and its parents, Washington, D.C., press release PR-22-2007.

Federal Deposit Insurance Corporation. 2007b. Moratorium on certain industrial bank applications and notices. *Federal Register,* 72, no. 23.

Federal Deposit Insurance Corporation. 2007c. FDIC extends moratorium on industrial loan company (ILC) applications by commercial companies for one year. Will move forward on applications from financial companies, press release PR-7-2007.

Fitch, Thomas. 2000. *Dictionary of banking terms.* Hauppauge, NY: Barron's Educational Services.

Government Accountability Office. 2005. Industrial loan corporations: Recent asset growth and commercial interest highlight differences in regulatory authority. Report to the U.S. House, Committee on financial services, Washington, D.C., no. 05–621.

Haubrich, Joseph, and João Santos. 2003. Alternative forms of mixing banking with commerce: Evidence from American history. *Financial Markets, Institutions, and Instruments* 12:121–164.

Hillman, Richard (Government Accountability Office). 2006. Industrial loan corporations: Recent asset growth and commercial interest highlight differences in regulatory authority. Testimony before the U.S. House, Committee on Financial Services, Washington, D.C., no. 06–961T.

Jones, Douglas (Federal Deposit Insurance Corporation). 2006. Industrial loan companies: A review of charter, ownership, and supervision issues. Statement before the U.S. House, Committee on financial services, Washington, D.C.

Jorde, Terry. 2006. Keys to the kingdom. *Independent Banker,* June, 11.

──────. 2003. Banking and commerce in the financial marketplace. Paper presented at *The future of banking* symposium held by the FDIC, July 16.

Kaufman, George, and Larry Mote. 1990. Glass–Steagall: Repeal by regulatory and judicial interpretation. *Banking Law Journal* 107: 388–421.

Kaufman, George, and Larry Mote. 1989. Securities activities of commercial banks. *Research in Financial Services* 1: 223–262.

Kohn, Donald (Federal Reserve Board of Governors). 2007. Industrial loan companies. Testimony before the U.S. House, Committee on Financial Services, April 25.

McWilliams, Gary. 2007. Wal-Mart plans to sell debit card from Visa. *Wall Street Journal*, June 20, B2.

Nolan, Kevin. 2006. Wal-Mart's industrial loan company: The risk to community banks. *North Carolina Banking Institute* 10: 187–207.

Reich, John (Office of Thrift Supervision). 2007. Industrial loan companies. Statement before the U.S. House, Committee on Financial Services, Washington, D.C., April 25.

State of Utah, Commissioner of Financial Institutions. 2006. Report to the Governor and the Legislature of the State of Utah, Salt Lake City, UT.

State of Utah, Commissioner of Financial Institutions. 1987. Report to the Governor and the Legislature of the State of Utah, Salt Lake City, UT.

Sutton, George. 2006. ILCs—A review of charter, ownership, and supervision issues. Testimony before the U.S. House, Committee on Financial Services, Subcommittee on Financial Institutions and Consumer Credit, no. 109–106.

——— 2002. Industrial banks. *Consumer Finance Law Quarterly Report* 56: 178–181.

U.S. House of Representatives, Committee on Financial Services, 2006, ILCs—A review of charter, ownership, and supervision issues: Hearing, *Congressional Record*, 109th Congress, 2nd Session, July 12, no. 109–106.

Utah Association of Financial Services and California Association of Industrial Banks. 2006. Response to the request for public comment on industrial corporations issued by the FDIC on August 29, 2006, report.

Volcker, Paul. 1987. Statement before U.S. Senate, committee on banking, housing, and urban affairs, January 21, 1987. *Federal Reserve Bulletin* 73: 199–205.

Wal-Mart Stores Inc. 2006. Comment submitted to FDIC, October 20. *www.fdic.gov.*

Wal-Mart Stores Inc. 2005. Federal deposit insurance application to FDIC, July 18. *www.fdic.gov.*

Weiss, Eric. 2007. Report to Congress: Industrial loan companies/banks and the separation of banking and commerce: legislature and regulatory perspectives, Washington, D.C.: *Congressional Research Service Report for Congress*, updated January 3.

Wilmarth Jr., Arthur. 2007. Wal-Mart and the separation of banking and commerce. Connecticut *Law Review* 39: 1539–1622.

2

Banking and Commerce: What Difference Did Wal-Mart Make?

*Christine E. Blair**

Introduction

We are once again engaged in debate over banking and commerce. The focus of the current debate is commercial ownership of industrial loan companies or industrial banks—commonly referred to as ILCs. Despite its seemingly narrow focus, this debate will have broad implications for how affiliations between banking, financial, and commercial firms will be regulated and supervised.

Today, the ILC is the only insured depository institution that can be chartered by commercial firms. ILCs have general banking powers and can only be chartered in a limited number of states. They are regulated and supervised by their state chartering authorities and the Federal Deposit Insurance Corporation (FDIC), which is their primary federal regulator. In 1987, the Competitive Equality Banking Act (CEBA) established an exemption for certain ILCs from the definition of "bank" in the Bank Holding Company Act (BHCA).[1] When the conditions of this exemption are met, the corporate owners of ILCs are not subject to consolidated supervision by the Federal Reserve. In some states, ILCs may be owned by commercial firms.

Over the past decade, the ILC industry has experienced rapid asset growth—primarily in ILCs owned by financial firms. More recently, large retailers and other commercial firms have expressed interest in obtaining ILC charters. These trends have caused policymakers to reappraise how the

ILC industry is regulated and supervised and to reconsider the extent to which affiliations between banking, financial, and commercial firms should be permitted and the ways in which they should be regulated.

This chapter revisits the banking and commerce debate and examines how current events—in particular, the recent interest on the part of commercial firms in the ILC charter—are affecting public policy.[2] The first section looks at the pressures for mixing banking and commerce and at the process of regulatory change. The next section describes the current debate—reactions to the 2005 application by Wal-Mart Stores Inc. for an ILC charter and the response of the regulators and Congress. The chapter then turns to the broader banking and commerce debate and explores the underlying issues and concerns about commercial affiliation. Questions for policymakers and an analysis of the Wal-Mart episode complete the chapter.

Banking and Commerce and the Process of Regulatory Change

The U.S. bank regulatory framework has evolved considerably over the last half century. Regulatory reforms have been introduced in stages—waves—that have transformed the regulation of interest rates, lifted restrictions on where a bank may conduct business, and expanded the products and affiliations available to banks and banking organizations.[3] In each case, reform has addressed regulations that have become outmoded in light of market pressures, changing demand, and technological innovation. Each stage required legislative action and resulted in new regulations that "modernized" or changed the face of the financial services industry. These regulations have often been phased in or introduced with limitations designed to maintain safe-and-sound banking, protect the deposit insurance system, and prevent a spillover of the safety net to the owners and affiliates of insured institutions.

One lesson that can be drawn is that the market will continue to drive innovation and change in the financial system. The next wave of change likely will affect how banking and commerce will mix. Current forces—such as the unbundling of banking services, the democratization of credit, and the unleashing of the information revolution—are already altering how financial services are delivered to consumers. Nonfinancial firms are finding ways to provide bank-like financial services to their customers, and financial and commercial firms are incorporating the ILC into their business strategies.

For nonfinancial firms, expanding into financial services can provide a new line of business that utilizes existing distribution networks and may not require significant additional capital investment. For example, the supermarket giant Kroeger Co., which operates over 2,000 supermarkets in 31 states, has entered the financial services business by marketing branded products, including mortgages, home-equity lines of credit, and several types of insurance, in its stores.[4] Customers can obtain loan and insurance brochures in the checkout lines and apply for such products by phone or on the company's personal finance Web site. Kroeger also leases space throughout its network of stores to commercial banks.

Wal-Mart Stores Inc. has also expanded its financial services offerings. It has created separate MoneyCenter desks in its stores where financial services such as check cashing, money transfers, branded credit cards, and bill payment are available to its customers.[5] In 2007, it launched the Wal-Mart MoneyCard, a stored-value card issued with GE Money using the Visa card network. The MoneyCard can be reloaded—card holders can have their pay transferred directly onto the card—and can be used to withdraw cash at ATMs, purchase goods through the Visa network, or pay bills. These nonbank services are expected to be very attractive to the roughly 9 percent of the U.S. population who are currently "unbanked." Wal-Mart has plans to further expand its financial services offerings—in store and online.[6] In leases with its in-store banks, the company has reserved the right to offer various financial services in its stores, including mortgages, consumer loans, home-equity loans, and investment and insurance products.

Another example is PayPal Inc.—the payments division of eBay Inc. PayPal is a safe, global, real-time payment service that enables any individual or business with an e-mail address to securely and quickly send and receive payments online. It operates on a large scale—with over 100 million account members and operations in over 190 countries and regions of the world. In May 2007, PayPal announced that Luxembourg had granted it a banking license for the European Union.[7] For its European operations, its banking license will allow it to bypass other banks and retain member account balances instead. As a deposit broker in the United States, it uses the banking system to provide pass-through FDIC insurance on member account balances. (PayPal was rumored to be interested in an ILC, but has not filed an application for deposit insurance with the FDIC.[8])

The use of cell phone technology to transmit payments outside of the banking system is another example of network synergies at work. The technology permits low-cost, real-time transfers of balances on a network that is accessed by cell phone. The cell phone functions as a smart card, allowing payments to be sent and received by consumers and businesses—without the use of a bank as intermediary.[9] The technology is expected to be used on a large scale by microfinance borrowers and as a secure alternative to bank remittances. Several U.S. banks, including Citibank, Bank of America, and Wachovia, have embraced this technology and now offer a service that allows customers to access many online banking services via cell phone.[10]

As recent trends show, financial and commercial firms have incorporated the ILC charter into their business plans. Unlike banking companies subject to the BHCA, the parent companies of ILCs may engage in commercial activities. They are not required to be supervised by the Federal Reserve, and some of them are not subject to any other form of consolidated supervision.[11] And it is the perceived need for expanding the reach of "consolidated" supervision that is one of the major issues in the debate. (The structure of the ILC industry and ILC powers and supervision are discussed in the appendix to this chapter.)

The rapid growth in ILC industry assets—from $11.5 billion at year-end 1995 to approximately $225 billion by midyear 2007—has been driven by a small number of ILCs owned by financial firms, including Merrill Lynch, Morgan Stanley, UBS, and American Express (see appendix, figure 2.1, and table 2.1). In 1996, American Express moved its credit card operations from its Delaware credit card bank to its Utah ILC, increasing the assets in the industry to $22.6 billion by year end. In 1999, Merrill Lynch began using its Utah ILC for its deposit sweep program, which places its brokerage's customers' cash management accounts in insured deposits.[12] Since then, several other financial firms associated with ILCs have offered their clients the option of holding their cash balances in insured deposits that are placed in the firms' ILCs through deposit sweep programs.

As of June 30, 2007, about 25 percent of ILCs were owned or controlled by parent companies that may be considered nonfinancial or commercial, including General Motors, General Electric, BMW, Target, and Toyota. These ILCs generally support the operations of the parent company in some way—their business model is not retail banking. For example, Target uses its ILC to issue proprietary commercial credit cards to business customers of Target Stores. Automakers generally use their ILCs to finance sales of their vehicles. Some commercial parents, such as Target, also own significant credit card issuing banks as allowed under CEBA. Some are unitary thrift holding companies that own a thrift institution overseen by the Office of Thrift Supervision (OTS). More recently, large retailers, notably Wal-Mart and Home Depot, and other commercial firms have sought ILC charters.

Increasingly, nonbank firms are finding ways to provide their customers with financial services, whether through an insured ILC or outside the banking industry. Will these and other forces for change trigger a fourth wave of regulatory reform? It will depend on how the banking industry, its regulators, and Congress respond in the face of these market-driven changes. They should consider whether current regulatory structures should be reopened to consider the mixing of banking and commerce and what consequences might result if they are not reopened.

ILCs and the Banking and Commerce Debate

ILCs have been the focal point for the banking and commerce debate before. In 2003 the issue was the regulation and supervision of ILCs by their chartering state and the FDIC, their primary federal regulator. At that time, Congress was considering giving ILCs additional powers in two areas: de novo interstate banking and the payment of interest on business transaction accounts.[13] The debate turned on whether a bank-centric supervisory approach provided sufficient protection for the ILC, the deposit insurance fund, and the safety net.[14] Commercial ownership, per se, was not the primary concern.

Differences in the scope of supervisory authorities was the focus of the FDIC Office of Inspector General (OIG) in 2004.[15] The OIG evaluation report pointed to differences in the supervisory powers granted to the FDIC and the Federal Reserve and expressed concern about the lack of regulatory oversight (consolidated supervision) of some ILC parent companies. The OIG noted that the FDIC lacked the authority to impose capital requirements on the parent company and had not formally adopted the principle of source of strength, which argues that parent companies should serve as a source of financial and managerial strength to their subsidiary financial institutions. The OIG concluded "that ILCs may pose additional risks to the deposit insurance fund by virtue of the fact that these depository institutions' parent holding companies are not always subject to the scope of consolidated supervision, consolidated capital requirements, or enforcement actions imposed on parent organizations subject to the BHCA."[16]

The following year the U.S. Government Accountability Office (GAO) expressed concerns about the rapid growth of ILC assets and the lack of consolidated supervision at the federal level.[17] It reported to Congress on the differences in the supervisory and regulatory powers exercised by the Federal Reserve and the OTS as consolidated supervisors and by the FDIC as primary federal regulator of ILCs. The GAO report concluded that ILCs may pose a greater risk of loss to the deposit insurance fund—not because they are operationally riskier than other insured depository institutions but because the FDIC's supervisory authority over the parent company is less extensive than that of federal consolidated bank supervisors.[18] The report recommended that Congress consider strengthening the regulatory oversight of ILCs. It also suggested that Congress more broadly consider the issue of mixing banking and commerce.[19]

ILCs continue to drive the banking and commerce debate, although the underlying concerns are focused less on regulatory oversight of the ILC and more on commercial ownership. The ILC industry is widely accepted to be well regulated and supervised, and ILCs are not considered to pose unique risks to the deposit insurance fund.[20] There is still concern about the oversight of the parent, and this has been heightened by the recent interest of commercial firms in the ILC charter. (These concerns were not an issue when, for example, Target or Toyota chartered their ILCs in 2004.) Rather than promoting additional powers for ILCs, Congress is now considering whether the ILC exemption from the BHCA should be limited or closed.

What difference did Wal-Mart make?

Essentially, the debate was renewed when, in July 2005, Wal-Mart Bank (In Organization)—a proposed ILC headquartered in Salt Lake City, Utah— submitted an application for deposit insurance to the FDIC. (After much public debate, Wal-Mart withdrew its application from consideration on March 16, 2007.) The proposed ILC would have been used to process electronic checks, and debit and credit transactions for the parent, Wal-Mart Stores Inc. Wal-Mart Bank would have eliminated the need to process payments through another bank, saving a small sum—the transaction cost or processing fee—on each payment. Revenue of $10 million was expected by the end of the bank's third year of operation. The proposed business plan did not include retail banking, and Wal-Mart indicated on numerous occasions that it would not seek to open branches in its stores.

The Interagency Notice of Change in Control filed on May 8, 2006, by Home Depot Inc. also raised concerns about commercial ownership. The notice filed with the FDIC indicated Home Depot's intention to acquire EnerBank USA, an ILC chartered in Utah. EnerBank USA specializes in home-improvement lending and is currently owned by CMS Energy Corporation. Under the plan, home-improvement contractors would refer their clients to Home Depot Bank for home-improvement loans. On January 25, 2008, the Home Depot withdrew their application, ending their bid to acquire the Utah ILC.

Both Wal-Mart's application and Home Depot's notice drew considerable attention. Their business plans were criticized, and concern was expressed about the risks posed to the deposit insurance fund and the financial safety net. On the Wal-Mart Bank application alone, the FDIC received an unprecedented number of letters—over 13,000—from the banking industry and its trade associations, consumer advocacy groups, bank regulators, members of Congress, academics, and the public at large. In response, the FDIC held three days of public hearings in April 2006 in order to gain insight into the issues raised by the application.[21]

In the comment letters and during the hearings, the ILC charter and the Wal-Mart application were both broadly criticized and defended. On the one hand, concerns were raised about the character and fitness of management, Wal-Mart's legal problems, and the independence of the bank from its parent. Wal-Mart's size and the impact it allegedly has had on small businesses and communities—affecting jobs and wages—were raised. Because Wal-Mart leases space in its stores to over 300 banks (many of them community banks), concerns were expressed about the possible effects on competition. It was asserted that a Wal-Mart bank would dodge its Community Reinvestment Act obligations; open retail branches in Wal-Mart stores, contrary to its business plan; and engage in predatory pricing and preferential lending. On the other hand, Wal-Mart's good character was defended, as was the legitimacy of the ILC charter. The continued safe-and-sound operation of the ILC industry was also noted.

Broader criticisms of the ILC industry were also voiced. In particular, the absence of consolidated supervision of the parent by the Federal Reserve was cited by some commenters as evidence that those ILCs were not adequately supervised. The ILC exemption from the BHCA crafted in CEBA was deemed a loophole, and commercial affiliations were said to violate a long-held principle of separating banking from commerce.

Wal-Mart had made previous attempts to enter banking. One plan was to open branches of a family-owned thrift in its stores. Another plan proposed a partnership with a bank, using Wal-Mart's clerks as tellers. Neither plan was approved by regulators. A later attempt to acquire a California ILC also failed. In that case, California revised its laws to prohibit commercial firms from owning ILCs. Although its most recent application for deposit insurance was withdrawn, Wal-Mart has reiterated its intent to provide expanded financial services to its customers and has not ruled out chartering an ILC in the future.[22] Several states have responded by passing laws that block commercial firms from using ILCs to offer in-store banking services. Colorado also has prohibited commercial ownership of an ILC.[23]

Further doubts were cast on Wal-Mart's claim that it would not enter retail branch banking, when, in November 2006, it established a retail banking presence in Mexico. Mexico's Ministry of Finance approved a banking license for Wal-Mart's Mexican subsidiary that permits it to provide basic banking services in its retail stores to the general public—many of whom are underserved by the country's banking system.

Regulators and Congress respond

In July 2006, the FDIC board of directors voted to impose a six-month moratorium on any action to accept or act upon ILC-related applications for deposit insurance and notices of changes in bank control.[24] The moratorium was declared to give the FDIC time to review the issues, facts, and arguments raised with respect to the ILC industry, including its recent growth and the trend toward commercial ownership. Other issues included whether there were emerging safety-and-soundness issues or risks to the deposit insurance fund and whether statutory, regulatory, or policy changes should be made to the FDIC's oversight of the industry.[25]

In connection with the moratorium, the FDIC published a request for public comment on ILCs and their ownership, which asked about the current legal and business framework of ILCs and the possible benefits, risks, and supervisory issues associated with ILCs.[26] Of the comments that specifically responded to the questions posed by the FDIC (many did not), 60 percent were generally positive toward ILCs.[27] In particular, the ILC charter was not believed by those commenting to pose greater risk or other possible harm than any other insured institution charter. Nevertheless, concerns were expressed about ILC ownership and the proposed business plans. Again, the absence of consolidated supervisory requirements for the parent companies of ILCs, the absence of an obligation by the ILC parent companies to keep the ILCs well capitalized, and differences in the scope of authority to examine affiliate relationships were noted.

On January 31, 2007, the FDIC extended the moratorium for one year for ILCs that would be owned or controlled, directly or indirectly, by companies engaged in commercial activities.[28] The FDIC also proposed a new regulation that would expand its supervisory authority over certain ILCs and their parent companies. The ILCs affected would be those that would become subsidiaries of companies engaged solely in financial activities but not currently subject to consolidated supervision by the Federal Reserve or the OTS.[29] The proposed regulation would modify Part 354 of the FDIC's Rules and Regulations to establish a set of comprehensive safeguards that would identify and avoid or control, on a consolidated basis, risks posed to the safety and soundness of the institution and to the deposit insurance fund. The proposed rules would assure, through reporting and examinations, that the FDIC had the ability to obtain transparency with respect to a parent company and its subsidiaries. Commercial owners were not addressed by the proposed regulation.

The FDIC has stated that commercial ownership is a policy question that Congress must resolve. Taking a neutral position, FDIC chairman Sheila Bair noted, "The question of whether banking and commerce should be mixed and . . . if at all . . . to what degree, needs answering. This is a fundamental policy decision that should be made by elected officials. And it's now up to Congress to decide where do we go from here."[30] Although the moratorium on commercial ownership was extended for one year, the FDIC cautioned that it could not defer action on outstanding applications and notices of change in control indefinitely. The moratorium expired on January 31 , 2008 and was not renewed.

The chartering, ownership, and supervision of ILCs are the subject of proposed legislation introduced by Representatives Paul Gillmor (R-OH) and Barney Frank (D-MA) in January 2007. Their bill, H.R. 698, the Industrial Loan Holding Company Act of 2007, would amend the Federal Deposit Insurance (FDI) Act to establish holding company regulation for ILCs. The bill would define an industrial bank holding company that would be subject to federal consolidated supervision and would recognize four consolidated supervisors: the Federal Reserve, the FDIC, the OTS, and the Securities and Exchange Commission (SEC). The bill would also limit commercial ownership of ILCs. In particular, commercial firms would not be allowed to directly or indirectly control ILCs. For these purposes, a "commercial firm" would be defined as an entity that derives 15 percent or more of annual gross revenues, on a consolidated basis, from activities that are not financial in nature or incidental to a financial activity.[31] Grandfather provisions for certain ILCs and commercial firms are included in the bill.[32] The House Committee on Financial Services held hearings on H.R. 698 and related ILC issues on April 25, 2007.[33] The bill was passed by the House of Representatives on May 21, 2007, and was referred to the Senate Committee on Banking, Housing, and Urban Affairs.

In May 2007, the bill S. 1356, the Industrial Bank Holding Company Act of 2007, was introduced in the U.S. Senate.[34] As would H.R. 698, the bill would amend the FDI Act to establish industrial bank holding companies and would strengthen the FDIC's authority to regulate and supervise ILCs and industrial bank holding companies (with the exception of those subject to consolidated supervision by the Federal Reserve, the OTS, or the SEC). Commercial firms that do not meet a revenue test would not be allowed to own or control an ILC. The Senate bill incorporates the same revenue test and grandfathering provisions found in H.R. 698. for certain ILCs and commercial owners.[35]

At the Wal-Mart public hearings, former senator Jake Garn (R-UT) defended the ILC charter and emphasized that the exception in CEBA had been purposely crafted, although it had not been anticipated that the charter would be acquired by large commercial—that is, retail—firms.[36] In light of recent trends—the growth of financially owned ILCs and the applications from commercial retailers—it is not surprising that efforts would be made to restrain the industry, perhaps irrespective of the actual risks posed to the deposit insurance fund and the safety net.

The Separation of Banking and Commerce

Restrictions on bank powers and permissible activities have generally existed in some form throughout American banking history. They were included in early bank corporate charters and in the definition of the "business of banking," as found in state legislation and the National Bank Act.[37] Yet, despite such regulations and prohibitions on certain activities and forms of control, this separation has been far from complete.[38] For example, the law has always permitted individuals to own both a bank and a commercial firm, and it has always permitted nonbank corporations to own some type of bank.[39] Moreover, extensive links between banking and commerce have existed and continue to exist and have often been facilitated by the use of arrangements very similar to those that have been prohibited by law.[40]

Since the banking crisis and economic depression of the 1930s, Congress has prohibited certain affiliations and permitted others. In 1933, responding to the general belief that the nation's banking and economic problems had been caused by conflicts of interest between banks and their securities affiliates, Congress passed the Glass-Steagall Act, which prohibited affiliations between commercial banking and investment banking companies.[41] This act, however, did not address the more general issue of separating commercial banking from nonbanking activities—that is, from commerce.

Two decades later, a general and long-standing distrust of large banking conglomerates led to the passage of the BHCA in 1956, which separated banking from commerce by further restricting the activities of owners and affiliates of banks. Prior to its enactment (with the Glass-Steagall exception), any nonbank corporation could own any number of commercial banks. The current restrictions on bank ownership and affiliation stem from the BHCA (and its amendments)[42] and the GLBA of 1999. ILCs remain an exception to that legislative framework.

Mixing Banking and Commerce: Concerns Raised by Commercial Affiliations

There are two general views on whether banking should be separate from commerce with different implications for how banks, their owners, and their affiliates would be regulated. One view argues that a line of separation must be maintained because the risks of allowing them to mix outweigh the possible benefits. The failure to maintain a separation, especially in terms of ownership and control of banking organizations, is argued to have potentially serious consequences, ranging from conflicts of interest and the lack of impartiality in the credit decision-making process to the unintended expansion of the financial safety net. The other view sees the mixing of banking and commerce as the market at work, finding new ways to benefit consumers, businesses, and the economy. From this perspective, mandating a separation of banking and commerce unnecessarily protects an inefficient status quo, prevents the benefits of affiliation from being realized, and can result in an inefficient allocation of resources.

The remainder of this section reviews the potential risks of affiliation and the regulatory and supervisory structures designed to mitigate risk and manage affiliations.

The potential risks of affiliation

The case for separating banking and commerce is built on the premise that affiliations between banking and commerce would lead to conflicts of interest and concentrations of economic power and to actions on the part of owners and affiliates of the insured entity that could threaten its solvency and lead to an unintended expansion of the safety net.[43] However, those potential risks are not unique to commercial affiliations, but are applicable to financial affiliations as well, such as those permitted in the current regulatory framework.[44] In the current debate, the ILC exemption is also said to provide a competitive advantage relative to banks subject to the BHCA.[45] These potential risks and how they are managed under current law and regulation are discussed below.

Conflicts of interest that could result from transactions between the bank and its affiliates have traditionally raised concern.[46] In the ILC debate the risk would be that an ILC affiliated with a commercial firm could deny loans to the affiliate's competitors, lend preferentially to its commercial affiliate(s), or illegally tie loans to purchases of the affiliate's products. However, in banking, such conflicts are generally controlled through the use of firewalls and prudential supervision. For example, Sections 23A and 23B of the Federal Reserve Act restrict the amount and terms under which banks, including ILCs, can lend to their affiliates. Similarly, banks, including ILCs, are prohibited from engaging in anticompetitive tying practices. Nonetheless, critics argue that when the ILC is owned (or controlled) by a commercial entity, these protections would be insufficient. Again, the lack of federal consolidated supervision of the commercial parent by the FDIC is cited as the reason.

The concentration of economic and financial power has traditionally been argued to be a reason for separating banking and commerce.[47] The fear is that commercial affiliations could lead to unacceptable levels of economic aggregation and power within the financial sector, resulting in monopolies and the potential for an expansion of the federal safety net that could expose the taxpayer to losses. It is also argued that permitting banking and commerce to mix would run counter to the U.S. ideals of separation and dispersion of political and economic power and would exacerbate the current trends of consolidation in banking and other industries.[48] Comparisons to the Japanese *keiretsu* system (conglomerate groupings in which banks are linked to their client companies through equity ownership) and the banking problems experienced by Japan and other Asian countries since the 1980s have been made. Although the close ties among the government, commercial firms, and banks found in the Japanese *keiretsu* are unlikely to be replicated in the United States, the possibility that the combined firm could nonetheless exert significant economic and political power remains a concern for many.[49] Although the fear of monopoly power in banking has deep roots, the question for policymakers is whether those fears are sufficient reason to prohibit all affiliations between banks and commercial firms.[50] Certainly, concentrations of economic and political power, regardless of their source, are likely to continue to raise concerns and warrant the attention of policymakers. These concerns have traditionally been (and are best) addressed by Congress.

It is also argued that because they are exempt from the BHCA, ILCs have an unfair competitive advantage over other insured depository institutions that are subject to holding company regulation. Concerns are raised that a large commercial entity with monopoly power, as Wal-Mart is often perceived to be, could enter banking and use its power to displace its banking competitors. However, a large commercial bank—not just a large commercial firm—could similarly displace its banking competitors in any given market. It is also possible that commercial owners could bring beneficial competition to banking markets.[51] These fears persist despite the fact that Congress, in the GLBA, permitted combinations of large banks with large securities and insurance firms, seeming to acknowledge that the potential for monopoly power is of less concern today than formerly and does not provide a rationale for separating banking and commerce.[52]

Safety-net issues arise when the bank and its affiliates (including its parent) have an opportunity or incentive to act in ways that threaten the solvency of the bank; as would be the case when an insured bank enters into transactions (e.g., loans, guarantees, or other obligations or transfers) for the benefit of an affiliated person or organization *and* those actions endanger the safety and soundness of the bank.[53] For example, the parent organization could shift funds from the ILC to its nonbank affiliates, or the ILC could buy assets from the affiliate at inflated prices or provide a capital infusion to the affiliate through a loan at below-market rates. As a result, the parent could shift potential losses to the ILC.[54] In today's debate, if transactions between the ILC and its affiliates were to threaten the solvency of the ILC, the fear is that the creditors of the ILC's commercial parent would be protected as losses were shifted to the ILC.[55] The effect on the ILC could range from minimal harm to failure, which would impose costs on the deposit insurance fund and potentially the taxpayer.

Unchecked, such behavior would raise doubts about permitting banks to affiliate with nonbank entities, whether financial or commercial in nature. It is precisely because these loss-shifting transactions raise safety-and-soundness concerns and potentially threaten the safety net that they have been made illegal under existing law. Regulatory discipline through the enforcement of firewalls and the prudential supervision of the insured entity have been regulators' tools to contain the potential harm to the deposit insurance fund and the safety net, and they have been quite successful.

Managing the risks: firewalls and prudential supervision

The primary means of controlling abuse and ensuring the safety and soundness of the banking system is through the supervisory process. The goal is to balance prudential supervision with the need of banks (and banking organizations) to pursue activities and affiliations by which they can generate profits, attract capital, and enhance their competitiveness.

Firewall restrictions are applicable to all insured depository institutions, including ILCs, and are enforced by primary banking regulators. Their purpose is to ensure that actions on the part of the parent and other nonbank affiliates do not threaten the solvency of the insured institution. Firewalls are contained in Sections 23A and 23B of the Federal Reserve Act, Section 106 of the BHCA, and Regulation O of the Federal Reserve Board. Sections 23A and 23B ensure that transactions between an insured bank and its nonbank affiliates, including its parent holding company, are on market-related, arm's-length terms. Section 106 protects the bank from harm that may result from illegal tying, and Regulation O governs the transactions between insiders and the bank.

Other prudential safeguards include requirements that the bank's investment in any operating subsidiary be deducted from regulatory capital, that the bank be well capitalized following that deduction, and that the corporate separateness of the bank be protected. To achieve adequate separation, the insured entity should be financially separate—that is, it must be separately funded and have no commingled assets, and all transactions with affiliates must be at arms length. The insured entity must also be perceived by the market to be operated separately and to be legally separate— that is, not responsible for the liabilities of its affiliates.[56] When approving deposit insurance applications, the FDIC has the authority to impose various conditions intended to ensure the independence and separateness of the insured institution from its owners and affiliates.[57]

All insured institutions are examined periodically by their primary regulator for safety and soundness and compliance with regulatory standards, including firewalls. Bank and thrift holding companies are examined on a consolidated basis. Off-site monitoring provides a check on the institution between examinations. In combination, prudential supervision and the enforcement of regulatory standards and firewalls protect the bank and help ensure the safety and soundness of the banking system.[58] These regulatory tools must be effective enough to ensure that the risk to the insurance funds is minimal and flexible enough to allow institutions to explore the opportunities presented by affiliations with nonbank entities.[59]

The Current Regulatory Framework

The current regulatory framework includes prudential supervision of the insured entity and consolidated supervision of the organization. How commercial affiliations fit into this regulatory framework is an important aspect of the banking and commerce debate. This section examines the effect of the GLBA on banking organizations and discusses differences in bank-centric and consolidated forms of supervision. It concludes with a discussion of the role for commercial affiliations in the current regulatory framework.

GLBA framework—oversight of the organization

When Congress enacted the GLBA, it opened the door for banking organizations to engage in nonbank financial activities through affiliations with securities and insurance firms. The GLBA is important to the banking and commerce debate because it made expanded affiliations possible for banking organizations and placed limits on commercial ownership of thrift organizations.

First, the GLBA lifted the Glass-Steagall prohibitions and provided for affiliations between qualifying BHCs—called financial holding companies (FHCs)—and securities and insurance firms. The Federal Reserve Board was designated the umbrella supervisor of the FHC and in that capacity has various authorities, including the power to examine the holding company, to require certain reports, and to set consolidated capital standards for the banking organization (except with respect to certain functionally regulated subsidiaries). Bank, securities, and insurance subsidiaries of the FHC are supervised on a functional basis by their respective primary regulators. Functionally regulated nonbank affiliates are not subject to bank-like supervision by the Federal Reserve. In performing the role of the umbrella supervisor, the Federal Reserve is directed to rely primarily on the information provided by the nonbank affiliates' functional regulators.[60]

The GLBA also granted the Federal Reserve primary responsibility for determining permissible activities for the FHC and its subsidiaries. Beyond an initial set of permissible activities, which includes merchant banking, the GLBA authorizes the Federal Reserve Board, in conjunction with the secretary of the treasury, to determine additional activities that are financial in nature or incidental to financial activities for FHCs.[61] In doing so, they are directed to evaluate a set of factors, including whether the activity is consistent with the purposes of the BHCA and the GLBA and with changes or reasonably expected changes in the marketplace in which FHCs compete and in the technology for delivering financial services.[62] The Federal Reserve alone is authorized to determine the set of commercial activities that is complementary to financial activities.[63]

The GLBA placed new restrictions on the mixing of banking and commerce by ending the ability of a commercial firm to own a single thrift institution in what is termed "a unitary thrift holding company."[64] Existing unitary thrift holding companies were grandfathered, with restrictions.[65] As do ILCs, unitary thrift holding companies operate outside of the BHCA and Federal Reserve oversight. Unitary thrift holding companies are subject to consolidated supervision by the OTS and firewall restrictions and have long operated without raising safety-and-soundness concerns or posing undue risk to the safety net.[66] By eliminating this corporate structure, the GLBA narrowed the options available for mixing banking and commerce. Again, the remaining way is through the ILC charter.

When the GLBA enabled qualified BHCs to affiliate with financial firms and redefined the set of permissible activities and the mechanism that determines additional activities, the line separating banking from commerce became a line separating finance and commerce. The task for regulators is to determine what is financial but not commercial—a difficult problem given changing markets and technology.[67] As a governor of the Federal Reserve Board noted, "GLB grants the agencies authority to move toward mixing banking and commerce at the margin as markets and technology begin to dim the already less than bright line between them."[68] In short, the GLBA has effectively endorsed a slow but accelerating integration of banking and commerce. As a result, it is argued that the policy rationale for separating banking and commerce has been undermined.[69] By contrast, the elimination of the unitary thrift option is offered as evidence that the GLBA underscored congressional intent to maintain a separation between banking and commerce. The ILC exemption from the BHCA, however, was not changed by the GLBA.

The GLBA framework has benefited the banking industry through expanded powers and the ability to affiliate with financial firms. Large U.S. banking corporations—many globally active—have taken advantage of the FHC structure and the synergies that can result from combining banking, securities, and insurance under one organization. The GLBA also gave financial firms an ability to acquire a commercial bank, although many large securities and insurance firms have not chosen that option. Instead, they operate outside of the GLBA framework, without constraints on affiliation and without umbrella supervision by the Federal Reserve.[70]

It was expected that, as regulators expanded the set of permissible activities, banks would face new competition from firms whose services closely resembled those in the expanded set.[71] However, the set of permissible activities has changed very little since the GLBA was enacted, while competition from nonfinancial firms that have expanded into bank-like financial services has increased. The bottom line is that we can expect the distinctions between banking, finance, and commerce to continue to blur and that it will be increasingly difficult to maintain a separation of banking (or finance) and commerce.

Differences in supervisory authorities—bank-centric and consolidated supervision

The philosophy and supervisory approach of primary regulators and consolidated supervisors play a significant role in the current policy debate.[72] Primary regulators employ a bank-centric approach that focuses on the insured entity.[73] Supervisory tools—implementing regulatory standards and firewalls described above—are applied at the bank level to protect the insured entity from the risks and conflicts that arise from affiliations and to ensure legal and financial separation. If these safeguards are adequate, then affiliations—commercial or financial—need not threaten the safety and soundness of the insured entity or the deposit insurance fund. Bank regulation remains focused on the insured entity, and mixing banking and commerce becomes possible.

Consolidated supervisors are responsible for determining whether the parent holding company is operated in a safe-and-sound manner and whether its financial condition threatens the viability of affiliated insured depository institutions. Consolidated supervision oversees the organization as a whole—from the top down—viewing all parts of an organization as one financial entity.[74] It supplements bank-centric supervision because firewalls and prudential supervision are perceived to be inadequate. The ability of firewalls to prevent harm to the insured entity yet permit the economic advantages of affiliation is questioned, as is the ability of firewalls to ensure corporate separateness.[75] Because this approach requires all affiliates of the bank, including its parent, to be subject to some form of bank regulatory oversight, commercial affiliations raise concerns.

The FDIC's ability to effectively supervise ILCs has been criticized, in part, because it does not have the same explicit powers as consolidated supervisors.[76] Although it may lack certain authorities, the FDIC has argued that its ability to preserve the safety and soundness of insured depository institutions, including ILCs, and to protect the deposit insurance fund is as effective as that of consolidated supervisors.[77] This view may be supported by the GAO's recent report, which found that "the contributions consolidated supervision programs make to the safety and soundness of financial institutions could not be assessed separately from other agency programs."[78] It noted that the stated goals for consolidated supervision often were the same as those for the agency's primary supervision programs. Without clear program objectives, the value added by an additional layer of supervision was difficult to discern.

To date, the supervisory experience of the FDIC with respect to commercially owned ILCs has been favorably compared to that of the OTS with respect to diversified thrift holding companies. Neither experience suggests that commercial ownership has presented safety-net concerns or otherwise threatened the banking system.[79] Of the insured ILCs that have failed since the mid-1980s, none were owned by a commercial parent and only two were owned by holding companies. They did not fail as a result of self-dealing, conflicts of interest, or improper actions by their owners.[80] Moreover, the bankruptcy in 2002 of Conseco Inc. did not result in the failure of either of its insured institutions—an ILC and a state-chartered credit card bank.[81]

Despite the supervisory tools available to the FDIC and its supervisory track record, concerns are raised that a commercially owned ILC would have a strong incentive to take risks that otherwise could not be been taken or that it might engage in illegal tying conduct in order to aid its commercial parent or affiliates. The FDIC allegedly could not detect these misdeeds without the ability to monitor the parent on a consolidated basis. Thus, the transparency of the commercial parent company, which is not subject to consolidated oversight, has been raised in the current debate.[82] (Both the FDIC's proposed regulation, which would extend its supervisory powers over certain financial owners of ILCs, and H.R. 698 and S. 1356, which would impose federal consolidated supervision on the owners of ILCs, attempt to address this concern.)

However, the degree of complexity within an organization, rather than its affiliation alone, might be a better determinant of the need for organizational oversight or monitoring. For example, organizations that combine banking and finance, where business lines may cross the legal boundaries, might warrant greater oversight than organizations that combine banking and commerce, where the insured entity is clearly separate. If the necessary transparency can be achieved without requiring the organization (parent and affiliates) to be subject to umbrella or consolidated supervision, it is more likely that nonbank economic activity associated with the commercial affiliations would continue to be driven by the market rather than by regulation.

Moreover, extending consolidated supervision to commercial affiliations would change the long-standing relationship between the federal banking agencies and the nonbank sector as commercial activities would increasingly be subject to regulation designed to protect the financial safety net. If the signal to the market is that regulators expect affiliates to be managed as integrated entities, then ensuring effective separation of the insured entity from the risks posed by its affiliates may become harder.[83] As a result, it is argued, consolidated supervision could lead to the unintended extension of the federal safety net to the owners and nonbank affiliates of the insured entity.

The costs of imposing bank-like regulation on firms that historically have not been subject to such regulation needs to be weighed against any perceived benefits provided to the insured institution.[84] As the then Federal Reserve chairman Alan Greenspan once told Congress, "The case is weak, in our judgment, for umbrella supervision of a holding company in which the bank is not the dominant unit and is not large enough to induce systemic problems should it fail."[85]

The banking industry enjoyed a period of extraordinary economic stability between 1999, when the GLBA made expanded affiliation among banking, finance, and insurance companies possible, and 2007. As a result it has been unclear how FHCs would fare under duress—to what extent umbrella oversight of the organization would protect the safety net. Critics of commercially owned ILCs similarly argue that it is unclear how well the bank-centric supervisory approach would work.[86]

What should be done about commercial affiliations?

The concerns raised by commercial affiliations are not new and have been analyzed and debated at great length over the years. Policymakers have discussed the potential for conflicts of interest, illegal tying, concentrations of economic or financial power, unfair competition, and actions that might threaten the solvency of the insured institution and ultimately the safety net. The analysis shows that these potential problems are not unique to commercial affiliations. Congress and the regulators have developed prudential supervisory tools and firewalls designed to mitigate potential risks.

What happens if commercial affiliations are prohibited? Congress can eliminate the ILC exception or otherwise prohibit the relationship. Current proposals, such as the House bill, move in this direction.[87] Although a prohibition would prevent the potential benefits of the affiliation from being realized and could result in an inefficient allocation of resources, it would not affect nonbank firms that are providing financial services—some of which may substitute for insured deposits. Moreover, would the prohibition be tenable in the face of market-driven change? Experience with other prohibitions or restrictions, such as those on interest rates or interstate banking, have not held.

The decision to permit or prohibit commercial affiliations should depend on the relative benefits and risks posed by affiliation. If regulatory controls are not sufficient to protect the insured depository and the safety net from abuses by its parent and affiliates, then not only should commercial affiliations be prohibited, but banking and finance affiliations should also be reconsidered. However, if regulatory controls are sufficient, then commercial affiliations could be permitted if the market wants them and customers can benefit from them. The task for policymakers is to determine the extent to which affiliations will be permitted. The key to that determination is in identifying whether the risks posed by these affiliations can be controlled.[88]

The current regulatory framework—defined by the GLBA and its provisions for affiliation between banking and finance—has been referred to as a "world with legally defined outer limits on permissible activities."[89] The ILC exception is a crack in that world—because it allows nonbank firms to enter banking without consolidated oversight of the parent by the Federal Reserve. Outside the GLBA framework there are many firms—diversified and commercial—that are not subject to the same limitations or oversight by the Federal Reserve (although some are subject to consolidated oversight by another federal regulator). Many of these firms control insured depository institutions and have been leaders in financial innovation.[90]

Further integration of banking and commerce is likely to occur within the GLBA framework and include some form of consolidated supervision of the bank's owners. However, over time, it is likely that the regulatory framework itself will be subject to change. A question for policymakers is whether the regulatory framework is flexible enough to accommodate market-driven change.

Conclusion—What Difference Did Wal-Mart Make?

This chapter has revisited the banking and commerce debate and posed the question, What difference did Wal-Mart make? Concerns raised about commercial affiliations with banks have been heightened by Wal-Mart's attempt to enter banking by chartering an ILC. Long-standing arguments have been raised again, some directly related to the application (e.g., whether ILCs should be permitted at all) and some obliquely related (e.g., the scope and meaning of consolidated supervision). Attention has been focused not only on the ILC exception to the current regulatory framework, but also on the ways in which market demand and technological innovations are changing the financial services landscape (e.g., as nonfinancial firms increasingly find ways to provide financial services to their customers—often in competition with commercial banks).

The Wal-Mart application unleashed a torrent of criticism and dire warnings about how the financial system might be affected by that mixing of banking and commerce. The FDIC and Congress responded to the unprecedented outpouring of comments. The FDIC imposed a moratorium on commercial applications and notices of change in control for ILCs through January 2008 and issued a notice of proposed rulemaking that would expand the FDIC's oversight of certain financial owners of ILCs. The Senate and the House of Representatives each introduced legislation that would limit commercial ownership of ILCs and put them under holding company regulation.

But Wal-Mart did make a difference. The current legislative direction does not seem to have the momentum to eliminate ILCs. In some form, they are here to stay. But, it would further limit the ability of commercial firms to engage in banking activities and expand the role of consolidated supervisors. An unintended consequence of the current push to limit commercial ownership of ILCs, and more generally separate banking and commerce, may be that basic financial services—including substitutes for insured deposits—will increasingly be provided to the consumers (especially the underserved) without the protections of deposit insurance and the safety net. The bifurcation of the financial services industry will likely continue.

Twenty years ago, the then FDIC chairman L. William Seidman argued that to serve the public interest, policymakers should craft a viable and competitive financial services industry that would meet the following objectives: the banking system should be operated in a safe-and-sound manner, customers should realize benefits from enhanced competition, and the system should be flexible enough to respond to technological change. Consistent with these objectives, he argued that the regulatory and supervisory structure should be the simplest and least costly one available.

The question facing policymakers then was—and continues to be—whether these objectives can be met without restricting the ability of banks to choose the corporate structure that best suits their business needs. As Seidman noted, "The pivotal question . . . is: Can a bank be insulated from those who might misuse or abuse it? Is it possible to create a supervisory wall around banks that insulates them and makes them safe and sound, even from their owners, affiliates and subsidiaries"?[91] If so, then the banking and commerce debate should focus on how affiliations should be regulated so that the public interest is met. Policymakers should ensure that regulators are given sufficient powers to regulate the relationship between the bank and its owners rather than prohibit it.[92]

Appendix

The industrial loan company: Structure, powers, and supervision

A review of industrial loan company (ILC) history reveals an industry that has provided banking services to a well-defined niche and has operated in a safe-and-sound manner.[93] In existence since the early 1900s, ILCs typically operated like finance companies, providing consumer loans to industrial workers who could not otherwise access banking services. ILCs currently operate in just seven states.[94] The majority are chartered in Utah and California, and only California, Nevada, and Utah have recently chartered new ILCs.

Today's ILC industry is a product of legislation that was enacted in the 1980s. In 1982, the Garn-St Germain Act expanded ILC eligibility for federal deposit insurance and brought more ILCs under federal regulation. In 1987, the Competitive Equality Banking Act (CEBA) established an exemption for certain ILCs from the definition of "bank" in the Bank Holding Company Act (BHCA). In particular, CEBA exempts any company that controls one or more ILCs from the BHCA generally if the ILC received a charter from one of the limited number of states issuing them and the state required federal deposit insurance at that time. One of three conditions must be met to retain the exemption: (1) control of the ILC may not have been acquired by any company since August 10, 1987, (2) the ILC may not accept demand deposits, or (3) the ILC must maintain total assets of less than $100 million.[95] This exemption was not modified by the Gramm-Leach-Bliley Act (GLBA) and remains intact today.

The ILC charter has been an attractive choice for companies that are not permitted to, or choose not to, become subject to the activity and supervisory regulation of the BHCA. The parent companies of ILCs include a diverse group of financial, and where permitted, commercial firms. And although not required for the ILC per se, some parent companies of ILCs have chosen corporate structures that are supervised on a consolidated basis by the Federal Reserve, the OTS, or the Securities and Exchange Commission (SEC).

As of June 2007, there were 59 ILCs with approximately $225 billion in assets, accounting for less than 1 percent of the nearly 8,615 FDIC-insured insured depository institutions and approximately 1.8 percent of insured depository assets. Of the 59 ILCs, 44 are either widely held or controlled by a parent company whose business is primarily financial in nature. These ILCs hold approximately 85 percent of total ILC assets and 89 percent of total ILC deposits. The remaining ILCs are owned by parent companies that may be considered commercial or nonfinancial. The rapid growth in the industry since 1996, when total assets were $11.5 billion, is accounted for by a small number of ILCs owned by financial services firms.[96] As of March 31, 2007, of seven ILCs with assets in excess of $10 billion, only one was controlled by a nonfinancial owner. (See table 2.1.)

ILC powers are determined by the chartering state and may vary by state and may be different than the powers granted to banks. Originally ILCs engaged primarily in consumer lending. Over time, however, the states have broadened ILCs powers so that ILCs generally have the same powers as state-chartered commercial banks. Today, ILCs are authorized to engage in traditional financial activities that are available to all charter types. They may make all kinds of consumer and commercial loans and may accept federally insured deposits, although some states do not permit ILCs to offer demand deposit accounts. They may be original issuers of Visa or MasterCard credit and debit cards and may fund their operations with Federal Home Loan Bank borrowings. If an ILC is organized as a limited-purpose or credit-card institution, its products and services are limited to those specified by its charter. Funding sources include retail deposits, wholesale deposits, money center operations, and borrowings.[97]

ILCs are subject to regular examination by their state chartering authority and by the FDIC. ILCs are examined for safety and soundness, consumer protection, community reinvestment, information technology, and trust activities. They are subject to FDIC Rules and Regulations (including Part 325, pertaining to capital standards, and Part 364, pertaining to safe-and-sound standards of operation) and are subject to restrictions under the Federal Reserve Act governing transactions with affiliates and tying practices, as well as consumer protection regulations and the

Community Reinvestment Act. ILC management is held accountable for ensuring that all bank operations and business functions are performed in a safe-and-sound manner and in compliance with federal and state banking laws and regulations.

As the primary regulator of ILCs, the FDIC has supervisory powers designed to ensure the safety and soundness of the ILC and, by extension, the deposit insurance fund. The FDIC has the authority to restrict or prohibit an ILC from engaging in activities with an affiliate or any third party that may cause harm to the insured institution. Section 8(b) of the Federal Deposit Insurance Act (FDI Act) gives the FDIC the authority to place limitations on the activities or functions of an insured institution and affiliated parties, including parent and nonbank subsidiaries (when the parent is not a BHC). Section 38 of the FDI Act gives the FDIC authority under certain circumstances to obtain guarantees of capital plans from the ILC's parent company. Under certain circumstances, the FDIC can require divestiture if doing so would improve the ILCs condition and prospects. The FDIC also has the authority to examine both sides of transactions between the ILC and its affiliates and to examine the ILC and any affiliate, including the parent, as may be necessary to determine not only the relationship between the ILC and the affiliate but also the effect of such relationship on the ILC. In addition, the FDIC's back-up authority allows it to examine any affiliate of an insured institution, including that institution's parent company, as may be necessary to determine the relationship between the insured entity and

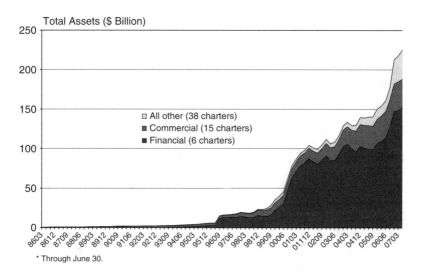

* Through June 30.

Figure 2.1 Assets of 59 current ILCs, 1986–2007*

Table 2.1 Industrial loan companies (institution financial data as of June 30, 2007)

Insured	Institution	Total Assets	Total Deposits	State	Parent
10/31/1988	MERRILL LYNCH BANK USA	60,879.3	51,601.1	UT	Merrill Lynch
5/25/1990	MORGAN STANLEY BANK	27,391.0	19,535.0	UT	Morgan Stanley
8/2/2004	GMAC BANK	23,451.0	10,740.1	UT	Cerberus/GMAC
3/20/1989	AMERICAN EXPRESS CENTURION BANK	23,419.5	2,791.5	UT	American Express
9/15/2003	UBS BANK USA	23,090.8	20,222.2	UT	UBS AG
7/6/2004	GOLDMAN SACHS BANK USA	15,028.0	13,341.9	UT	Goldman Sachs
9/24/1984	FREMONT INVESTMENT & LOAN	10,767.5	9,754.4	CA	Fremont General Corporation
4/1/2003	CAPMARK BANK	6,616.8	4,918.9	UT	Capmark Financial Group / GMAC
9/27/1996	USAA SAVINGS BANK	6,346.3	326.2	NV	USAA Life Company
10/20/2000	CIT BANK	4,065.6	3,078.7	UT	CIT Group
8/24/2005	LEHMAN BRO. COMMERCIAL BANK	3,431.7	2,849.1	UT	Lehman Brothers Holdings Inc.
11/12/1999	BMW BANK OF NORTH AMERICA	2,365.0	1,815.3	UT	BMW Group
2/12/1993	GE CAPITAL FINANCIAL INC	2,217.3	214.6	UT	GE (General Electric)
12/16/1991	ADVANTA BANK CORP	2,011.4	1,408.2	UT	Advanta
8/2/2004	BEAL SAVINGS BANK	1,505.8	62.0	NV	Beal Financial Corporation
10/5/1984	FIRESIDE BANK	1,437.0	1,210.8	CA	Unitrin Inc.
9/22/1997	MERRICK BANK	1,119.0	880.0	UT	CardWorks, LP
6/1/1998	WRIGHT EXPRESS FINL SERVICES	1,108.2	927.2	UT	Wright Express
11/28/2005	SALLIE MAE BANK	807.3	611.9	UT	Sallie Mae
11/3/1989	CENTENNIAL BANK	673.1	524.8	CA	Land America Financial Group
1/16/1998	PITNEY BOWES BANK INC	664.3	532.2	UT	Pitney Bowes
6/4/1984	FINANCE FACTORS LTD	661.7	484.7	HI	Finance Enterprises
7/21/2003	EXANTE BANK	524.8	403.0	UT	UnitedHealth Group
8/29/1991	TAMALPAIS BANK	520.4	369.9	CA	Epic Bancorporation
10/1/1998	TRANSPORTATION ALLIANCE BK	507.0	423.7	UT	Flying J Inc.

11/12/1999	REPUBLIC BANK INC	482.4	428.8	UT	No affiliation
9/10/1985	COMMUNITY COMMERCE BANK	339.9	213.2	CA	TELACU
12/22/2003	MEDALLION BANK	323.1	268.0	UT	Medallion Financial
8/26/1988	SILVERGATE BANK	306.5	184.2	CA	Silvergate Capital
4/3/2000	SECURITY SAVINGS BANK	303.8	192.7	NV	Stampede Capital LLC
1/10/2002	VOLKSWAGEN BANK USA	288.0	239.8	UT	Volkswagen
8/16/2004	TOYOTA FINANCIAL SAVINGS BANK	272.2	68.6	NV	Toyota
1/22/1990	CIRCLE BANK	211.6	139.7	CA	New West Bancshares
7/3/1986	BALBOA THRIFT & LOAN ASSN	184.7	166.8	CA	Hafif Bancorporation
12/1/2003	WORLD FINANCIAL CAPITAL BANK	177.4	108.4	UT	Alliance Data Systems
11/5/1985	5 STAR BANK	160.6	125.3	CO	Armed Forces Benefit Association
6/3/1985	HOME BANK OF CALIFORNIA	159.3	104.1	CA	La Jolla Savers and Mortgage Fund
7/21/1987	FIRST FINANCIAL BANK	152.5	29.2	CO	First Data Corp.
6/28/1989	FIRST SECURITY THRIFT CO	152.5	91.3	CA	First American Corp
6/3/2002	ENERBANK	150.1	127.1	UT	CMS Energy
2/25/1986	GOLDEN SECURITY BANK	138.9	110.4	CA	No affiliation
3/1/2001	CELTIC BANK	119.5	97.9	UT	Celtic Investment Inc.
12/17/1984	FINANCE & THRIFT CO	118.5	94.6	CA	F&T Financial Services Inc.
12/17/1984	RANCHO SANTA FE TH & L ASSN	100.0	69.2	CA	Semperverde Holding Company
8/25/1997	EAGLEMARK SAVINGS BANK	51.6	4.2	NV	Harley-Davidson
9/28/1987	HOME LOAN INDUSTRIAL BANK	48.3	39.1	CO	Home Loan Investment Company
8/1/2005	ALLEGIANCE DIRECT BANK	45.3	37.3	UT	Leavitt Group Enterprises Inc.
11/3/1999	ESCROW BANK USA	33.6	1.0	UT	Capmark Financial Group / GMAC
8/7/1986	MINNESOTA 1ST CREDIT & SVG INC	26.2	19.2	MN	Minnesota Thrift Company
1/26/2006	LCA BANK CORPORATION	24.9	18.7	UT	Lease Corporation of America
5/15/1997	WEBBANK	22.5	13.9	UT	Steel Partners II, LP
5/14/2007	FIFTH STREET BANK	18.7	4.6	NV	Security National Master Holding Company
9/27/2004	TARGET BANK	15.3	6.5	UT	Target Corporation

(Continued)

Table 2.1 (Continued)

Insured	Institution	Total Assets	Total Deposits	State	Parent
10/5/2000	FIRST ELECTRONIC BANK	14.0	8.1	UT	Fry's Electronics
9/22/1997	AMERICAN SAVINGS INC	4.5	2.5	MN	Waseca Bancshares
1/12/2001	TRUST INDUSTRIAL BANK	2.8	0.6	CO	FISERV
New	CAPITALSOURCE BANK			UT	CapitalSource Inc.
New	MARLIN BUSINESS BANK			UT	Marlin Business Services Corp.
New	ARCUS FINANCIAL BANK			UT	WellPoint Inc.
n		225,059.1	152,042.5		

Source: FDIC Call Reports.

the affiliate, and the effect of the relationship on both of them.[98] When the parent is subject to the reporting requirements of another regulatory body (e.g., the SEC or a state insurance commissioner), the FDIC has agreements in place to share information with that regulator.

The FDIC has statutory authority to grant or deny federal deposit insurance to depository institutions, including ILCs. In making this decision, the FDIC must evaluate seven statutory factors: the financial history and condition of the institution, the adequacy of the institution's capital structure, the future earnings prospects of the institution, the general character and fitness of the management of the institution, the risk presented by the institution to the deposit insurance fund, the convenience and needs of the community to be served by the institution, and the consistency of the institution's corporate powers with the purpose of the FDI Act. In addition, the FDIC must evaluate the application to determine compliance with any applicable requirements of the Community Reinvestment Act, the National Environmental Protection Act, and the National Historic Preservation Act.

The FDIC also has the authority to impose reasonable conditions through its order approving the application. Specific conditions are based upon the FDIC's assessment of the application and may consider issues such as the complexity and perceived risk of the proposed business plan, the adequacy of capital and management, relationships with affiliated entities, and the sufficiency of risk-management programs. Conditions may be time-specific or may impose continuing requirements or restrictions that must be satisfied on an ongoing basis. Conditions that impose ongoing requirements remain in effect as long as the FDIC determines that the condition is necessary to ensure the safe-and-sound operation of the institution. The FDIC can also require written agreements with the institution and its parent that address capital maintenance, liquidity, and other matters as appropriate.[99]

Notes

*The author is a senior financial economist in the Division of Insurance and Research at the FDIC. An earlier version of this chapter was presented at the Western Economic Association International (WEA) meeting in Seattle, WA, June 30, 2007. The author thanks Missy Craig, Rose Kushmeider, Arthur Murton, Jack Reidhill, Bernard Shull, Ken Spong, Larry White, and WEA session participants for their comments. The views expressed in this chapter are solely those of the author and not necessarily those of the FDIC.

1. The exemption in CEBA and characteristics of the ILC industry are discussed in the appendix.

2. This chapter draws extensively on Blair (2004a).
3. In 1980, the Depository Institutions Deregulation and Monetary Control Act phased out interest-rate ceilings on time and savings deposits, although a prohibition on paying interest on demand deposits remained. Restrictions on interstate and intrastate banking were phased out by the states in the latter half of the 1980s. Federal law followed with the Riegle-Neal Interstate Banking and Branching Efficiency Act of 1994, which phased in interstate banking and branching. Restrictions on affiliations among banks, securities and insurance firms were lifted by the Gramm-Leach-Bliley Financial Modernization Act of 1999.
4. *American Banker* (2007a).
5. *Wall Street Journal* (2007).
6. *Financial Times* (2007a,b). The MoneyCard joins Wal-Mart's branded credit card, which is issued by the Discovery network and offers discounts on gasoline purchases at Wal-Mart and Sam's Club, and its money transfer service offered through MoneyGram.
7. PayPal Corporate Web Site (2007).
8. *Dow Jones Newswires* (2007a).
9. The development of this technology by Suvidha Starnet, India, was discussed by Charles Calomiris at the Federal Reserve Bank of Chicago Conference on Bank Structure and Competition, May 17, 2007. He noted that this technology could easily be utilized by retailers using an internal network of accounts, debit cards, and phones. The benefits to consumers could be delivered without regulatory reforms.
10. *The New York Times* (2007) and *The Birmingham News* (2007). Citibank and Bank of America each have a large remittance business.
11. The Office of Thrift Supervision (OTS) is the consolidated supervisor for many financial companies that own ILCs, including Merrill Lynch, American Express, and UBS. OTS-supervised holding companies controlled about 65 percent of ILC assets (approximately $115 billion) as of December 31, 2006.
12. See FDIC (2006a).
13. In April 2003, the U.S. House of Representatives passed both H.R. 758 and H.R. 1375. The former was the proposed Business Checking Freedom Act, which would allow banks to pay interest on business demand deposits and would permit ILCs to offer their corporate customers interest-bearing negotiable order of withdrawal (NOW) accounts. The latter was the Financial Services Regulatory Relief Act of 2003, which would remove the remaining regulatory barriers to interstate de novo banking: banks and ILCs would be allowed to use start-up branches to cross state lines. In March 2004, the House amended H.R. 1375 to restrict the ability of certain ILCs to branch interstate: only ILCs that had been established before October 1, 2003 and were owned by companies such that no more than 15 percent of income is derived from nonfinancial sources would be permitted to branch interstate. The amendment effectively would have prevented commercial firms such as Wal-Mart from using the ILC charter to develop a branch banking business. Neither bill was addressed by the Senate.

14. See Blair (2004a) for a discussion of the factors underlying banking and commerce debate at that time.

15. FDIC Office of Inspector General (2004).

16. Ibid., 3. The OIG also concluded that the FDIC had established controls to help mitigate any risks posed by the mixing of banking and commerce in the ILC charter. Also in 2004, the FDIC adopted modifications to improve its ILC supervisory program. See West (2004).

17. GAO (2005). The report cites the rapid growth in ILC assets and noted that three of six new ILCs approved in 2004 were chartered by commercial firms.

18. GAO (2005), 24.

19. Responding to the GAO report's findings, the FDIC emphasized that its legal authorities allowed it to insulate the insured depository from risks posed by the parent or other affiliates. The FDIC cautioned that a consolidated supervisory approach could endanger legal-entity distinctions and raised the possibility of extending the federal safety net beyond the insured depository. GAO (2005), 92–7. These points are further discussed in a later section of this paper.

20. See FDIC (2006a).

21. The FDIC press release on the public hearings includes the final agenda and list of presenters. See, http://www.fdic.gov/news/news/press/2006/pr06038.html

22. *Dow Jones Newswires* (2007b). Wal-Mart observed that their ILC business strategy had become less attractive because the processing fees they were being charged by banks had been lowered. That is, the proposed Wal-Mart Bank had affected the competitiveness of the market. See, *American Banker* (2007c).

23. *American Banker* (2007b).

24. On July 12, 2006, the FDIC testified before the U.S. House of Representatives Committee on Financial Services on ILC charter, ownership and supervision issues (see FDIC [2006a]). The moratorium was imposed on July 28, 2006 (see FDIC [2006b]).

25. See FDIC (2006b), 43483. The FDIC was to consider changes in its oversight with the purpose of protecting the deposit insurance fund or "important Congressional objectives." Throughout the moratorium period, the FDIC studied these issues although a formal report was not prepared.

26. The notice and request for comment was published on August 23, 2006. See FDIC (2006c).

27. Of the over 12,600 comment letters received by the FDIC, 12,485 comments were generated by what appears to be organized campaigns either supporting or opposing the proposed Wal-Mart Bank or the acquisition of EnerBank by The Home Depot. The remaining comments were sent by individuals, law firms, community banks, financial services trade associations, existing and proposed ILCs or their parent companies, the Conference of State Bank Supervisors and two members of Congress. See FDIC (2006c), 5219.

28. See FDIC (2007b).

29. See FDIC (2007a). Financial firms not subject to consolidated supervision that currently own an ILC are grandfathered under the proposed rules. The proposed regulation does not apply to commercial owners of ILC, which remain the subject of the moratorium.

30. FDIC (2007d).
31. See H.R. 698, Section 2(b).
32. In general, the restrictions would not apply with respect to any ILC which became insured before October 1, 2003, if there has been no change in control after September 30, 2003. The restrictions would apply to commercial firms that became Industrial Bank Holding Companies by acquiring an ILC on or after October 1, 2003, and before January 29, 2007, and meet certain other conditions. See, H.R. 698 Section 2(b).
33. The FDIC's Chairman testified at the hearings. See FDIC (2007c).
34. See, S. 1356 Section 2(b).
35. S. 1356 was referred to the Senate Committee on Banking, Housing, and Urban Affairs in May 2007. As of June 2008, the Senate has not taken final action on the pending bills.
36. Utah Association of Financial Services (2006). Senator Garn's statement was presented on behalf on the Utah Association of Financial Services. Responding to questions from the panel, he noted that in crafting CEBA, the interest of large retailers in the ILC charter may not have been anticipated.
37. See Blair (1994). The policy derived from the view that banks were often not simply private firms, but served as instruments of public policy. The original underlying concern was that the affiliation between banks and government often found in early bank charters would provide competitive advantages over commercial firms that were on their own. The affiliation implied support—a safety net—as well as supervision and regulation. (Comments received from Bernard Shull at the Western Economic Association International Meetings, Seattle, WA, June 30, 2007.)
38. There is an extensive literature that discusses the extent to which banking and commerce have mixed or have remained separate throughout U.S. banking history. For example, see Golembe (1997) for an overview of the policy issues. See also Blair (1994, 2004a), FDIC (1987a), Halpert (1988), Hammond (1936, 1957), Haubrich and Santos (2003), Huertas (1988), Shull (1999), and Symons (1983).
39. See Huertas (1988), 744–45.
40. For example, certain charter types—including limited-purpose consumer banks and ILCs—permit a mixing of banking and commerce. Grandfathering provisions in CEBA and the Gramm-Leach-Bliley Act have allowed certain commercially owned insured institutions to continue operating, including some nonbank banks and unitary thrifts. Moreover, banks exercise control over commercial firms, and commercial firms over banks, in a variety of ways. See Haubrich and Santos (2003) for a discussion of the alternative ways in which banking and commerce have intersected throughout U. S. history.
41. Sections 16, 20, 21, and 22 of the Banking Act of 1933 are referred to as the Glass-Steagall Act. See Benston (1990) for an analysis of the act.
42. The Bank Holding Company Act (BHCA) of 1956 separated banking from commerce by restricting the activities of owners and affiliates of banks. It defined the bank holding company (BHC) and established the framework for its regulation by the Federal Reserve. A BHC was defined as a corporation

owning at least 25 percent interest in two or more commercial banks. Commercial firms were able to own a single commercial bank until the BHCA was amended in 1970 and its restrictions were extended to one-bank holding companies. The 1970 amendments also redefined a bank for the purposes of the BHCA to be an entity that made commercial loans and accepted demand deposits. Banks that only performed one of these functions became known as nonbank banks and could be owned by commercial firms. In 1987, CEBA again redefined the term "bank" to include all insured banks, closing the so-called nonbank bank loophole. ILCs, credit-card banks, trust banks and grandfathered nonbank banks remained exempt from the BHCA restrictions.

43. The potential risks and benefits from mixing banking and commerce are discussed in Blair (2004a), 102–07. See also, Halpert (1988), Saunders (1994), Shull and White (1998) and Walter (2003).

44. Wallison (2000, 2003) elaborates on this point.

45. See Board (2007). The ILC exemption is claimed to promote competitive and regulatory imbalances in the banking system.

46. See Blair (2004a), 102–4. Conflicts of interest are also discussed in FDIC (1987a), Halpert (1988), and Walter (2003).

47. Halpert (1988), 505, notes that Americans have had a longstanding fear and distrust of banks—particularly large money center banks. "Like the owners of large railroads and armaments manufacturers, bankers have been suspected of pursuing clandestine, antisocial ends and, despite their relatively small numbers, of having wielded enormous political influence." These suspicions have likely contributed to arguments for separating banking and commerce.

48. See FDIC (2003), 60–73, for the viewpoint of community bankers.

49. Such comparisons, however, may be misleading, for the close ties among the government, commercial firms, and banks found in the Japanese *keiretsu* (and between European universal banks and commercial firms) are unlikely to be replicated in the United States. For example, corporations are not dependent on banks for funding (capital markets are an important funding source) and U.S. banking law prohibits banks and commercial firms from being both creditors and shareholders. As an example, if Citigroup were acquired by General Electric (or vice versa), the bank subsidiary (or affiliate) would continue to be prohibited from owning stock in the other.

50. U.S. Department of the Treasury (1991), 57, noted that the allocation of credit and the concentration of economic power were best addressed by means other than prohibiting the mixing of banking and commerce.

51. To the extent that there are few barriers to entry in that market, the argument that a large commercial or banking competitor would be able to exert monopoly power is weakened. Saunders (1994), 239, notes that "there is no reason to expect, a priori, that the competitive behavior of the banking industry would be eroded by eliminating the commerce-banking separation. Indeed, it may be that such a policy could have a pro-competitive effect, as the number of potential entrants and potential competitors expands."

52. Wallison (2000, 2003) argues that the GLBA, in effect, says that none of the reasons advanced against commercial ownership of banks are valid.

53. Transactions with affiliates—commercial or otherwise—need not pose safety-net concerns. For example, up streaming dividends to the bank's parent organization would be acceptable, provided the dividends were reasonably related to the bank's existing capital and earnings potential. However, when transactions benefit a related party and are detrimental to the viability of the insured bank, the safety net can be threatened. See FDIC (1987a), 87.

54. Reasons for doing so include protecting the reputation of the parent company or allowing the parent to take advantage of limited liability. Incentives to do so can exist when the creditors of the bank or the ILC do not impose discipline. If the bank's creditors are aware of the potential for loss shifts, they should demand higher interest rates when they perceive a higher risk of such shifts. However, if deposit insurance creates moral hazard—as can occur when deposit insurance is mispriced—it is less likely that the creditors of the bank will impose discipline by demanding higher interest rates and more likely that losses will be shifted to the bank than to a nonbank affiliate. See Blair (2004a) and Walter (2003) for a discussion of these safety net concerns. For a discussion of moral hazard as it applies to deposit insurance, see Hanc (1999), 3ff.

55. Conversely, the parent could engage in activities that benefited the bank at the expense of its affiliates. It is argued generally that this conflict is of less concern because fewer safety-and-soundness issues surround most nonbanking firms. When the bank is allowed to affiliate with other businesses or to own nonbank subsidiaries, that affiliate or subsidiary can be sold to generate a source of added capital for the bank. See, for example, FDIC (1987a), chap. 5, "Conflicts of Interest." See Jones and Kolatch (1999) for a discussion of the relative benefits of the bank subsidiary model.

56. See FDIC (1987a), 65–69.

57. FDIC (2006a) discusses the applications process in the context of ILCs. Also see Sections 6 and 7 of the Federal Deposit Insurance Act.

58. The enforcement of capital standards, the monitoring of loan quality and the capability of management to run the bank, reporting requirements and disclosure standards, and the use of enforcement tools such as cease-and-desist orders and civil-money penalties, are among the supervisory tools that are used by the FDIC to protect the insured entity from excessive risk.

59. Firewalls are constructed to allow some synergies to be realized. Although impenetrable firewalls can be constructed, they may not be desirable. For example, as enacted in 1956, Section 6 of the BHCA achieved the complete isolation of banks within a holding company by effectively prohibiting transactions between affiliated banks. The 1966 amendments to the BHCA repealed the prohibition. See Shull and White (1998), 15.

60. See, Blair (2004a), 109–10.

61. Unlike the "closely related to" standard of the BHCA, newly defined permissible activities under GLB must be "financial in nature or incidental to," and they do not need to meet a net-public-benefits test. Once defined as permissible, an activity is open to FHCs and financial subsidiaries with only a post-entry notification to the Federal Reserve required. As a result, subsequent competitive evaluations are not possible. See Shull (2002).

62. The final factor is whether the activity is necessary or appropriate to allow a FHC and its affiliates to: compete effectively with any company seeking to provide financial services in the United States; efficiently deliver information and services that are financial in nature through the use of technological means, including any application necessary to protect the security or efficacy of systems for the transmission of data or financial transactions; and offer customers any available or emerging technological means for using financial services or for the document imaging of data. (GLBA Title 1, Section 103.) See Shull (2002), 42.

63. The Federal Reserve is directed to ensure that complementary activities do not pose a substantial risk to the safety and soundness of the insured institution or to the financial system. As an example of a complementary activity, the Federal Reserve has approved physical commodity trading activities as complementary to engaging as principal in commodity derivative activities. See, Board (2003).

64. The Savings and Loan Holding Company Act of 1967 limited ownership by a diversified holding company to one thrift institution—thus creating the unitary thrift holding company. The Act also authorizes the OTS to examine and supervise the companies that own, directly or indirectly, savings associations. The scope of this authority includes the savings association, its holding company and other affiliates, and subsidiaries of the savings association. See Blair (2004a), 112. Also see: http://www.ots.treas.gov/docs/4/480208.html

65. Existing thrift holding companies that (a) owned a single savings and loan or other thrift institution, (b) were in existence before May 4, 1999, and (c) continued to meet the qualified-thrift-lender test were grandfathered. However, they may not engage in any new commercial activities or transfer their right to mix banking and commerce. See Blair (2004a), 111.

66. Thrifts that were part of diversified holding companies have tended to outperform other thrifts because of the greater diversification of their revenue streams, loan and asset portfolios, and funding sources. They were not significant sources of losses during the savings and loan crisis of the 1980s. See Blair (2004a), 111–12, Shull and White (1998).

67. Shull (2002) discusses the dynamics of permissible activity expansion, generally, and the lengthy regulatory process by which the Federal Reserve has considered whether real estate brokerage should become a permissible activity.

68. Meyer (2001), 6.

69. See, for example, Wallison (2000, 2003). Shull (2002) also expresses concern about whether a separation of banking and commerce can be maintained.

70. Absent the requirements of consolidated supervision, these firms may have greater flexibility to adapt to a rapidly changing financial environment and to best meet the needs of their customers. See, FDIC (2003), 41–49.

71. Shull (2002), 53.

72. Blair (2004a), 109–14, discusses these differences.

73. A bank-centric supervisory approach is used by the FDIC, the Federal Reserve, the Office of the Comptroller of the Currency (OCC) and the OTS in their supervision of state-chartered nonmember banks, state-chartered member banks, national banks and thrift institutions, respectively. The Federal Reserve

also employs a bank-centric approach in its supervision of branches of foreign banks operating in the United States.

74. Consolidated supervision of the banking organization is performed by the Federal Reserve for BHCs and FHCs and by the OTS for thrift holding companies. The Federal Reserve also serves as the umbrella supervisor of FHCs. As the umbrella regulator of FHCs, the Federal Reserve must rely on examination of functionally regulated subsidiaries conducted by the functional regulator of the subsidiary, and must make certain findings before conducting an independent examination of such a subsidiary. However, there appears to be little difference in practice between consolidated supervision and umbrella supervision. See Kushmeider (2006), 17.

75. Cases exist in which limited-liability law has been shown to be less than perfect. In particular, the courts have occasionally disregarded limited liability—or pierced the corporate veil—when a corporation has been shown to have engaged in conduct such that creditors were led to understand that the shareholder was the true debtor. Certain safeguards can be applied to ensure that the bank and its affiliates are viewed as separate; they include separate management and record keeping for the bank and any affiliates, and boards of directors that are not identical. See, for example, Walter (1996), and FDIC (1998).

76. See FDIC Office of Inspector General (2004) and GAO (2005). The FDIC lacks explicit authority to set capital requirements for the parent company, to set limits on or prohibit activities that may be conducted in the parent company's nonbank subsidiaries, and to require the divestiture of affiliates that are deemed to pose a safety-and-soundness risk to the insured depository institution. For a comparison of powers available to bank regulators versus holding company regulators see West (2004).

77. GAO (2005), 92. The FDIC noted that "[t]he core of each banking agency's statutory mandate for supervision is preserving the safety and soundness of insured depository institutions. With respect to the ability to achieve this goal, the FDIC's authorities, supported by case law, are functionally equivalent to those of consolidated supervisors."

78. GAO (2007), 34.

79. See Blair (2004a), 111–12 and Douglas (2006).

80. Douglas (2006) notes that the failures of Pacific Thrift and Loan and Southern Pacific Bank cost the FDIC roughly $100 million and were caused by poor risk diversification, imprudent lending and poor controls, and not by self dealing, conflicts of interest or improper actions on the part of their owners. By contrast, the failures of banks in BHC structures have cost the FDIC much more.

81. See Blair (2004a), 114, Douglas (2006), and West (2004). ILCs that failed between 1986 and 1996 operated as finance companies and had assets of less than $60 million. They were primarily located in California, were not commercially owned and were not part of holding companies.

82. For example, the FDIC noted that " . . . financial companies that are not subject to consolidated federal supervision that own [ILCs] may not provide the same level of transparency or the same opportunity for supervisors to deal with the risks." See, FDIC (2007a), 5222.

83. Edwards (1996), 161, deemed consolidated supervision "a vote of no confidence in firewalls." Requiring the parent company to serve as a source of strength for its insured depository subsidiaries also may make it more difficult to maintain corporate separateness. See Blair (2004a), 111 ftnt 74, and Bradley and Jones (2006). By making investments in bank equities less attractive, the policy could have the effect of raising the organization's cost of capital. And because the policy is directed primarily at the corporate owners of banks, it would lead to the differential treatment of individual owners, for presumably they would not be held to the standard.

84. See Comments from the FDIC. GAO (2005), 93.

85. Board (1997). In further testimony on financial modernization in 1999, Chairman Greenspan noted the following. "It seems wise to move first toward the integration of banking, insurance, and securities, and employ the lessons we learn from that important step before we consider whether and under what conditions it would be desirable to move to the second stage of full integration of commerce and banking." See Board (1999).

86. FDIC (2007a), 5222. When resolved, the problems emanating from the subprime crisis and turmoil in the financial markets may provide some evidence on these questions.

87. The ILC parent would be limited a small basket of commercial activities and ILC-commercial affiliations in existence before 2003 would be grandfathered.

88. Over the years, different regulatory approaches have been advocated. For example, Litan (1987) proposed the narrow bank as an approach to financial modernization. It would allow banking organizations to diversify their product and service offerings through holding companies. The insured depositories would be restricted to investing insured deposits in safe-and-liquid securities and lending would be funded through the uninsured securities markets. In 1991, the U.S. Department of the Treasury published an interagency study that made recommendations for modernizing the financial system (see U.S. Department of the Treasury [1991], 54–61). The study recognized the benefits of lowering the barriers between banking and commerce, but it did not recommend lowering them evenly. Affiliations between banking and commercial firms were recommended partly as a way to infuse capital into a then-weak banking system. The study recommended that commercial firms be allowed to own banks indirectly through a financial services holding company, although banks and bank holding companies were not to be permitted to acquire commercial firms as subsidiaries or hold equity claims on commercial firms on their balance sheets. Banks and financial firms would have been able to affiliate with each other.

89. Muckenfuss and Eager (2007), 3, refer to this as a bifurcated financial services industry—or two worlds of finance. There is the GLBA-regulated world on the one hand and "the rest of the world" where financial services are provided without similar limitations on affiliation or consolidated oversight.

90. These include commercial companies and securities and insurance firms that may own or control an ILC, thrift, trust or credit-card bank. Examples include GE, GM, Toyota, Target, Nordstrom, BMW, Merrill Lynch, Morgan Stanley, and American Express.

91. See FDIC (1987b), 3.
92. Also see the remarks by L. William Seidman at the 2003 FDIC Symposium on Commercial Affiliations. FDIC (2003), 139–47.
93. For information on ILCs see: Blair (2004a), FDIC (2006a), and West (2004). The FDIC's experience as supervisor of ILCs and state-nonmember banks is comparable in terms of examination experience and managing problem institutions. FDIC (2006a). The GAO noted in its 2005 report on ILCs that " . . . from an operational standpoint, ILCs do not appear to have a greater risk of failure than other types of insured depository institutions." GAO (2005), 24.
94. Until the 1940s ILCs once operated in most states. Today ILC operate in California, Colorado, Hawaii, Indiana, Minnesota, Nevada and Utah.
95. Bank Holding Company Act section 2(c)(2)(H), 12 U.S.C. 1841(c)(2)(H).
96. See FDIC (2007c). In 1996, American Express moved its credit card operations from its Delaware credit card bank to its Utah ILC. Also in that year, a number of financial services firms began using their ILCs in conjunction with sweep deposit programs in their brokerage businesses. The effect was a substantial increase in total ILC assets.
97. See FDIC (2007a), ftnt 32, 5221.
98. [12 U.S.C. §1820(b)(4)].
99. For information on the FDIC's authorities for processing deposit insurance applications see the Federal Deposit Insurance (FDI) Act , Section 6 [12 U.S.C. 1816] sections 303.20–25 (Deposit Insurance) of the FDIC Rules and Regulations, and the FDIC Statement of Policy on Applications for Deposit Insurance. The processing of a notice for a change in control is performed in accordance with Section 7 of the FDI Act and sections 303.80–86 (Change in Bank Control) of the FDIC Rules and Regulations.

References

American Banker. 2007a. Kroeger in financial services: How its approach is evolving? February 16.

———. 2007b. 7 More states take up ILC branch debate, March 7.

———. 2007c. Post-ILC, Wal-Mart discusses strategy, March 19.

Benston, George. 1990. *The separation of commercial and investment banking: The Glass-Steagall Act revisited and reconsidered.* New York and Oxford: Oxford University Press.

Blair, Christine. 1994. Bank powers and the separation of banking and commerce: An historical perspective. *FDIC Banking Review* 7: 28–38.

———. 2004a. The mixing of banking and commerce: Current policy issues. *FDIC Banking Review* 16: 97–120.

———. 2004b. The separation of banking and commerce: Evidence versus myth. Unpublished manuscript, FDIC.

Board of Governors of the Federal Reserve System (Board). 1997. Testimony of Chairman Alan Greenspan on supervision of banking organizations before the Subcommittee on Capital Markets, Securities, and Government Sponsored

Enterprises of the Committee on Banking and Financial Services, U.S. House of Representatives. 105th Congress, 1st Session.

———. 1999. Testimony of Chairman Alan Greenspan on the need for financial modernization before the Committee on Banking, Housing, and Urban Affairs, U.S. Senate. 106th Congress, 1st Session.

———. 2003. Press release, http://www.federalreserve.gov/boarddocs/press/orders/2003/20031002/default.htm

———. 2007. Testimony of Governor Donald L. Kohn on industrial loan companies before the Committee on Financial Services, U.S. House of Representatives. 110th Congress, 1st Session. http://www.federalreserve.gov/boarddocs/testimony/2007/20070425/default.htm

Bradley, Christine, and Kenneth Jones. 2007. Protecting the deposit insurance fund: An assessment of the source of strength policy and the cross-guarantee authority. Unpublished manuscript, FDIC.

Cell-phone banking coming to Wachovia, 2007, *Birmingham News*, November 14.

Corrigan, E. Gerald. 1987. *Financial Market Structure: A Longer View* (Federal Reserve Bank of New York).

Douglas, John. 2006. Testimony on behalf of the American financial services association on ILCs—A review of charter, ownership and supervision issues before the U.S. House Committee on Financial Services, Subcommittee on Financial Institutions and Consumer Credit. 109th Congress, 2nd Session.

Dow Jones Newswires. 2007a. eBay has mulled ILC charter for PayPal division, February 21.

———. 2007b. Wal-Mart CEO doesn't rule out seeking ILC bank charter, March 27.

Edwards, Franklin. 1996. *The new finance: Regulation and financial stability*. Washington D.C.: AEI Press.

FDIC Office of Inspector General. 2004. The division of supervision and consumer protection's approach for supervising limited-charter depository institutions, Evaluation Report No. 04–48.

Federal Deposit Insurance Corporation. 1987a. *Mandate for Change: Restructuring the Banking Industry*. Washington D.C.: FDIC.

———. 1987b. Testimony of L. William Seidman, FDIC chairman, on financial services reform legislation before the U.S. Senate Committee on Banking, Housing, and Urban Affairs. 100th Congress, 1st Session.

———. 1998. Testimony of Donna Tanoue, FDIC chairman, on financial modernization, before the U.S. Senate Committee on Banking, Housing, and Urban Affairs. 105th Congress, 2nd Session. http://www.fdic.gov/news/news/speeches/archives/1998/sp25june98.html

———. 2003. Symposium on the future of banking: the structure and role of commercial affiliations. http://www.fdic.gov/news/conferences/future_transcript.html#Seidman

———. 2006a. Testimony of Douglas H. Jones, FDIC acting general counsel, on industrial loan companies: A review of charter, ownership, and supervision issues before the U.S. House Committee on Financial Services, Subcommittee on Financial Institutions and Consumer Credit, 109th Congress, 2nd Session.

———. 2006b. Notice on the imposition of a moratorium on certain industrial loan company applications and notices. *Federal Register* 71: 43482–84.

———. 2006c. Notice and request for comment on industrial loan companies and industrial loan banks. *Federal Register* 71: 49456–59.

———. 2007a. Notice of proposed rulemaking on industrial banks subsidiaries of financial companies. *Federal Register* 72: 5217–28.

———. 2007b. Notice of the limited extension of a moratorium on certain industrial loan company applications and notices. *Federal Register* 72: 5290–94.

———. 2007c. Testimony of Sheila C. Bair, FDIC chairman, on industrial loan companies: a review of charter, ownership, and supervision issues before the U.S. House Committee on Financial Services. 110th Congress, 1st Session.

———. 2007d. Remarks by Sheila C. Bair, FDIC chairman, at the Federal Reserve Bank of Chicago's 43rd annual conference on bank structure and competition. http://www.fdic.gov/news/news/speeches/chairman/spmay1707.html

Financial Times. 2007a. Retailer's alternative to small change, June 6.

———. 2007b. Wal-Mart in prepaid card move, June 6.

Golembe, Carter. 1997. Separation of banking and commerce: A myth that's ripe for debate. *Banking Policy Report* 16: 12–17.

Government Accountability Office. 2005. Industrial loan corporations: Recent asset growth and commercial interest highlight differences in regulatory authority, GAO-05–521.

———. 2007. Financial market regulation: Agencies engaged in consolidated supervision can strengthen performance measurement and collaboration, GAO-07–154.

Halpert, Stephen. 1988. The separation of banking and commerce reconsidered. *Journal of Corporation Law* 13: 481–533.

Hammond, Bray. 1936. Free banks and corporations: The New York Free Banking Act of 1838. *Journal of Political Economy* 44: 184–209.

———. 1957. *Banks and Politics in America from the Revolution to the Civil War.* Princeton, NJ: Princeton University Press.

Hanc, George. 1999. Deposit insurance reform: State of the debate. *FDIC Banking Review* 12: 1–26.

Haubrich, Joseph, and João Santos. 2003 Alternative forms of mixing banking and commerce: Evidence from American history. *Financial Markets, Institutions & Instruments* 12: 121–59.

Huertas, Thomas. 1988. Can banking and commerce mix? *Cato Journal* 7: 743–62.

Jones, Kenneth, and Barry Kolatch. 1999. The federal safety net, banking subsidiaries, and implications for financial modernization, *FDIC Banking Review* 12: 1–17.

Kushmeider, Rose. 2006. Restructuring U.S. federal financial regulation, Unpublished manuscript, FDIC.

Litan, Robert. 1987. *What should banks do?* Washington D.C.: The Brookings Institution.

Meyer, Laurence. 2001. Remarks by Governor Laurence H. Meyer before the American Law Institute and American Bar Association. http://www.federalreserve.gov/boarddocs/speeches/2001/20010215/default.htm

Muckenfuss III, Cantwell, and Robert Eager. 2007. The ILC debate and the separation of banking and commerce: A work still in progress, Gibson, Dunn & Crutcher, LLP.

The New York Times. 2007. Cellphone banking is coming of age, May 24.

Office of the Comptroller of the Currency. 2007. *Comptroller's licensing manual.* Washington D.C.: Office of the Comptroller of the Currency.

PayPal Corporate Web Site. 2007. PayPal expands European growth with bank charter and new European headquarters. http://www.shareholder.com/paypal/releaseDetail.cfm?ReleaseID=243295&Category=US.

Saunders, Anthony. 1994. Banking and commerce: An overview of the public policy issues. *Journal of Banking and Finance* 18: 231–54.

Shull, Bernard. 1999. The separation of banking and commerce: An examination of the principal issues, E&PA working paper WP99–1, Office of the Comptroller of the Currency.

———. 2002. Banking, commerce, and competition under the Gramm-Leach-Bliley Act. *Antitrust Bulletin* 47: 25–61.

——— and Lawrence White. 1998. Of firewalls and subsidiaries: The right stuff for expanded bank activities. Working paper, CLB-98–017, Center For Law And Business, New York University.

Symons Jr., Edward. 1983. The "business of banking" in historical perspective. *The George Washington Law Review* 51: 676–726.

USA Today 2007 Wal-Mart to offer payment cards; Prepaid Visa-branded cards to target customers who don't have bank accounts, June 7.

U. S. Department of the Treasury. 1991. *Modernizing the financial system: Recommendations for safer, more competitive banks.* Washington D.C.: U.S. Department of the Treasury.

Utah Association of Financial Services. 2006. Statement at the FDIC's public hearing regarding the federal deposit insurance application of the proposed Wal-Mart bank presented by Edwin J. "Jake" Garn, Mimeo.

Wallison, Peter. 2000. The Gramm-Leach-Bliley act eliminated the separation of banking and commerce: How this will effect the future of the safety net, presentation at the Federal Reserve Bank of Chicago's *Annual conference on bank structure and competition*, Mimeo.

———. 2003. The Gramm-Leach-Bliley Act eliminated the rational for the separation of banking and commerce. Comments at the FDIC's symposium *The future of banking: the structure and role of commercial affiliations*, July 16, in Washington D.C. http://www.aei.org/news/newsID.17994,filter./news_detail.asp

Wall Street Journal. 2007. Wal-Mart pushes financial-services menu, June 6.

Walter, John. 1996, Firewalls, Federal Reserve Bank of Richmond. *Economic Quarterly* 82: 15–39.

———. 2003. Banking and commerce: Tear down this wall? Federal Reserve Bank of Richmond. *Economic Quarterly* 89: 7–31.

West, Mindy. 2004. The FDIC's supervision of industrial loan companies: A historical perspective. *FDIC Supervisory Insights* 1: 5–13.

3

Managing Financial Failure in an Evolving Economic and Financial Environment

Eva H. G. Hüpkes[*]

Introduction

Increased international linkages within and across institutions may make crises more broad-ranging and complicated to deal with. This underscores the importance of policymakers continuing to ensure that national legal, regulatory, and supervisory arrangements evolve to cope with the increasingly globalized nature of institutions. The emergence of large and complex financial institutions (LCFIs) poses significant challenges for managing and resolving financial failures. The complexity of these institutions makes effective supervisory oversight harder. The vulnerability of the financial system to the complexity that they entail is illustrated by the unfolding of the subprime crisis. Weaknesses associated with the manner in which the "originate to distribute" model has been implemented gave rise to serious disruptions. To engage in off-balance sheet maturity transformation, a number of financial institutions sponsored the establishment of separate legal entities ("conduits" and structured investment vehicles or SIVs). These entities funded purchases of asset backed securities (ABS) and corporate bonds by issuing shorter-term commercial paper and medium-term notes (MTN). When liquidity dried up in the markets in which the entities funded themselves, the sponsoring institutions did not abandon them. Instead they provided funding even though the conduits are separate legal entities and could have been allowed to fail. Corporate form failed to follow corporate function.

The Nature and Objectives of Insolvency Procedures

A key component of a dynamic market

Insolvency procedures[2] are designed to deal with circumstances in which a shortfall of financial resources prevents an economic agent from meeting all of its financial obligations on time and in full. If a legal entity's assets are insufficient to pay all its creditors and a *concursus creditorum* occurs (i.e., there are competing creditors), measures need to be adopted to resolve the multiple creditors' claims in an equitable and predictable manner. Properly designed insolvency procedures provide a kind of Darwinian mechanism to ensure that weak firms are culled and newer, more dynamic ones can emerge. This triage is essential for the effective operation of a dynamic market economy. However, it must be applied in an evenhanded manner to all companies, large and small, financial and nonfinancial. Otherwise, there is a risk of distortions to competition.[3]

A good insolvency procedure provides efficient and welfare-maximizing outcomes both across actors and over time.[4] The predictability of the insolvency process[5] shapes the behaviour of contracting parties ex ante. The prospect of recovery in bad times and certainty about the ranking of economic agents' claims increases their willingness to enter into contracts. Ex post, an efficient insolvency procedure will permit the orderly, predictable, and rapid reallocation of economic resources in a manner that fosters growth and increases welfare.

Insolvency procedures serve a broad array of functions. These include

- maintaining strong incentives to meet contractual obligations,
- providing an effective and predictable means to regularize situations in which economic agents cannot meet their contractual obligations because they lack the financial means,
- treating different similarly situated creditors (domestic and foreign) in an equitable manner (pari passu principle),
- preventing intercreditor competition from reducing the value of the defunct firm ("increase the size of the pie"),
- channeling resources from less productive to more productive uses,
- preventing adverse social consequences resulting from financial failure ("permit insolvent agents to meet basic needs and retain the implements of their trade"), and
- maintaining the positive externalities associated with the operation of the insolvent firm.

There are tensions and trade-offs among these different objectives. The weight given to specific objectives varies over time and across countries.

In centuries gone by, the emphasis was on ensuring contract performance. The literature of earlier periods—whether it be Shakespeare's description of an attempt to enforce a collateral agreement in the *Merchant of Venice* ("a pound of flesh") or Dickens's account of the squalid and forlorn conditions in the debtors' prison in which his father spent several years of his life—illustrates the importance accorded to this particular feature. The emergence of the limited liability company and provisions that permit a bankrupt individual to retain his home and the tools of his trade were reactions to this.

In modern times the emphasis has been on increasing the size of the pie and preserving positive externalities. This has been done by addressing the collective action problem.[6] If there is no mechanism to restrain an individual creditor from exercising his contractual rights and no mechanism to ensure the equitable distribution of the proceeds of legal action by an individual creditor, there is a strong incentive for each creditor to seek satisfaction individually, aggressively, and quickly. Such action can quickly lead to the closure of the firm and the dispersal of its assets even when the firm would be worth more if it were kept intact, reorganized, and sold. Insolvency procedures address this collective action problem by limiting the capacity of individual agents to take action and by pooling the proceeds of the liquidation of the bankruptcy estate. Their principal purpose is to resolve conflict between private parties, that is, the creditor and the debtor, as well as among competing creditors. In other words, insolvency procedures essentially seek to achieve comity among the interests of those private agents who have a claim on or contractual relation with the firm.

Public interest considerations

Besides the defunct firm's creditors, there may be other private agents who would be affected by the insolvency of the firm. If the firm is a major employer in the region, its demise could depress economic activity. Or, if the firm is a provider of an essential service, its disappearance could cause welfare losses, at least until an alternative supplier emerges. The insolvency procedure needs to protect the interests of these other private agents and to preserve the positive externalities associated with the continued functioning of the firm. This raises a broader collective action problem that led to the inclusion of public interest provisions such as employment, economic development, and financial stability in the insolvency laws as competing objectives.

Public interest may be used as an argument for the provision of public support or for a reorganization instead of liquidation. Some jurisdictions, such as Italy, have modified their insolvency procedures in light of these considerations and have introduced special procedures for large companies in which public interest considerations are more likely to arise. It is not uncommon that government entities assume a role in insolvency procedures with a significant public interest dimension. As such, the Ministry of Industry plays a role in the Italian large-firm special reorganization.[7] Public interest concerns sometimes lead governments to exempt firms from the operation of insolvency law by providing public support. To avoid distortions in the level playing field, the European Union (EU) introduced rules to limit the extent to which failing firms may receive official support.[8]

Objectives of procedures to resolve financial failures

In broad terms, the objectives of procedures to resolve financial failures are the same as for failures of nonfinancial businesses. However, their relative importance varies. First, there is a greater need for speed in handling the resolution of financial failures, and second, financial failures of large financial institutions can generate significant negative externalities and therefore give rise to public interest concerns.[9] The goal to achieve comity among private (creditor and debtor) interests is therefore affected by the need to take account of the public interest.

Financial institutions only operate efficiently to the extent that market participants have confidence in their ability to perform the roles for which they were designed. The more sophisticated the economy and the greater its dependence on financial promises, the greater is its vulnerability to failure of the financial system to deliver against its promises. Even when they are solvent, financial institutions can quickly become illiquid if something happens to cast doubt on their ability to meet their payment obligations. This is because the liquidity mismatch between assets and deposits gives rise to the risk that depositors run to withdraw their funds. A run can be triggered by bad news about the value of bank assets or by any unexplained fear. In either case, there may be a loss, since illiquid assets will be sold at a discount. Moreover, a bank failure can eventually trigger a signal on the solvency of other banks, leading to a systemic crisis. What changes in the case of an LCFI is merely the nature of the counterparties and the nature of the financial contracts, namely commercial paper, structured products, and other wholesale instruments, the treatment of which in insolvency is largely untested.

The need for speed and the potential for financial failure to result in systemic instability explain why crisis procedures for financial firms differ from ordinary insolvency procedures. In the case of financial institution failures, the goal under ordinary insolvency law to maximize the outcome for creditors competes with the goal to preserve financial stability.

In some jurisdictions, the legislator provides for an explicit override of the public interest in financial stability over creditors interests. For example, Section 141 of the Statement of Principles: Bank Registration and Supervision of the Reserve Bank of New Zealand (January 2006), which governs statutory management, provides that

> statutory managers are required to have primary regard to the need to maintain public confidence in the operation and soundness of the financial system, and the need to avoid significant damage to the financial system. They are also required to have regard to the need to resolve the difficulties of the registered bank as quickly as possible and to preserving the position and maintaining the ranking of creditors' claims, to the extent that this is not inconsistent with the primary objectives specified in the Act.

In the United States, the goal of bank insolvency resolution is set out explicitly in the law. The Federal Deposit Insurance Corporation (FDIC) must choose a resolution method that is "least costly to the deposit insurance fund."[10] Under the systemic risk exception, the FDIC is exempted from the least cost resolution requirement if adhering to it and imposing losses on uninsured creditors "would have serious adverse effects on economic conditions and financial stability and any action or assistance . . . would avoid or mitigate such adverse effects."[11] As pointed out by Robert Bliss and George Kaufman (2006), the FDIC is directed to "fully consider adverse economic impact."[12]

In the United Kingdom, the Memorandum of Understanding of March 22, 2006, between HM Treasury, the Bank of England, and the Financial Services Authority states in the section governing financial crisis as the main aim the avoidance of wider financial or economic disruption and thus subordinates other objectives to this overarching goal.[13]

Introducing public interest considerations into the procedures for dealing with distressed financial institutions should not hamper the operation of forces that permit a dynamic market economy to work. It must not result in distortions of the financial system. For that reason, legislators have put in place procedures that attempt to reduce those distortions by ensuring early action before solvency or liquidity problems become serious and provide for speedy resolution minimizing disruptions to financial operations.

Changing Economic and Financial Conditions and Implications

Emergence of LCFIs

A number of factors have led to increasing consolidation and conglomeration in the financial sector and the emergence of a small number of

LCFIs.[14] The factors at work include technological advances, which lead to economies of scale in risk management, the delivery of products to retail customers and other services such as custody and research; deregulation, which reduces cross-border barriers and cross-sector restrictions; and increased competition in the financial industry arising from the above factors. Changes in the financial landscape are focusing attention on one specific trade-off: the need to maintain incentives that permit the operation of a dynamic market economy versus the need to preserve the positive externalities that are created by LCFIs.

LCFIs have several common characteristics apart from being big:

- Their operations span different segments of the financial market. They are not confined just to banking or insurance or to any one activity.
- Their group structures are complex. Even though they may brand their produces with a single name, the groups are composed of multiple legal entities that are regulated by different authorities or may not even be regulated at all.
- They operate in a multiplicity of jurisdictions.
- They can easily become providers of systemically important (critical) functions in particular market segments.

Shortcomings of existing failure regimes

Given the changes described above the question arises whether the frameworks that are in place today to deal with insolvencies in the financial sector are still capable of fulfilling the functions of insolvency procedures.

Market discipline

A function of the insolvency process is to maintain strong incentives to meet contractual obligations. The perception that LCFIs may be too big to fail reduces market discipline. As a result, bank managers may feel confident that public officials will bail them out of crises, even those of their own making. A concrete manifestation of these distortions is the support ratings given by Fitch and other rating agencies that seek to reflect the probability of official support in a crisis and seem to indicate that large firms may, in fact, enjoy a "too big to fail" premium.[15] As a result they can attract and retain funding at a price that assumes protection; therefore, too much risk is taken on by such organizations. Linkages of the LCFI with the rest of the financial sector and the resulting spillover effects of potential problems within an LCFI on the institution's counterparties and the financial markets as well as the complex organizational setup and centralization of key business functions make it impractical to put an LCFI into liquidation.[16] The complex web of interdependent corporate subsidiaries and convoluted legal structures gives rise to uncertainty concerning the costs of a default. Supervisors, even consolidating supervisors, cannot exercise powers with respect to an entire LCFI and apply a structured early intervention and resolution SEIR approach on a group-wide basis.

Effectiveness and predictability
The insolvency procedure should provide an effective and predictable means to regularize situations in which economic agents cannot meet their contractual obligations. In the absence of a legal regime for the winding down of corporate groups, much uncertainty remains about the applicable law. Most jurisdictions do not have any provisions addressing the insolvency of a group of companies and will claim jurisdiction over the local part of the group's insolvency to the benefit of the creditors of that jurisdiction. The legal framework is further complicated by the fact that different components of a group may be subject to different regulatory regimes. The conduct of individual procedures with respect to individual group companies is likely to give rise to multiple intragroup claims ranging from contractual to extracontractual, tort, fraudulent conveyance (pauliana), and mismanagement, which are likely to divert resources from the more significant goal of resolving the crisis in the most efficient manner.

Equitable treatment of (different classes of) creditors
The insolvency procedure should treat different similarly situated creditors (domestic and foreign) in an equitable manner. If a large financial group fails, the application of different legal frameworks is likely to result in differing treatment of creditors belonging to the same classes depending on the competent jurisdiction and applicable law. Intragroup debts may be dealt with in a number of different ways in the jurisdictions concerned.[17]

Preventing intercreditor competition
Insolvency mechanisms should prevent intercreditor competition from reducing the value of the defunct firm. If a large financial group fails, a number of authorities will claim competence over parts of the group. This leads to competition among different functional regulators and judicial or administrative bankruptcy authorities. While competition can be looked at positively in that it ensures that intervention occurs early enough when an institution still has a positive net value, it favors a territorial approach. It may precipitate an early closure and makes an early restructuring and preservation of critical functions less likely.[18]

Channelling resources from less productive to more productive uses
A function of the insolvency process is to ensure that resources are allocated from less productive to more productive uses. Supervisory powers to manage financial failure focus on individual financial institutions and are sector-based. They cannot be applied across a group and thus achieve a group-wide reorganization. In the absence of effective means to reorganize, the threat of liquidation may give rise to forbearance and an expectation that the LCFI be bailed out. As observed by Alan Greenspan, "The perception that all creditors of large banks, let alone of their affiliates, are protected by the safety net is a recipe for a vast misallocation of resources and increasingly intrusive supervision."[19]

Preventing adverse social consequences and maintaining positive externalities
Another function of the insolvency process is to maintain the positive externalities associated with the operation of the insolvent firm. The existing processes do not adequately address the need to preserve critical functions performed by such groups or any other entity.[20] Functional specialization within the banks does not always follow the national and legal divisions. If critical functions are performed not just by one but a number of legal entities belonging to a group, effective crisis resolution will be complicated by the fact that a financial group whose financial condition is impaired may be split up into numerous legal entities, each of which is subject to separate regulatory, corporate, and general bankruptcy laws.

Way Forward—the Three Pillars of an Effective Crisis Resolution Framework

A primary challenge of resolving an LCFI arises from the fragmented supervisory and insolvency frameworks. In fact, even within the same jurisdiction, individual entities belonging to a group may become subject to different crisis resolution mechanisms administered by different authorities. For instance, in the United States banks, broker-dealers, and insurance companies are subject to special insolvency regimes, whereas a holding company is subject to federal bankruptcy law. Fragmented regimes also exist in the EU. In the EU, there is a winding-up directive for banks and a separate one for insurance undertakings, but there is no comparable directive for securities firms or financial holding companies.

Another challenge relates to the legal structure of financial groups. There is a mismatch between economic reality and legal form. In other words, legal form does not necessarily follow functions and functions are not embedded in individual legal entities. This makes it difficult to resolve integrated financial groups under applicable insolvency laws. Existing laws are designed to resolve individual legal entities with little regard to the many interdependencies that may exist. Regardless of whether or not a legal entity forms an integral and functional part of a group of companies, it is legally considered as a stand-alone body, solely liable for its debts with no claim on the assets of other group companies.[21] Indeed, in some cases, part of the rationale for creating a separate legal entity within a group is to make it bankruptcy remote. For instance, many LCFIs use special purpose vehicles (SPVs) to raise cash and enhance credit. If creditors are misled to believe that the assets that were diverted to the SPV are part of the entire estate on which they relied for its financial strength, then it would not be fair to leave these creditors with all the bad assets. Other creditors, however, may claim that they were assured that the SPV will stay out of any bankruptcy event. Even some integral parts of the group that are not separate legal entities may be separated from the group in insolvency. This is frequently the case in a cross-border situation. Whereas foreign branches normally constitute an integral part of the headquarters, some jurisdictions will ring fence a foreign bank's branch along with the foreign bank's assets located in their jurisdiction and treat it as if it were a separate legal entity. In the United States, which applies a separate entity doctrine,[22] a foreign branch of an insolvent or near-insolvent foreign bank will be treated as if it were a separate entity. When a branch or agency of a foreign bank becomes insolvent, a U.S. administrator can attach all of the foreign parent's assets in the United States even if they are part of a different non-bank subsidiary. The U.S. court or administrator would ring fence those assets and use them to satisfy domestic claims, paying any surplus to satisfy creditors in any foreign proceedings. Individual transactions may be subject to different rules depending on the status of the counterparties.[23]

To overcome these challenges arising from the fragmented legal and supervisory framework on the one side and the mismatch between legal form and function on the other, this chapter identifies three lines of action that complement each other:

- Crisis resolution frameworks should be closer aligned with the concept of comprehensive consolidated supervision in order to be able to allow for supervisory intervention and implement the SEIR approach with respect to LCFIs.[24]
- For LCFIs, there is a high degree of legal uncertainty regarding the resolution framework. Several legal frameworks may apply simultaneously. The resulting concern that LCFIs cannot be resolved in an orderly fashion may give rise to moral hazard and the expectation that governments will bail out a failing institution. The absence of a

credible and predictable bankruptcy procedure may undermine effort to prevent a crisis or resolve it at an early stage.

- As long as the supervisory and insolvency frameworks remain fragmented, national authorities need to consider how they can deal with a crisis in their jurisdiction in the most effective manner. They will need to take action, either ex ante or ex post, to minimize the impact of a financial failure on the domestic financial system. To this end, they may require financial institutions to align their legal structure more closely to their operational structure and make their internal governance more transparent.

Aligning Supervisory and Crisis Resolution Frameworks

As long as a financial group remains solvent, the fact that—and the manner in which—it is formally divided into several legal entities is not of material significance. In a supervisory context, the financial group is viewed as a single economic entity. Internationally accepted standards governing the supervision of cross-border banking make the home supervisor responsible for the supervision of the consolidated banking group. The concept of comprehensive consolidated supervision means that the home-country supervisor is responsible for monitoring a banking group's risk exposure and capital adequacy on the basis of the totality of its business wherever it is conducted. The underlying idea is that an international banking group composed of various independent legal entities is to be looked at as one economic unit. Financial difficulties in one member of the group can trigger a loss of confidence in the group as a whole and thereby affect other members. Moreover, there may be a legal or de facto obligation on the part of the other members to come to the rescue of the failing member.[25] For that reason, the home supervisor generally adopts a universalistic approach and treats the group as a single economic entity.

This universalistic approach does not apply in a crisis. Herein lies the problem. Crisis resolution frameworks are not aligned with the concept of comprehensive consolidated supervision. When supervision is organized in silos in which each sector-based supervisor independently carries out its own responsibilities, effective consolidated supervision of LCFIs and more so the resolution of crises become a challenge.[26] Effective supervision of an LCFI presupposes that the supervisors are able to monitor risk in both a cross-border and a cross-sectoral context and to this end are in contact with supervisors responsible for other parts of the group.[27] To facilitate cross-sectoral supervision at a national level, a number of countries have moved away from a system of sector-based supervision to one in which there is a single integrated financial regulator. Currently, there are integrated supervisory authorities in 12 of 27 EU member states. Other jurisdictions, such as the United States and the other EU member states, retain a system of functional regulation comprising separate sectoral supervisory agencies. Where different regulators continue to exist, laws such as the Gramm-Leach-Bliley Act (GLBA) need to be enacted to enable supervisors to take a global and comprehensive overview of the group, the risks that it poses, and its financial soundness.[28]

At the international level, principles for cooperation and information sharing within a financial group are set out in a number of documents. The formulation of principles regarding cross-border supervision began with the creation of the Basel Committee. In fact, one of the main reasons for establishing the committee was the recognition of the need for cooperation among regulators in the aftermath of the Herstatt Bank collapse in 1974. This gave rise to the formulation of the Basel Concordat. Subsequent revisions clarified the roles of both home- and host-country supervisors. The principles of consolidated supervision, which were laid down in the 1983 Basel Concordat and the 1992 Minimum Standards, place the major supervisory responsibilities for both the headquarters or parent and foreign branches on the home-country supervisor. The Joint Forum has developed principles that set out a general framework for facilitating information sharing between supervisors of regulated entities within internationally active financial groups or conglomerates.[29]

At present, there are no binding international agreements governing crisis situations. Supervisory authorities of a number of jurisdictions have entered into bilateral and multilateral memoranda of understanding (MoU) that set forth a number of principles of and practical issues regarding cooperation and information exchange in a crisis:

An example is the MoU signed in May 2006 by the De Nederlandsche Bank (DNB), the Belgian Banking, Finance and Insurance Commission (CBFA), and the National Bank of Belgium (NBB) on cooperation in the area of supervision and in case of a possible financial crisis. The MoU stipulates that a crisis management committee consisting of the three authorities will be convened if an emergency situation arises. This committee deals with the consultation and coordination between the authorities, collects information, coordinates actions, and maintains contacts with the institution and market participants. In addition, the MoU aims at making specific information available in case of a crisis. The financial institution must then be able to immediately generate this information. Through this MoU, the three authorities will bring about more pronounced cross-border cooperation, as required under the new EU Capital Requirements Directive.

A similar arrangement was signed by the Nordic supervisors Sweden, Finland, Norway, and Denmark in 2001 and updated in 2004. In June 2003, the Nordic central bank governors signed an agreement on the management of financial crises in a Nordic bank with activities in two or more Nordic countries. The agreement contains procedures for the coordination of crisis management among the central banks. The MoU provides that in a financial crisis the central banks would establish a crisis group responsible for providing joint and rapid access to and management of information. The first EU-wide MoU on cooperation in crisis management situations was adopted in March 2003 under the auspices of the Banking Supervision Committee (BSC) of the European System of Central Banks (ESCB). This MoU was designed to contribute to effective crisis management by ensuring a smooth interaction between the authorities concerned. In particular, this MoU sets out specific principles and procedures for the identification of the authorities responsible for the management of a crisis in the EU and details the practical arrangements for sharing information across borders. A second MoU was adopted in May 2005. The main difference between this MoU and the 2003 MoU relates to their scope. While the 2003 MoU deals with cooperation between EU banking supervisors and central banks only, the 2005 MoU addresses cross-border cooperation involving the EU finance ministries as well. The 2005 MoU was extended and updated in 2008. The update, which took effect on June 1, 2008, defines procedures and practical arrangements for the involvement of all relevant parties in a crisis situation and sets out common principles and practical arrangements for cooperation among the authorities responsible for preserving financial stability.

A weakness that is often cited in connection with MoUs is their nonbinding character. Their stipulations may be observed in good times and breached in bad times. The reputational damage of not honoring a commitment arising from an MoU can, however, be significant, in particular in a context where supervisory authorities are committed to achieving convergence of supervisory practices through close cooperation and coordination as is the case in the EU. Thus, the shortcoming of an MoU is less the apparent lack of enforceability but more its limited scope. An MoU cannot create any new rights and responsibilities. For instance, it is not an appropriate legal instrument to achieve the extraterritorial recognition of supervisory action, that is, a mechanism that ensures that supervisory action ordered in the home country can be effectively applied with respect to legal entities located in host countries. An MoU can only achieve commitment of home and host supervisors to coordinate their actions. The recognition and enforcement of official action across borders can only be agreed upon by a binding legal instrument, either by national law, as with the national implementation of the Winding up Directive,[30] or by supranational law that is directly enforceable, such as the European Insolvency Regulation.[31]

Options for improved supervisory cooperation

Increasingly, the operational structure of financial groups is becoming less congruent with their legal structure. Important decisions are no longer made by separate entities within the group, but at the group level. Supervisors have a number of important powers under the existing frameworks for the management of financial failures. These include the power to temporarily assume the administration of the failing institution (or to appoint administrators to that end), to suspend financial activities, to transfer assets and liabilities, to make changes in the capital structures, and to impose haircuts on creditors. As strong as these powers are, they can be exercised only with respect to those institutions under their oversight and not with respect to group companies that are unregulated or subject to another supervisory and insolvency regime. A designated coordinating or lead supervisor does not have powers that reach beyond its remit. Even the lead supervisor designated under the Conglomerates Directive cannot use the intervention powers granted to it with respect to other group companies within the same territorial jurisdiction. The Winding-up Directive for banks and the directive governing the winding-up of insurance undertakings limit the EU-wide recognition of intervention measures to branches located in other member states.[32]

In view of the limited intervention powers of the lead or coordinating supervisor, there is reason to question whether it would be possible to achieve effective, early resolution of a crisis affecting globally active institutions with diverse financial activities carried out through separate legal entities.[33] As seen in the following, a number of different approaches are being discussed in the EU context. They aim at formalizing the framework for consolidated supervision by conferring formal powers to a European lead regulator or, alternatively, by creating an EU-body with respective supervisory and crisis resolution powers. However, unless recognition of lead supervisory powers extends beyond the borders of the EU, supervisory and crisis resolution powers with respect to globally active LCFIs will continue to be fragmented.

Supervisory colleges for individual banks
The classic approach that has been followed in a number of past cases is to establish specific standing committees for individual cross-border banking groups. These standing committees, also referred to as supervisory colleges, comprise representatives from the relevant supervisors. In the Bank of Credit and Commerce International (BCCI) case, supervisory colleges were established to cooperate in order to disentangle the complexities of this defunct bank.[34]

The Financial Stability Forum (FSF) recently recommended that a college of supervisors be put in place for each of the largest global financial institutions and that, in addition, the supervisors and central banks most directly involved establish a small group to address cross-border crisis management planning issues specific to the structure of the individual firms.[35] Such groupings could serve as fora to forge an ex ante agreement on resolution modes and the procedures to follow in a crisis. Such an arrangement will need to be tailored to the specific nature of the group and regularly reviewed and adapted to changes in its structure and operations.

Currently, there are two institution-specific MoUs in the Nordics. They relate to cooperation in the supervision of the Nordea Group and the Sampo Group and have been concluded between Kredittilsynet (the Banking, Insurance, and Securities Commission) in Norway; Finansinspektionen (the Financial Supervisory Authority) in Sweden; Rahoitustarkatus (the Financial Supervision Authority) in Finland; Vakuutusvalvontavrastu (the Insurance Supervision Authority) in Finland; and, in the case of the Nordea MoU, but not the Sampo MoU, Finanstilsynet (the Financial Supervisory Authority) in Denmark. Both MoUs are organized along similar lines and contain the same main provisions.[36] The German BaFin signed such an MoU with the German Bundesbank and its UK and U.S. counterparts to coordinate the supervision of a globally active German financial group. With respect to the supervision of two large Swiss institutions, UBS and Credit Suisse, the Swiss Federal Banking Commission as their home regulator conducts regular trilateral meetings with its U.S. and UK counterparts without having formalized that arrangement.

Arrangements for close cooperation and coordination in a crisis may be built upon the existing arrangements and tailored to the specific circumstances of individual financial groups. They are flexible and may be quickly adapted to changes in the group structure. A shortcoming of this approach may however be that such arrangements lack the necessary legal robustness to hold in a crisis.

The EU Commission's White Paper on Financial Services Policy (2005–2010) identified among the key challenges the need to clarify and optimize home-host responsibilities and to explore the delegation of tasks and responsibilities. It notes that home-country control is still the core concept for supervision in Europe and that any evolution of prudential supervisory structures in the EU away from the current arrangements would raise complex issues of political and financial accountability, especially when support from the public purse might be called upon.

Following an EU-level crisis simulation exercise in April 2006, the Economic and Financial Affairs Council (ECOFIN) stressed that EU arrangements for financial stability need to correspond to the develop-ments in the financial markets.[37] The council reaffirmed the importance of actions set out in the commission's White Paper on Financial Services Policy in developing EU arrangements for financial stability and invited the European Financial Committee (EFC) to further develop procedures and, as appropriate, general principles for resolving cross-border finan-cial crises in the EU. In its recently issued concluding statement in the context of the 2007 Article IV consultations with the Euro-area coun-tries, the IMF mission recommends that the financial stability frame-work should be built upon a foundation of joint responsibility and joint accountability for large cross-border financial institutions.[38] The com-mon principles for cross-border crisis management set out in the 2008 MoU stipulate that the "objective of crisis management is to protect the stability of the financial system in all countries involved and in the EU as a whole and to minimize potential harmful economic impacts at the low-est overall collective cost." They further provide that if public resources are involved in the resolution of the crisis "direct budgetary net costs are shared among affected Member States on the basis of equitable and bal-anced criteria, which take into account the economic impact of the crisis in the countries affected and the framework of home and host countries' supervisory powers".

Formalizing the position of the lead supervisor
The existing lead regulator model works well in the supervision of sound financial institutions. However, the incentives for cooperation change when an institution becomes insolvent. In a world where the supervision of financial institutions remains national, each of the various authorities will be obliged to act in accordance with its own statutory obligations.[39] These obligations may bring the authorities into conflict with each other and discourage cooperation.[40] Financial supervisors have the statutory obligation to protect domestic depositors (or to protect the deposit insur-ance fund)[41] and to maintain financial stability in their domestic financial systems. The obligation to achieve least cost outcomes does not extend to costs that fall outside the country.

   To enhance the home country's responsibility the home supervisor would need to be given additional powers not only for the group but also for all its foreign subsidiaries.[42] For this approach to be effective the powers of the lead regulator would need to be formalized and the laws and regula-tions of the home country extended to the financial group as a whole. Orders issued by the lead regulator need to be enforceable in both the home and host jurisdictions. This is not the case under the current regime of con-solidated supervision. For this approach to work in Europe, the current

Winding-up Directive, which provides for the recognition of home regulator action with respect to branches, would need to be extended to include subsidiaries.[43]

This approach is not without challenges. It could lead to a fragmented supervisory landscape and result in banks in one country being governed by laws from different nations. Legal regimes would change if a parent institution is taken over by a bank from another country. A foreign subsidiary could be subject to both home- and host-country regulation.

There is also an inherent conflict of interest. National authorities are accountable to their national government and legislature for the defence of their own national interests (financial stability). Conflicts of interest may arise between acting in the interest of the home country and acting in the interest of wider cross-border stability concerns and the interests of depositors in both the home and host countries.

A less radical approach would be to rely on existing supervisory regimes and establish joint responsibility and accountability of European supervisors for financial groups in the EU. This approach may be implemented by the creation of a special charter and single prudential regime for financial groups headquartered in the EU.[44] The single prudential regime would provide for harmonized supervisory powers and could be made mandatory at least for those groups that are regarded systemically important at the EU level.

A supranational body

Another solution discussed at the EU level is to focus some authority on a European level to deal with the relatively limited number of most important cross-border banks. Stefan Ingves (2007) proposes the establishment of a new pan-European body, a European Organization for Financial Supervision (EOFS). The EOFS would exclusively focus on truly cross-border banking groups and not deal with banks having a predominately national character. The EOFS would be established directly by the EU countries and would have an obligation to report to the European Parliament. It would employ staff from all EU countries and have local offices in the national financial centres. Its main task initially would be the assessment of the risks and vulnerabilities of cross-border banking groups. At a later stage, the EOFS could become a full-fledged European supervisor—a future European Financial Services Authority (FSA). As for crisis resolution, Ingves suggested setting up a deposit insurance fund for the largest cross-border banks, possibly within the framework of the new European supervisory agency, akin to the FDIC in the United States. The agency that would be operating the fund would also have the power to reconstruct banks.

Codifying Insolvency Regimes for Corporate Groups

An effective failure regime consists of two components: a framework for supervisory intervention and a formal insolvency procedure. Even if financial failures tend to be resolved within the supervisory framework through early intervention the existence of an insolvency framework is important. It has a significant effect on ex ante behaviour of stakeholders.

It would seem that just as is the case for comprehensive consolidated supervision the economic reality, and not the legal structure, should determine the approach to insolvency. An insolvency proceeding over any part of the group has the ability to affect the other parts of the group. For instance, the liquidation of only one particular component of the group may have a damaging effect upon the reputation of the rest of the group and result in a "domino effect" leading to a total shutdown. Conversely, when a certain subsidiary is a burden on the others, in order to stabilize the business it may be necessary to close it down.

Most national laws lack a codified legal framework to deal with the special case of insolvency of groups. There are a number of reasons:

- There is a tension between the desire to optimize the insolvency process and traditional corporate theory, which stipulates that the integrity and distinctiveness of the corporate form be respected.
- It is generally recognized that corporations and their shareholders and affiliates are separate legal entities with their own separate assets and liabilities and that creditors of one member of a corporate group generally are not entitled to assert their claims against other members of the group.
- Treating companies as other than separate legal entities would introduce significant uncertainty and undermine the capacity of market participants to make choices about risk.

A group insolvency may take many forms that may call for different resolution approaches and are difficult to codify in a single legal framework. Depending on whether only one subsidiary fails or a number of subsidiaries or the entire group and depending on the degree of integration of functions and intragroup contagion one resolution approach may be appropriate for one case but completely inadequate for another. An integrated and centrally managed and controlled group with a high degree of interdependence would suggest a pooling of assets, whereas great autonomy of the individual components may suggest imposing an insolvency solution to each insolvent part as a separate process. Since there is no single set of creditors of a single debtor, creditors' interests will diverge. Authorities representing the interests of local creditors of local entities of the group have their own narrow interests or national mandates that may undermine a more global solution that could benefit the stakeholders as a whole.

Given the existence of significant differences in the legal frameworks agreeing on a global regime for a group insolvency faces additional difficulties.[45] For instance, one of the jurisdictions involved may provide for a reorganization process under the oversight of the supervisor, while another provides the supervisor with only limited intervention powers and relies heavily on the corporate insolvency law framework.

The failure of an LCFI will most likely trigger multiple cross-border claims and elicit local creditors opening separate proceedings in different places around the world. Individual companies of the group may have claims against each other. Creditors may have claims against several companies regarding the same debt (as a consequence of cross-guarantees for instance). An administrator appointed to resolve an individual company of the group which in fact was related to a wider business with operations (through subsidiaries) across the globe may attempt to expand control over cross-border assets and subsidiaries in order to be able to design a workable plan for the business or to maximize value for creditors in any possible way. However, since each of these administrators is appointed to supervise a company rather than the entire group, such intentions are likely to result in extensive litigation and disputes with other administrators appointed to supervise affiliates' proceedings.

The absence of a framework on the international level is therefore not surprising. The UNCITRAL Model law does not address the insolvency of groups of companies, nor does the EU regulation include any specific provisions for dealing with such cases.[46] The only current approach addressing the matter is found in the ALI Principles.[47] These principles however limit themselves to encouraging coordination between concurrent proceedings of affiliated companies and, for instance, suggest that joint filings for affiliates should be permissible.

The current debate about the insolvency of groups of companies distinguishes two approaches: (1) joint proceedings or administrative consolidation and (2) substantive consolidation. Both approaches, though radically different, contain elements that may inform the approach to be used to resolve a global LCFI.

Joint proceedings

Coordinating proceedings against group companies and handling them jointly and not as separate insolvencies could facilitate a coordinated resolution, reduce inefficiencies arising from disputes regarding the control of assets and subsidiaries' proceedings and achieve a more efficient resolution of claims and disposition of assets. While each company in the group would be dealt with as a separate legal entity, issues common to each of the members of a group would be considered in the same proceeding. This would make it easier to assess the feasibility of a rehabilitation and coordinate decisions with regard to a reorganization. Procedural (or administrative) consolidation should enable the authorities to obtain the records of many or all group companies and to negotiate sales of all or part of a business that extends across more than one legal entity in an efficient and cost-effective manner. To determine the best possible solution it should be possible to consider the "group scenario," so as to provide a solution that will serve creditors in general. Such general oversight could be exercised jointly by all authorities in charge, both domestically and internationally. Such an approach would facilitate sharing and transferring information between affiliates' administrators or liquidators and the competent authorities and reduce the need to seek data that were already gathered by another authority.

Substantive consolidation

As financial institutions increasingly concentrate different functions, such as funding, liquidity management, risk management, and credit decision making, in specific centres of competence in order to reap the benefits of specialization and economies of scale, subsidiaries and branches, domestically and abroad, are becoming much less self-contained. In case of the insolvency of financial groups with a number of centralized operations and entangled financial dealings among individual corporate entities that would not be able to subsist on their own, it would seem sensible to sanction the dissolution of corporate separateness and engage in substantive consolidation. The group as a whole would have greater value than the sum of its components. The sale, restructuring, or liquidation of the consolidated assets of the group would be more equitable for creditors who dealt with the group companies as single entity. It would also facilitate actions to preserve critical functions when the performance of the function depends on several individual legal entities of the group.

At the same time, it would be unrealistic to expect the emergence of a regime that did not accord due respect for the existence of corporate boundaries. Counterparties legitimately expect that separate incorporation will make a legal entity remote from insolvency of related parties. The consolidation of all the assets and liabilities of companies belonging to the same financial group would violate the expectation of corporate separateness that underlies limited corporate liability and the existence of a separate legal personality.

Under certain circumstances it would seem equitable to pool assets of companies belonging to the same group, as in the case of an LCFI with closely integrated, highly interdependant, or even totally commingled operations. If the companies comprising the group are highly interdependent, an apparently solvent component may in fact be totally dependant on the support of its parent company or other members in the group and could not be considered as a stand-alone entity. The apparent worth of its assets may be unrealistic. A joint administration or procedural administration cannot solve this problem of entanglement since the rights and obligations of the group's members would still be left intact. Therefore, a mechanism that would allow for the pooling of assets (substantive consolidation) would seem the most adequate solution in order to promote both a fair and efficient result. At the same time, it should not be a fixed rule that an integrated group should always conduct a centralized process. When affiliates comprising the group had significant autonomy it should be possible to have local proceedings. When an LCFI was not operated or regarded as a "de facto" one entity there is no justification to pool all assets and disregard the corporate form. All relevant interests should be taken into account and components that are not strongly integrated with the rest should not take part in a pooling mechanism. In other cases, it should be permissible to compensate creditors who otherwise will be harmed in the course of the consolidation. It is important to set out the conditions in which a pooling of assets may occur. Otherwise the predictability that is essential for economic contracting would be impaired. The following criteria could be used.

- The affairs of the parent and subsidiaries are entangled to such a degree that they constitute a single operational entity.
- The creditors genuinely thought and were led to believe that they were dealing with the business as a whole (although, formally there is more than one entity). Determining factors may be corporate branding and the way the enterprise was structured and operated.
- Respecting corporate boundaries would be inequitable. Consolidation may be warranted where respecting corporate boundaries would be inequitable, for instance, in cases where insiders have systematically siphoned off the subsidiaries' equity.
- The benefits of consolidation in the aggregate outweigh the costs to a particular creditor or creditor group. If the potential injustice is significantly lower compared with the advantage to the creditors in

general, substantive consolidation could be justified. An important benefit of consolidation could be the preservation of certain operations that are critical in the financial system.

This approach should not interfere with the concept of corporate separateness. Only in those cases where the integration between the constituent companies was so strong, so that it is neither efficient nor fair to treat it separately, should a pooling of assets be an option. In implementing this approach it is necessary to take into account the factors that determine the choice of corporate form in the first place. Regulatory requirements may call for separate incorporation to avoid conflicts of interests. Often tax considerations determine the choice of corporate form and prompt the group to create SPVs. Finally, separate incorporation may also be chosen to ensure separation in insolvency.

To apply a "complete" substantive consolidation the entire proceedings would need to be placed under a single legal regime. Judgments given in this respect would need to be internationally recognized and enforceable in other states where the parties are located. Such a global approach will not be for tomorrow. It is bound to pose some degree of threat to the fundamental concept of "limited liability" and national interests.

In some jurisdictions, some solutions are already available to treat financial groups differently in insolvency from single entities. These range from joint insolvency proceedings, the appointment of special administrators to ensure proper coordination and exchange of information, to consolidation of assets and liabilities of different group members. Examples of procedural consolidation are found in Italian and Norwegian legislation. In both jurisdictions, the supervisor can initiate an administration procedure not only with respect to the distressed bank but also any other firm or holding company that belongs to the same group. Whereas the procedures remain legally separate, the authority administering them is the same and is therefore able to coordinate them by applying compatible measures. In both jurisdictions, a group company may become subject to an administration procedure if it forms part of a bank-dominated group and if either the parent company or another group company that is a bank has been subjected to such procedure.

There are only few examples where it was possible to agree on a "pooling" or "consolidation" solution. In the case of BCCI, the provisional liquidators devised a number of agreements of which the most significant was the "pooling agreement." The idea was to create a structure under which all BCCI assets would be pooled; hence, the tracing and recovery of assets would be a joint enterprise and creditors in each of the liquidations would receive the same level of dividend from a central pool. Despite the existence of this pooling arrangement, the liquidators did not achieve an equitable distribution among all creditors. The reason was that some jurisdictions ring fenced BCCI assets and did not adhere to the pooling arrangement. The assets in those jurisdictions were liquidated to satisfy claims of local creditors before any other creditors. As a result, creditors in those jurisdictions obtained a significantly higher dividend.[48]

Aligning the Legal Structure and Operational Structure—Form Follows Function

As long as the supervisory and insolvency frameworks remain fragmented, national authorities need to consider how they can deal with a crisis in their jurisdiction in the most effective manner. They will need to take action, either ex ante or ex post, to minimize the impact of a financial failure on the domestic financial system. To this end, they will seek to maximize control over assets and operations in insolvency and impose measures that ensure the continued performance of critical functions in their financial system. Supervisory authorities may require financial institutions to align their legal structure more closely to their operational structure and make their internal governance more transparent.[49] This has three benefits. First, it will achieve greater predictability in resolving LCFIs under national law. Second, it will enable the preservation of critical functions. Third, it will help reduce moral hazard and weaken the "too big to fail" argument. To implement this approach, the national (or the regionally or globally integrated) regulator needs to establish clear rules on the use of corporate form. These rules should seek to reduce the gap between the institutions' operations and their effects on jurisdictional matters. Borrowing a term from the design profession, this approach may be described as "form follows function." More and more we observe that functions (or business units) in a financial group ignore form and span many legal forms (separately incorporated entities), which despite being legally autonomous are not functionally autonomous. The recent crisis that was triggered by difficulties in the U.S. subprime mortgage market highlighted another angle of this apparent mismatch between legal form and economic reality. Financial institutions found themselves obliged to provide credit or capital to affiliated entities, including hedge funds, even when they were under no explicit legal obligation to do so. This raises the question of whether such stand-alone vehicles should not be consolidated with the sponsoring institutions.

When imposing restrictions on the way in which financial groups structure their operations it is necessary to carefully weigh the gain in efficiency against greater dependency on foreign operations and the risk of failure. Requiring major financial institutions to operate on a stand-alone basis may significantly reduce banking efficiency to the extent that it forces them to rely on more costly and less expert in-house resources. On the positive side, outsourcing can reduce the probability of failure through diversification and access to greater expertise and capital. Limits on how LCFIs structure their operations could make their operations less efficient. However, it would increase predictability of how the individual entities would be handled in a failure situation. In a crisis situation the ability to transfer assets from or to individual entities in a financial group can be critical for the resolution of a crisis. Asset transfers from one entity to another of the same banking group may be used to avoid any deterioration of situations. On the other hand, national authorities may seek to prevent the transfer of assets in a crisis situation in order to maximize assets in their jurisdiction to protect domestic creditors' interests should the attempt to resolve the crisis fail. In certain jurisdictions, such as the United States,[50] intragroup claims will simply be disregarded in insolvency.

In a world with LCFIs cutting across banking, securities, and insurance sectors and operating in multiple jurisdictions, an entity-based approach pursued by different national regulators will not suffice to manage and resolve failures effectively. In the absence of appropriate procedures, LCFIs may easily come to regard themselves as either too big or too complex to fail. They may indeed be too critical to fail if the continued operation of the critical functions that these institutions perform would be threatened. The only way to keep moral hazard at bay is to create effective means to wind down these institutions without relying on public funds. The creation of a legal framework with clear, predictable, and expeditious procedures that operate across borders is therefore an important priority.

A global approach better reflects the LCFI's economic reality than one that is territorial, entity-based, and sector-specific. However, such is not for tomorrow. National governments are unlikely in the foreseeable future to agree to a unitary approach on a global basis. It is more realistic to achieve the objective of a more efficient and predictable crisis resolution framework that reduces moral hazard by building on existing national regulatory and insolvency regimes. Effective crisis management must take into account the economic reality of complex group structures through a combination of greater cooperation and coordination on the international level and an increase in the capacity of national authorities to resolve LCFIs under existing regimes.

To achieve such a framework this chapter proposes a three-pillar-approach. The first two pillars relate to the supervisory and insolvency framework. They seek to achieve greater clarity in the legal frameworks and powers of home and host authorities, moving beyond the existing legal entity-based and sector-specific regimes to a regime that is closer to the economic reality of a financial group. In so doing it builds on the concept of consolidated supervision. The third pillar complements the first two. It seeks to achieve a greater correspondence between legal form and economic reality and in this way to provide for predictable crisis resolution under existing national frameworks in circumstances where no binding cross-border arrangement provides for a group-wide solution. The three pillars are complementary. Where the degree of ex ante agreement on cooperation is low, authorities may put greater weight on having legal form and function more closely aligned so that the insolvency procedure will be clear, predicable, and expeditious. Where there is a high degree of cooperation, attention to corporate form may be less important.

Supervisory cooperation and coordination

Most crises affecting individual financial institutions are managed through the early intervention of supervisory authorities. For this reason supervisors need to have sufficient powers to intervene early and in a coordinated manner in an LCFI. Cooperation and coordination problems need to be resolved at a national level before they can be addressed at a global level. Accordingly, supervisory and crisis resolution responsibilities over a financial group must be clearly assigned at a national level. The national lead authority should act as a single counterpart for foreign regulators. National authorities would also need to agree on predefined modes for cross-border cooperation and coordination. One solution discussed at the EU-level is to let the home country take a leading position and to give it a formal mandate to act in the interest of all relevant authorities. An alternative approach would be to allot sufficient authority on a supranational level to deal with the relatively limited number of most important LCFIs.

An insolvency regime for groups of companies

Since the resolution of financial failures occurs in the shadow of the corporate insolvency framework, the existence of legal frameworks to resolve groups of companies would contribute significantly to the way in which a financial institution is resolved. It is important that an insolvency regime addresses matters concerning corporate groups in sufficient procedural detail to provide certainty for all parties to financial transactions with the groups and to speed the resolution. Creditors may be reluctant to accept any "joint process" if they are uncertain that their rights will be preserved. One way to create such a framework at a global level would be to conclude an international convention. Another, probably more realistic approach would be to develop a model law, similar to the UNCITRAL Model law on Cross-border Insolvency,[51] which would then be adopted by national legislators.

Corporate structure— aligning corporate form and function

While much attention has been given to the need for some form of framework for cross-border coordination and cooperation both in the earlier stages of crisis management and in the later stage of insolvency, relatively less attention has been given to the legal structures of the LCFIs and to how these structures affect the resolution process. To ensure effective crisis resolution under the existing imperfect conditions of fragmented supervisory and insolvency frameworks, it would be helpful to forge a closer link between the legal form of the LCFI and economic reality. Apart from adding transparency and logic to their operations, this would have three benefits. First, it would achieve greater predictability in resolving LCFIs under national law. Second, it would enable critical functions to be preserved. Third, it would help reduce moral hazard. To ensure that "form follows function," the national regulator (or the regionally or globally integrated regulator) would need to establish clear rules on the use of corporate form. These rules should seek to create a de facto correspondence between the locus of the institutions' operations, the corporate form, and applicable law and jurisdiction. Increasingly, the functions (or business units) in a financial group span many legal forms (separately incorporated entities), which are not functionally autonomous despite being legally distinct. Where there is a manifest disparity between corporate form and economic reality, it should be possible to "pierce the corporate veil." One possible approach is to apply "substantive consolidation" to some or all parts of the group even though they constitute separate legal entities. Another approach is to hold related companies responsible for the losses of other companies in the group in the state of insolvency. Rules and procedures that seek to mitigate the abuse of the corporate form by LCFIs will create an incentive for LCFIs to monitor the activities of companies within the group more closely and to intervene early in the case of financial difficulties of one of them. While an insolvency regime deals with LCFI behaviour only after the harm is done, such rules could reduce manipulation at an early stage of distress.

Conclusion

LCFIs create a significant challenge for the international regulatory community. Their complex group structures often consist of multiple legal entities operating in a variety of different jurisdictions. The close linkages among business areas within an LCFI increase the risks of contagion both from one business area to another and across jurisdictions. For these reasons it is urgent to develop effective measures that can be applied across the relevant jurisdictions to address the risk that their size and complexity will make them "too big to fail". Three types of action are needed. They are all based on the presumption that it is unrealistic to expect the creation of a global regulatory authority or an international insolvency framework in the foreseeable future. The first type of action is to ensure that national authorities have the necessary powers to cope with a crisis in an LCFI operating in their jurisdiction and that they have effective means to cooperate with their counterparts in other jurisdictions. The second type of action is to ensure that insolvency procedures for groups of companies in all the relevant jurisdictions are mutually consistent and operationally compatible. Finally, it is important that corporate structures correspond to economic reality. Regulators need to establish clear rules on the use of the corporate form.

The three types of action are complementary. In the absence of predefined modes for cross-border coordination, authorities may put greater weight on having legal form and function closely aligned so that the applicable resolution procedures in a crisis are clear and predicable. Where there is a high degree of cooperation, attention to corporate form may be less important.

Notes

*Eva Hüpkes is head of regulation in the Legal Department of the Swiss Federal Banking Commission. The views expressed here are those of the author alone. This chapter is based on a paper presented at the North American Economics and Finance Association conference "The Resolution of Bank and Financial Institutional Insolvencies" in San Diego in June 2006.

1. In the following the term "insolvency procedure" is understood as a collective procedure that allows a debtor, who is unable to pay creditors, to resolve the debt through reorganization or the division of the debtor assets among all creditors in an equitable manner. The term covers any formal bankruptcy or administration procedure for settling the debts of an insolvent borrower. In some jurisdictions, such as the United Kingdom, the term "bankruptcy" relates only to individuals and partnerships. Companies and other corporations enter into differently named legal insolvency procedures: liquidation, administration, and administrative receivership.

2. The European Community Guidelines on State aid for rescuing and restructuring firms in difficulty note that "State aid tends to distort competition and affect trade between Member States and impede or slow down the structural adjustment . . . "

Community Guidelines on State aid for rescuing and restructuring firms in difficulty (Notice to Member States including proposals for appropriate measures) (1999/C 288/02).

3. Hart (1999).
4. The outcome of the process may be highly unpredictable if it is the result of negotiations among creditors.
5. A "collective action problem" describes a situation in which everyone (in a given group) has a choice between two alternatives and where, if everyone involved acts in his own narrow interest, the outcome will be worse than if they had chosen the other alternative and then pooled the reward and shared it.
6. Amministrazione straordinaria delle grandi imprese (Special administration of large enterprises), Decree of 30 January 1979, No. 26.
7. See *supra* note 2.
8. Kelley (1997); Corrigan (1982).
9. 12 USC 1823 (c)(4)(A)(ii).
10. 12 USC 1823(c)(4)(G).
11. 12 USC 1821(h) (1).
12. See http://www.bankofengland.co.uk/publications/news/2006/037.htm (last accessed on 27 July 2006). Sec. 15 of the MoU provides that "in any such exceptional circumstances, the authorities' main aim would be to reduce the risk of a serious problem causing wider financial or economic disruption."
13. Group of Ten (2001).
14. Rime (2005).
15. Systemic risks arising from the activities of large and complex financial institutions have been the subject of a number of studies. See for example Richard Herring, 2002. International financial conglomerates: implications for bank insolvency regimes. Paper given at the Second Annual International Seminar on "Policy challenges for the financial sector in the context of globalization," Washington D.C., June 5–7, 2002.
16. Under some insolvency laws, intragroup transactions may become subject to avoidance proceedings. Other approaches involve classifying intra-group transactions differently from similar transactions conducted between unrelated parties (e.g. a debt may be treated as an equity contribution rather than as an intragroup loan), with the consequence that the intragroup obligation will rank lower in priority than the same obligation between unrelated parties.
17. Baxter et al. (2004).
18. Remarks by Chairman Alan Greenspan. The financial safety net At the 37th Annual Conference on Bank Structure and Competition of the Federal Reserve Bank of Chicago, Chicago, Illinois May 10, 2001.
19. An orderly wind-down should permit the preservation and continued operation of critical functions performed by a failing financial institution. See Hüpkes (2005).
20. Some jurisdiction provide for a departure from this principle where a corporation has only one shareholder. See § 2362 of the Italian Civil Code. *(Unico azionista:) "In caso d'insolvenza della società, per le obbligazioni sociali sorte nel*

periodo in cui le azioni risultano essere appartenute ad una sola persona, questa risponde illimitatamente".

21. See, for example, N.Y. Banking L. § 606 *et seq.*

22. This lack of homogeneity is illustrated by the EC Collateral Directive. Under the Collateral Directive, Member States may opt to exclude from the scope of the Collateral Directive financial collateral arrangements in which the collateral taker and the collateral provider do not both belong to one of the listed categories of financial institutions and public authorities. In a jurisdiction that opted for the most limited scope of application of the collateral directive, the identical contract could be governed by different rules depending on whether or not they are financial institutions within the meaning of the Directive. The same is true for the set-off protection, which may not be available with certainty to nonfinancial institutions governed by the Insolvency Regulation.

23. The mechanisms to preserve critical functions are discussed in Hüpkes (2005).

24. Under U.S. law, a holding company is required to act as a source of strength to its subsidiary banks (cf. 12 C.F.R. § 225.4). The law requires that holding companies use capital of subsidiary banks to cover the losses of each individual bank subsidiary. The law also gives the FDIC "cross-guarantee" provision, which it can use to defray the cost of liquidating a failed subsidiary bank with the capital of a healthy subsidiary. While in most jurisdictions a parent holding company cannot be held liable for its subsidiaries, regulators may require that regulated subsidiaries be at all times adequately capitalized and that failure to adequately capitalize a subsidiary bank may be amount to a violation of the requirement that controlling shareholders be fit and proper. As a consequence, the regulator may order a sale of the regulated subsidiary to a third party. For the purposes of defining the scope of consolidation a recent amendment to the Swiss Banking Ordinance sets forth criteria that give rise to a presumption that legally independent entities form a single economic entity and may come to rescue each other (Art. 12 of the amendment to the Banking Ordinance of 1972). Besides the existence of a control relationship due to ownership or other economic factors, personal or financial entanglement, the use of a common brand or name, a uniform market presence, and letters of comfort are conditions that among others may also serve as indicators for the existence of a de facto interdependence among legal entities. See also the decision of the Switzerland's Federal Supreme Court, BGE 116 Ib 337, 338, 339, 342 (finding that there is a de facto obligation (*"faktischer Beistandszwang"*) on the part of the other members to come to the rescue of the weak member).

25. The need for regulatory cooperation across industry groups was also taken up by the Group of Thirty in their report on reducing systemic risk. Global Institutions, National Supervision, and Systemic Risk (1997) examines the potential for systemic risk arising from the gap between the global operations of financial institutions and markets and nationally based systems of accounting, reporting, law, and supervision. The Group of Thirty argues that some of the large international financial institutions that dominate finance today need global, hands-on supervision. In the absence of a global agency, it suggests that someone at the center of the process needs to coordinate contacts among

supervisors and their sharing of information. The Group of Thirty believes that regulatory cooperation across borders and functions will come about only "*if supervisors recognise their mutual interdependence and adopt common supervisory techniques.*"

26. In Principles for the Supervision of Financial Conglomerates (1995), a document written by the Tripartite Group of bank, securities, and insurance regulators, which later became the Joint Forum, supervisory cooperation is touted as one of the eight major principles of financial supervision. This is because the financial activities of many financial conglomerates are subject to regulation from different regulators in one country and also often a number of regulators from other jurisdictions. The Joint Forum's Framework for Supervisory Information Sharing (Supervision of Financial Conglomerates), 1999 follows up the Tripartite Committee's recommendations. The paper outlines a framework to facilitate information sharing between regulators of financial conglomerates and is accompanied by Principles for Supervisory Information Sharing (1999). These principles were further elaborated on in ten key principles of information sharing issued by the G-7 finance ministers in May 1998.

27. To regulate conglomerates, the GLBA introduced the concept of a financial holding company (FHC) and placed the Federal Reserve in charge of consolidated supervision of such holding companies. Underneath the holding company, the Fed is to rely on the existing functional regulators, such as the Securities and Exchange Commission (SEC), for information about securities affiliates and insurance regulators for insurance activities.

28. See Joint Forum, 1999, Supervision of Financial Conglomerates, pp. 112–119 ("Coordinator Paper"). The Coordinator Paper provides to supervisors guidance for the possible identification of a coordinator or coordinators and a catalogue of elements of coordination from which supervisors can select the role and responsibilities of a coordinator or coordinators in emergency and non-emergency situations.

29. See *infra* note 31.

30. Council Regulation (EC) No 1346/2000 of May 29, 2000, on insolvency proceedings.

31. European Parliament and Council Directive 2001/24/EC on the reorganization and winding-up of credit institutions; Directive 2001/17/EC on reorganization and winding up of insurance undertakings.

32. This paper uses the Joint Forum's definition of financial conglomerate, which is "*any group of companies under common control whose exclusive or predominant activities consist of providing significant services in at least two different financial sectors (banking, securities, insurance).*" In contrast, the definitions applied in the European Union and in the United States are somewhat narrower. The EU Financial Conglomerates Directive defines a financial conglomerate as having at least one insurance or reinsurance undertaking in combination with at least one firm from one or both of the banking and securities sectors. In the United States, a financial conglomerate is any combination of a bank with at least one firm from one or both of the insurance or securities sectors.

33. The Committee on European Banking Supervisors (CEBS) recently published a paper describing the range of practices on supervisory colleges and home-host cooperation and a template for a multilateral cooperation and coordination agreement on the supervision of an individual financial group.
34. Report of the FSF on Enhancing Market and Institutional Resilience, 7 April 2008.
35. See description in Cihak and Decressin (2007).
36. See Press Release of the 2753rd Council meeting Economic and Financial Affairs Luxembourg, October 10, 2006.
37. Concluding Statement of the IMF Mission on Euro-Area Policies in the Context of the 2007 Article IV Consultation Discussions with the Euro-Area Countries, May 30, 2007, see also Euro Area Policies: 2007 Article IV Consultation, Staff Report, July 2007 IMF Country Report No. 07/260.
38. For this reason, the protection of local markets and local creditors' interests will take precedence over more global objectives, even if such an outcome would be superior in the sense that total costs would be lower. This is the underlying rationale for measures such as ring fencing and capital maintenance requirements that host regulators may impose on foreign bank branches in order to secure local creditors' claims in the event of the failure of the head office.
39. Holthausen and Ronde (2004).
40. 12 USC 1823 (c)(4)(A)(ii).
41. "Regulatory challenges of cross-border banking—possible ways forward. Speech by Stefan Ingves, governor of the Sveriges Riksbank, at the Reserve Bank of Australia, Sydney, July 23, 2007, BIS Review 83/2007.
42. In June 2007, the European Commission (Commission) launched a public consultation on the Reorganisation and Winding Up of Credit Institutions Directive (2001/24/EC). The Commission sought stakeholders' opinions, among others, on whether special provisions are needed to address the problems of cross-border reorganization and winding-up of banking groups and the obstacles to the transferability of assets in a crisis situation.
43. See Cihak and Decressin (2007).
44. These difficulties are illustrated by the Parmalat case. The Italian Dairy group of companies was operated in Europe, but also in many other parts of the world, including South America, South Africa, Canada, United States, and Australia. Proceedings were opened in different countries with no sufficient cooperation and no one single direction for the entire group. The mandate of the Italian extraordinary administrator was to try to design a global reconstruction plan for the group as a whole. The specific aim was to preserve the group as a going concern. However, one of the greatest threats the administrator faced was disintegration, brought on by local creditors opening separate proceeding in different places around the world.
45. As was expressly indicated in the Report Virgos/Schmit (1996) (para. 76)"[t]he Convention offers no rule for groups of affiliated companies (parent-subsidiary schemes). The general rule to open or to consolidate insolvency proceedings against any of the related companies as a principal or jointly liable debtor is that

jurisdiction must exist according to the Convention for each of the concerned debtors with a separate legal entity. Naturally, the drawing of a European norm on associated companies may affect this answer". The Report had been issued to serve as an interpretive guide to the Insolvency Convention of 1995, which five years later was altered to the Insolvency Regulation. The Report has been recognized as an unofficial guide to interpretation (see comments made in this regard in EU Regulation courts' decisions for instance *In re* Brac Rent-A-Car Inc [2003] EWHC (Ch) 128, [2003] BCC 504 and in Geveran Trading Co Ltd v Skjevesland [2003] BCC 209; see also Wessels (2003).

46. American Law Institute, Transnational Insolvency: cooperation among the NAFTA Countries (2003).
47. Baxter et al. (2004).
48. Hüpkes (2006).
49. Also see the 2004 UNCITRAL Legislative Guide on Insolvency Law, Part II, Chapter V, para. 92.
50. The texts of the UNCITRAL (United Nations Commission on International Trade Law) Model Law and Guide to Enactment are available through the UNCITRAL website at: www.uncitral.org/uncitral/en/uncitral_texts /insolvency/ 1997Model.html.

References

Baxter, Thomas, Joyce Hansen, and Joseph Sommer. 2004. Two cheers for territoriality: An essay on international bank insolvency law. *American Bankruptcy Law Journal* 78: 57–91.

Bliss, Robert, and George Kaufman. 2006. U.S. corporate and bank insolvency regimes: An economic comparison and evaluation. Federal Reserve Bank of Chicago working paper no. 2006–01.

Cihak, Martin, and Jörg Decressin. 2007. The case for a European banking charter. IMF working paper WP/07/173.

Corrigan,Gerald. 1982. Are banks special? In Federal Reserve Bank of Minneapolis *Annual Report*, 5–7. http://minneapolisfed.org/pubs/ar/ar1982a.html.

Group of Ten. 2001. Report on consolidation in the financial sector, www.imf.org/external/np/g10/2001/01/Eng/index.htm.

Group of Thirty. 1997. *Global Institutions, National Supervision and Systemic Risk*. Washington, D.C.: Group of Thirty.

Hart, Oliver. 2000. Different approaches to bankruptcy. Harvard Institute of Economic Research Paper No. 1903.

Holthausen, Cornelia, and Thomas Ronde. 2004. Cooperation in international banking supervision. European Central Bank working paper 316.

Hüpkes, Eva. 2005. "Too big to save": Towards a functional approach to resolving crises in global financial institutions. In *Systemic financial crisis: resolving large bank insolvencies*, ed. Douglas Evanoff and George Kaufman, 193–215. Singapore: World Scientific Publishing.

———. 2006. The legal framework for foreign bank entry. *Banks and bank systems* 1: 4–15.

Ingves, Stefan. 2007. Regulatory challenges of cross-border banking – possible ways forward. Speech at the Reserve Bank of Australia, Sydney, July 23, 2007, *BIS Quarterly Review* 83/2007.Joint Forum on Financial Conglomerates. 1999. Supervision of Financial Conglomerates. Documents jointly released by the Basel Committee on Banking Supervision, the International Organization of Securities Commissions, and the International Association of Insurance Supervisors, Basel.

Kelley Jr., Edward. 1997. "Are banks still special?" In *Banking soundness and monetary policy*, ed. Charles Enoch and John H. Green, 263. Washington D.C.: International Monetary Fund.

Rime, Bertrand. 2005. Do "too big to fail" expectations boost large bank issuer ratings? Paper presented at the banking and financial stability workshop on applied banking research, April 21, in Vienna.

Wessels, Bob. 2003. International jurisdiction to open insolvency proceedings in Europe, in particular against (groups of) companies, WP017, Working Papers Series, Institute for Law and Finance (Johann Wolfgang Goethe University).

4

The Political Economy of Burden Sharing and Prompt Corrective Action

Gillian G. H. Garcia[*]

Introduction

A number of writers have observed that problems exist in the safety net that the European Union (EU) currently has in place to ensure financial stability.[1] These deficiencies present a potentially serious international problem as banks increasingly cross state borders—a problem that has become more immediate as a result of the turmoil in the credit markets that started in the summer of 2007. While I am aware that safety-net deficiencies are a worldwide problem, this chapter confines its analysis to arrangements in the United States and the EU. Acceptance of the criticisms of the situation in the EU has provoked a lively discussion of how to improve it. Greater degrees of federalism and uniformity appear to be politically unacceptable in the EU at present (Ingves 2007), and especially after the Irish rejection of the EU Treaty in spring 2008, so proposals for sharing the cost of resolving cross-border failed banks across member countries (burden sharing) and for initiating prompt corrective action (PCA) by supervisors are being offered as alternative remedies. This chapter discusses these two ideas in the light of the U.S. experience.

The chapter also characterizes the evolution of the financial safety net in the United States as progressing from Phase 1 in which it was undefined and invited catastrophe, to Phase 2 in which the country was prepared for political reasons to fully compensate creditors and sometimes even owners in the name of avoiding financial and economic disaster. In Phase 3, which lasted until the subprime crisis of 2007–2008, policymakers in the United States acknowledged that bailouts encourage moral hazard, conflicts of interest, and other incentive problems and that these problems weaken the financial system in the long run. As a result they realigned incentives in order to minimize costs to the taxpayer, contain moral hazard, and strengthen both the financial system and the economy. While it is too early to be certain, it may be that the subprime debacle has caused the authorities to begin on a new era—Phase 4—with a round of nonbank bailouts.

The current safety-net arrangements in the EU appear to have the characteristics appropriate for Phase 1. Burden sharing—a policy currently under discussion in the EU—potentially belongs to the safety net's Phase 2, while a successful system PCA and early resolution would seem to be essential ingredients for achieving least cost resolutions in a Phase 3.

I begin by briefly examining the history of the three progressive phases in the provision of the financial safety net in the United States. In the next section, I summarize problems that currently exist in the EU's financial safety net and point out some disadvantages of burden sharing as a potential solution to these problems. Then, I note the role of PCA in enabling a country to move to Phase 3 and compare PCA as enacted in the United States with that proposed by the European Shadow Financial Regulatory Committee (ESFRC) for the EU. Next, I examine the political history of PCA in the United States by describing supervisory opposition to its enactment, by discussing the unusual political situation that helped to overcome this opposition, and by noting some questions about its implementation. Finally, I consider the likelihood of PCA's enactment in the EU, noting differences between, and similarities in, the financial environment in the United States 20 years ago and the EU today. I also observe, however, that PCA should not be regarded as a panacea for the EU, which also needs to reform its system of deposit insurance and failed bank resolution—at least for large complex financial institutions (LCFIs)—in order to achieve prompt and cost-effective remedial action.

Phases of the Financial Safety Net in the United States

With the exception of the First and Second Banks of the United States, banks in the United States were all chartered by the states until the Office of the Comptroller of the Currency was created in 1863 to charter and supervise national banks.[2] Subsequently, the United States has had a dual banking system with banks chartered and supervised by federal and/or state governments. It was not until the 1980s, however, that many banks, whether national or state, were able to move beyond their home state as separately chartered subsidiaries of a bank holding company (Garcia 2008). Moreover, few banks were able to branch across state lines until the 1994 Riegle-Neal Interstate Branch Banking and Efficiency Act (IBBEA) was widely implemented in 1997. Consequently, the United States has had to only relatively recently consider the problems arising from the failure of interstate banks.

When problems surrounding failures of interstate banks do arise in the United States, they are ameliorated by having a federal system of deposit insurance that is applied equally across all states and provides prompt reimbursement to insured depositors and hopefully speedy provision of estimated recovery values to the uninsured. In addition, the United States has a federal lender of last resort, a federal Treasury, to provide financial assistance nationwide when it is deemed to be unavoidably necessary and a federal agency, the Federal Deposit Insurance Corporation (FDIC), to resolve failed banks across the land. This tidy arrangement is violated somewhat, however, because the FDIC does not resolve holding companies, which remain the province of state laws and procedures (Bliss and Kaufman 2006).

Phase I: The Great Depression

The United States experienced periodic banking panics in the nineteenth century and suffered two major episodes of bank and thrift failures in the twentieth century. During the crisis of the early 1930s, the United States. can be described as having been in Phase 1 of the safety-net provision. It lacked policies, institutions, and procedures for dealing adequately with troubled banks. For example, while the Federal Reserve had existed since 1913, it failed as the monetary authority and lender of last resort to alleviate banks' problems and prevent them from spilling over to the macroeconomy. In addition, there was no system of federal deposit insurance and no federal resolution agency for failed banks. It is widely acknowledged that the inadequacy of the U.S. authorities' responses contributed significantly to the depth of the Great Depression (Friedman and Schwartz 1963; Bernanke 1983).

The undefined situation in Phase 1 is unsatisfactory partly because players do not know the rules of the game and so cannot act to successfully protect their own interests. Further, the authorities' delayed or ineffective responses can cause the public to lose confidence in the banking system and run from it in panic. Finally, the unplanned, ad hoc, hurried actions the authorities finally take (or fail to take) may discriminate unfairly among market participants. Moreover, decision-makers are unlikely to be held accountable for their inaction or mistaken actions. Adverse consequences ensue.

Phase 2: Rescuing failed banks in the 1980s

Having been burnt under such safety-net inadequacies during the Great Depression, U.S. policymakers subsequently moved to Phase 2 by enacting legislation, including the Glass-Steagall Act to curb opportunistic behavior, and by creating the FDIC to insure small deposits and resolve failed banks. In the next almost six subsequent decades policymakers used their discretion to do whatever they thought necessary to maintain stability in the financial markets in the short run and to avoid adverse repercussions on the economy. Such an approach could involve recapitalizing large failed banks in order to keep them operating.

In the 1984 rescue of Continental Illinois National Bank, for example, public assistance was offered to keep the bank open and operating. Protection was offered not only to insured depositors, but also to uninsured creditors and even to subordinated bondholders, although shareholders were penalized. The comptroller of the currency testified before Congress that regulators were afraid of spillover—for example, to banks that held correspondent accounts at Continental—and that they were reluctant to find out what would happen if they failed to protect all creditors. With the rescue of Continental Illinois the age of *too big to fail* had dawned in the United States and with it Phase 2 of the U.S. financial safety net.

Continental's rescue was immediately criticized in Congress and academia as being unfair to small banks. As a result the FDIC arranged the resolution of the more than 1,617 banks that failed between 1980 and 1994 in ways that protected almost all creditors—insured and uninsured—alike. Sometimes even shareholders benefited (Bair 2007). This period is, therefore, an era of extensive public support for failing banks that may be compared to the current proposal for the public sectors in member countries to share the costs of recapitalizing large failed banks that cross EU borders.

Phase 3: PCA and least cost resolution

By the 1990s U.S. academics and policymakers had concluded that such efforts to maintain stability in the short run exacerbated moral hazard in the longer term by encouraging those protected to take excessive risks that harmed financial soundness. They blamed the 2,912 bank and thrift failures that occurred between 1980 and 1994 on inadequate capital standards, lax accounting, fraud, and safety-net extensions beyond insured deposits.[3] The budgetary costs to the taxpayer (estimated by the FDIC at $150 billion) of resolving failed savings and loan associations (S&Ls) and the need for the FDIC to borrow from the Treasury in 1991 to meet its out-lays for commercial bank failures focused attention on the long-term costs of overgenerous protection.

Congress responded first by enacting the Competitive Equality Banking Act of 1987 to diminish preferential treatment when resolving large failed banks. The legislation gave the FDIC the ability to remove a bank's charter while keeping it open and operating as a bridge bank. Second, in the FDIC Improvement Act (FDICIA) of 1991, Congress shifted U.S. policy toward Phase 3: supervisors were instructed to practice prompt corrective super-visory action, and the FDIC was required to adopt a method of failed bank resolution that is least costly to the Bank Insurance Fund (BIF). PCA was intended to close failed banks before they incurred heavy losses, and least cost resolution sharply curtailed the FDIC's discretion to protect unin-sured creditors, who henceforth could expect to incur losses when their bank failed.

While FDICIA was under consideration, the FDIC expressed hesitancy about its own operational ability to resolve a large failed bank under least cost procedures.[4] Consequently, FDICIA included a systemic risk excep-tion that would allow the FDIC to protect uninsured creditors if it were determined that doing otherwise would "have serious adverse effects on economic conditions and financial stability," and that "any action or assis-tance under this subparagraph would avoid or mitigate such adverse effects" (U.S. Congress 1991: FDICIA Sec. 141[a][4][G]). To invoke this exception the FDIC would need a two-thirds majority of the boards of both the FDIC and the Federal Reserve and the approval of the secretary of the Treasury after he had consulted with the president. The banking industry would be required to pay the additional costs of a resolution under the sys-temic risk exception through a special assessment proportional to each bank's total liabilities, so that the costs would fall heavily on large banks, which typically rely heavily on uninsured funds, and not on the taxpayer. Thus, while there is still a possibility that the FDIC might rescue uninsured creditors and possibly even owners, bailout possibilities for commercial and savings banks in the United States have been considerably reduced, albeit not entirely eliminated.

In effect, since FDICIA the FDIC has met the least cost test in all of its resolutions and only insured depositors have been protected by the deposit insurance fund (Bair 2007).[5] According to its chairman, the FDIC has not invoked or even seriously considered the systemic risk exception. Although IndyMac Bank with assets of $32 billion failed on July 11, 2008, no mega bank had failed since 1991. The FDIC, recognizing that resolving a com-plex bank with over $100 billion in assets would be problematic, has been making preparations to meet the challenge.[6]

To preserve confidence and prevent spillover to the macroeconomy the FDIC needs to restore all depositors' access to their funds promptly so that they can continue to conduct business with little or no interruption. It does this by typically closing a bank on Friday afternoon and reopening it on Monday with insured depositors having virtually continuous access to their funds. The FDIC also attempts to give uninsured creditors prompt access to a substantial portion of their funds. The federal agency typically advances to uninsured creditors their pro rata share of the present value of the net amount it estimates that it will obtain by selling the failed bank's assets (Kaufman and Seelig 2002). It does this the day after it is appointed receiver, unless it is unable to estimate recovery values.[7] If the FDIC later recovers more than it expected, it makes a supplemental payment. If it overestimates, it takes the loss; consequently, it tends to estimate conservatively.

One of the operational problems the FDIC would face is imposing losses on uninsured creditors while giving them speedy access to their remaining funds in order to avoid a liquidity crunch that would harm the economy. If a large bank were to fail the FDIC would need to quickly decide what haircut would be appropriate for imposing on uninsured depositors and other creditors. Doing this currently would be difficult because bank records do not facilitate making an accurate distinction between insured and uninsured funds. Consequently, the FDIC is proposing that certain banks change their record systems to enable them to place a provisional hold on a small percentage of every depositor's uninsured funds, pending the FDIC imposing a haircut, while giving owners prompt access to the remaining bulk of their funds (FDIC 2006).[8]

The United States has accomplished Phase 3 of the safety-net provision, at least in principle. Whether the policies and procedures in place would in fact succeed in practice awaits the testing imposed by the failure of an LCFI. Large banks today are many times bigger than the largest banks the FDIC has ever resolved to date.[9] Further, bank operations have become highly complex and rely heavily on uninsured deposits and other sources of funds. So market participants may believe that the authorities will experience a time inconsistency problem; that is, they would "chicken out" into an extensive rescue should a large bank get into trouble.

Deficiencies in the EU's Financial Safety Net

On the basis of the studies listed in footnote 1 I conclude that the EU today is in Phase 1—euphemistically characterized as *constructive ambiguity.* Gillian Garcia and Maria Nieto (2005 and 2007) examine the deficiencies of the EU's financial safety net in detail, and their findings are summarized briefly as follows.

Supervision

Since the late 1980s the Second Market Directive has allowed EU banks to branch across the borders of member countries with the permission of the home supervisor, while cross-border subsidiaries are chartered by their host country. All EU banks are chartered and supervised by member countries—there is currently no bank with an EU charter and no EU regulator/ supervisor. The home country supervises the main bank and its consolidated entity, while the host oversees subsidiaries. Prudential data and supervisory practices vary across countries. Having several supervisors involved in overseeing a cross-border bank presents a problem for the home country to obtain a complete picture of the institution and for the host to be confident that the home country is supervising adequately. Unpublished and unenforceable memoranda of understanding (European Central Bank 2003 and 2005) aim to facilitate the timely exchange of information among the many supervisors, central banks, and treasury departments, but there is doubt whether they would succeed in doing so in a crisis.[10]

Liquidity assistance

Lending of last resort principally remains a task for the monetary authority of each member country together with the European Central Bank (ECB), which has responsibility for the payment system. It could easily provide liquidity to the markets in general during a market freeze and vigorously did so during the credit turmoil in 2007 and 2008. It is unclear whether the responsibility for providing liquidity assistance to individual cross-border banks falls on home or host country and whether either the home or host country would be willing, or able, to provide emergency liquidity assistance to a bank or a branch from another member country when the cost of that aid would ultimately devolve on its national budget.

Deposit insurance

The home country is responsible for deposit insurance for cross-border branches, except that the host deposit insurer may also be involved in cases in which the branch has topped up its coverage to the higher levels that the host country offers. Cross-border subsidiaries are insured by the host country. Some countries offer coverage above the EU's 20,000 minimum per depositor. It is unclear whether a home deposit insurer would in fact be willing to reimburse depositors in another country. Further, it is unclear whether a host country would be prepared to use its funds to support depositors in the topping-up branches and the subsidiaries of a cross-border bank, especially if it feels that the inadequacies of home-country supervision contributed to the failure.

Failed bank resolution

Responsibility for resolving a failed bank and its branches lies with the home country under the EU's universal approach in its 2001 Directive on Reorganization and Winding Up. Philosophies and laws regarding bankruptcy vary widely across member countries, and banks frequently do not have special laws covering their demise and are often subject to court action. Cross-border subsidiary banks are to be resolved by the host country that chartered them under its laws. It is unclear whether countries would be willing,[11] or small countries would be able, to provide funds to facilitate the resolution of cross-border banks. A deficiency in funding for resolutions could lead to forbearance followed by the ultimate liquidation of the failed bank rather than a preferred alternative form of resolution that allows a failed bank to continue its core operations under different owners and managers.

In any event, reimbursement of insured deposits would probably not be prompt either within or across borders—the 1994 directive on deposit guarantee schemes requires only that payment be made within three months and allows member countries to extend that period three times in exceptional circumstances (Directive 1994, Article 10). Moreover, uninsured creditors would need to wait for the liquidator to dispense the proceeds from selling the bank's assets.

Accountability

The crux of the cross-border dilemma is that countries are accountable to their own parliaments, not to an EU body, for their expenditures for supervision, liquidity assistance, deposit insurance, and bank resolution. Countries can be expected, therefore, to be reluctant to let their taxpayers' funds cross borders to another member country. At the same time, there is no "federal" fiscal authority in the EU that could provide resources to fund cross-border responsibilities. It is unclear, therefore, what would happen should an LCFI get into difficulties. Numerous authorities would need to agree on action, and it seems possible that unanimity will not be reached in a sufficiently timely fashion for it to be successful.[12] Such a situation could lead to the liquidation of the failed bank rather than to a preferable alternative form of resolution.

Some analysts welcome these uncertainties over responsibilities as serving to discourage moral hazard. Others disagree because they see constructive ambiguity as gambling that a problem will not arise and having to improvise a response if one should occur. The dissenters consider it to be asking for trouble—the financial system and the economy at large would suffer in the short run unless policymakers organize a rescue to avoid liquidating the bank and experiencing liquidation's unfortunate economic outcomes. It would be difficult to calibrate the extent of the rescue so that it contained the crisis without constituting a bailout. Overgenerous open-bank assistance could encourage undue risk taking and so weaken the system in the long run. Moreover, in the cross-border context it may well not be possible to agree on funding for a response quickly enough to avoid a damaging financial and economic crisis.

The press has reported that the EU has held exercises to test the resilience of its arrangements for crisis resolution, but the EU has not published the results of its simulations. The proposal for burden sharing may have arisen, however, as a result of concerns over inadequacies revealed in the crisis simulations. Further, Xavier Freixas (2003) has shown that there is likely to be an underprovision of recapitalization services where cross-border externalities are present, and Dirk Schoenmaker and Sander Oosterloo (2005) have demonstrated that such externalities are growing.

Burden sharing and PCA as solutions

The aforementioned concerns have prompted some analysts to call for a pool of funds to be made available to provide support should a cross-border LCFI get into difficulties (Boot 2007). The idea is to prevent an institution from being liquidated with the inherent loss of its going-concern value and disruption to the economy. Charles Goodhart and Stephen Smith (1993) propose a system of general burden sharing in which the ECB would use its seigniorage to fund rescues (with side arrangements for countries that are not members of the European Monetary Union). Goodhart and Schoenmaker (2006) and Wim Fonteyne (2007) propose specific burden sharing in which countries that would benefit most from the rescue pay most for it.

Getting agreement on a burden-sharing arrangement is proving politically difficult, however (Parker 2007). A question arises, therefore, whether the EU should expend its political capital on moving from Phase 1 into

Phase 2 if it agrees in fact that Phase 2 is only second best to Phase 3. Would it not be better to aim to move straight from the current ambiguity to an ultimately ideal solution and skip burden sharing? One strong disadvantage of burden sharing is that it might well make policymakers content to let matters rest after achieving such an agreement so that they would fail to take the many other steps that the EU could and should take to strengthen its financial system. The general burden-sharing scheme would also suffer from free riding. The specific burden-sharing scheme, in which countries that benefit from the rescue should pay for it, could impose major costs on host countries, even though the home country has responsibility for consolidated supervision and for deposit insurance and failure resolution for branches. Home countries might conduct these responsibilities more vigorously if they are expected to pay the costs of deficiencies in their performance.

Moving to Phase 3 would require that the EU make a number of improvements to its present safety-net arrangements. The principles that would underlie these changes are listed in table 4.1. In a nutshell, the discussion of burden sharing may be putting the cart before the horse. It would be preferable to avoid having any burden for anyone, especially taxpayers, to share. Table 4.1 offers a list of principles that the EU would need

Table 4.1   Principles to make burden sharing redundant

Avoid bailouts
Ensure strong supervision with mandatory prompt corrective action (PCA)
Make adequate prudential information publicly available
Let public know who is the LOLR that will lend to illiquid but solvent banks
Remove a critically undercapitalized bank's charter if it is not recapitalized promptly
The failed institution should not be allowed to have its charter removal reversed; instead
It should be able to sue for compensation if the charter is held to have been wrongfully removed
Require a bank resolution to be conducted at least cost to public (deposit insurance) funds
Have financial institutions cover the cost of limited depositor protection
Ensure deposit insurance funding is adequate
Pay insured depositors promptly (in a very few days)
Apply a haircut on uninsured credits so that their owners can also access their remaining
     funds quickly
Make sure that bank records and operations are adequate to do this
Use a low value for estimated recovery values when making the haircut
Payment to the uninsured can be increased later if actual recoveries exceed the estimated value
Deposit insurer should take the loss if it overestimates the values that will be recovered
State makes temporary back-up funds available if the deposit insurer's funds are insufficient
Arrange for insured institutions to repay any state advance ASAP
Supervisor, LOLR, deposit insurer, resolution agency accountable to home authorities
Make them also answerable to an EU body

Source: The author.

to adopt if it were to aspire to a Phase 3 safety net. PCA is a necessary condition in this set of principles, but it is not sufficient.

PCA as Enacted in the United States and Proposed for the EU

It is eminently sensible for bank supervisors to apply a set of increasingly stringent measures to a bank as its capital ratios deteriorate. The objective is to force owners and managers to correct the bank's deficiencies before it becomes nonviable. Such a process can be seen as "Prompt Corrective Action (PCA) light." For decades U.S. supervisors had sufficient authority to practice PCA light, but they "had a tendency to discard [it] under pressure" (Carnell 1995, p. 314). Some supervisors in the EU today, such as those in the UK, claim that they voluntarily conduct PCA already. The ESFRC (2007) has proposed that supervisors in the EU adopt a more exacting model of PCA—somewhat similar to that in use in the United States, but adapted to make it suitable for the EU. PCA in the United States and as proposed by the ESFRC is mandatory and therefore more onerous for supervisors. In fact, no EU member is listed as practicing mandatory PCA in table 1 of the paper by Nieto and Larry Wall (2006).

At the press conference at the start of the LSE/ESFRC conference on PCA for the EU a reporter asked if, and when, PCA would become mandatory in Europe. This chapter argues that PCA was enacted in the United States in response to a particular set of severe circumstances that existed in the early 1990s and which allowed Congress and the administration to join together in a bipartisan effort that overcame opposition from the nation's banking regulators.[13] It has often been said that it takes a crisis to engineer financial reform in the United States, and the same may be true for Europe. One step toward answering the reporter's question would be to find out whether banking regulators in the EU would be opposed to mandatory PCA—they might well be because it would diminish their discretion.[14] In this case, a banking crisis in the EU might be a prerequisite for overcoming their opposition. If national regulators in the EU are indeed opposed to mandatory PCA, then answering the reporter's "$64,000 question" requires assessing whether circumstances in the EU are similar to those in the United States in the period leading up to its crises 20 years ago—as is done in the concluding section.

Features of PCA

PCA, as it is conducted in the United States where it originated and as proposed by the ESFRC, is a much more demanding construct than PCA light.

Table 4.2 enumerates the features that make U.S. and ESFRC PCA more onerous for supervisors. In particular, U.S. PCA is enshrined in legislation—the FDICIA of 1991—that requires supervisors to take specified actions when a bank becomes less than well capitalized and to take increasingly punitive corrective measures as the bank falls below further capital trigger ratios. Supervisors are accountable for their actions.

In addition to requiring a rather detailed sequence of corrective measures that are described in table 10 of the paper by Robert Eisenbeis and George Kaufman (2006), U.S. PCA is notable first in that it was made mandatory for U.S. supervisors under FDICIA. As will be argued in the next section, PCA was mandated because during the bank/thrift debacle of the 1980s and early 1990s Congress and the public lost confidence that the actions of U.S. supervisors would serve the public interest. This distrust overcame supervisors' opposition to the diminution of their discretion. Making PCA mandatory in the EU would be contentious, because reducing

Table 4.2   Attributes of PCA

	U.S. PCA	*PCA in the ESFRC Proposal*
1	Supervisors are required to apply increasingly severe measures as a bank's capital declines	Supervisors would apply increasingly severe measures as a bank's capital declines
2	The nature of the corrective measures are mandated in legislation (FDICIA)	Similarly in a new EU directive and in national laws and regulations that implement the directive
3	Banks are divided into five groups: from (1) well-, (2) adequately, (3) under-, (4) significantly under-, to (5) critically undercapitalized	Banks could be similarly divided into 5 groups: ranging from well-capitalized to critically under-capitalized
4	Legislation requires two capital measures: the leverage ratio and a risk-based measure. Supervisors added a second risk-based measure by regulation	Groupings would be based on two capital measures: a risk-based and a leverage ratio
5	Increasingly severe corrective steps are taken when a bank fails to meet any of the 3 trigger ratios	Corrective steps would be taken when a bank falls below either of the trigger capital ratios
6	Closure is mandated at or below 2% capital to total assets (leverage ratio)	At the fifth stage the bank should be treated as insolvent under national law, if possible
7	Supervisors are held accountable by their agency's inspector general, Congress, and GAO	Make the EU's single banking license conditional on effective PCA, as adjudicated by an EU body.

Source: Author's analysis of FDICIA (1991) and the ESFRC proposal.

Table 4.3   PCA Capital measures

Capital Measure	Well Capitalized	Adequately Capitalized	Under Capitalized	Significantly Under Capitalized	Critically Under Capitalized
Total capital to	10	8	< 8	< 6	
risk assets	and	and	or	or	
Tier 1 capital	6	4	< 4	< 3	
to risk assets	and	and	or	or	
Leverage Tangible	5	4	< 4	< 3	2 or less
equity/assets					

Source: FDIC at www.fdic.gov

national supervisors' discretion would be seen as a repudiation of their integrity and judgment. Moreover, as Thomas Huertas (2007) argued at the LSE/ESFRC conference, enshrining mandatory action in legislation might weaken the set of corrective measures already available to supervisors.

PCA in the United States is also notable on a second account in that, although only two ratios are required under the legislation to categorize banks into five specified groups, supervisors use three different capital ratios.[15] Two of these are risk-based, while the third—the leverage ratio—is not, being required in the legislation and defined as the ratio of tangible equity capital to total assets. Table 4.3 reports the numerical ratios currently in effect in the United States.

The U.S. legislation is quite explicit, however, with regard to the leverage limit, which it defines as the ratio of tangible equity to total assets and sets the lower boundary for identifying a critically undercapitalized bank at not less than 2 percent. The FDIC is given the final "say" with regard to capital requirements for PCA, because the other regulators are required to obtain its concurrence. The ESFRC proposes to use a risk-based and a leverage measure for European PCA. The EU's Capital Adequacy Directive, enacted to implement Basel II, does not, however, include a leverage ratio. So mandating one might prove politically problematic.

The third notable feature of U.S. PCA is that it requires supervisors to close an institution within 90 days when its leverage ratio declines to 2 percent. (The 90 days can be extended twice to give owners a fair opportunity to recapitalize their institution.)[16] Experience during the U.S. bank/thrift crisis had shown that allowing institutions to continue to operate and gamble without their own capital at risk added substantially to the losses that they, and hence the insurance fund, incurred. The idea here was also that the market value of the capital to assets ratio would already be negative by the time the book-value ratio had reached 2 percent. Hence, the institution should be closed and quickly resolved by placing it in FDIC receivership.[17] A large institution could become a temporary bridge bank; other banks would be sold promptly in whole or in parts to new private owners or, as a last resort, liquidated. The objective of the resolution process is minimizing the cost of resolution to the Bank Insurance Fund while at the same time avoiding spillover and keeping the bank's services available to its customers.

Most (albeit not all) of the failed banks and thrifts in the United States in the 1980s and early 1990s were not large enough to present the FDIC with difficulties. The banking industry in Europe is more concentrated today than that in the United States 15 –20 years ago. It is well known that resolving a failed mega institution is a major challenge for the authorities, who may be tempted to bail it out, that is, recapitalize it without penalizing its owners and managers/ mismanagers. PCA, requiring owners to recapitalize before insolvency, appears to be a valuable alternative to open bank assistance/bailouts in the EU. However, the EU may be unable to replicate this early closure notion should it wish to do so. The reason, as Rosa Lastra and Clas Wihlborg (2007) point out, is removing owners before book-value insolvency is illegal, even unconstitutional, in some member countries.

A fourth feature of PCA in the United States is that regulators, while formally independent of the executive branch, are accountable to their agency's own inspector general and to Congress, which has oversight responsibility for the regulatory agencies. These agencies appear before Congress in periodic oversight hearings and for special investigations. Congressional oversight is boosted by the efforts of its research bodies, in particular those of the Government Accountability Office (GAO), which audits supervisory budgets. It can and does conduct investigations of supervisory deficiencies. In addition, inspectors general of the regulatory agencies have set high standards in their "material loss reviews" that are mandated by FDICIA when the FDIC suffers a serious loss in covering the insured deposits of a failed bank or thrift.[18] The Treasury Department's IG report on the failure of Superior Bank in 2002 is, for example, highly critical of the Office of Thrift Supervision and, in particular, of its trust in the owners' commitment to recapitalize the troubled institution (Rush 2002).

Accountability is aided by the Federal Financial Institutions Examination Council (FFIEC), which was created in 1978 among other things to standardize the quarterly "call report" balance sheet and income data that every insured depository institution submits to its supervisor (FDIC 1998). The primary regulator collects the information and conveys it to the FDIC, which then consolidates and collates it and makes it publicly available. GAO had access to and used these time series data in its accounting and investigative reports during the banking and thrift debacles. During the crisis, private data companies provided user-friendly software, data series and analysis so that the public—and congressional staffs—could conduct their own inquiries. Congressional staffs were then able to analyze the condition of weak and failing thrifts and to call forbearing supervisors, who might otherwise have concealed the information, to order. Supervisors, knowing Congress had these data, were correspondingly more circumspect.

Currently, accountability varies in the EU across member countries. The ESFRC proposes that an EU body would assess a country's conformance with a new EU directive that would mandate PCA. ESFRC also proposes to make the availability of the new single banking license conditional on certification of conformance. Eisenbeis and Kaufman (2006) make a slightly different proposal. They would grant a single license only to banks that agree to be "subject to a legal closure rule at a positive capital ratio established by the EU or the home country." Standardizing call report data and making it publicly available in the EU would facilitate accountability and would seem to be a sine qua non for the success of whatever body is tasked with certifying conformance with PCA.

The Political History of PCA in the United States

Proponents of PCA as a remedy for safety-net deficiencies in the EU need to be aware of three aspects. First, the regulators had resisted PCA when it was mooted in the United States—they opposed the diminution of their discretion (Carnell 1993 and Horvitz 1995). Second, this chapter argues that it was enacted only because of the severe problems that existed in the banking and thrift industries in the years immediately prior to its enactment. Third, since enactment, PCA has not been fully tested by serious banking problems and worked as well as had been expected when it has been used.

Supervisory resistance

PCA light is meritorious; however, although they had the power to so, banking and thrift supervisors did not practice it before or during the banking debacle, as Richard Carnell notes. As mentioned above, PCA was initially heavily resisted by the regulators because it diminished their discretion (Carnell 1993 and Horvitz 1995).[19] In addition, Eisenbeis and Wall (2002) question whether regulators have been fully conscientious in implementing it since its enactment. I would expect supervisors in the EU to be similarly reluctant to see their discretion diminished. Some such opposition was expressed at the ESFRC conference held at the London School of Economics.

Only exceptional circumstances permitted enactment

This chapter argues that PCA was enacted only because of the severity of the problems in the banking and thrift industries in the United States during the 1980s and early 1990s. The cost to the taxpayer of compensating the depositors of failed institutions was enough to overcome the opposition and allow the authorities to adopt a version of structured early intervention and resolution (SEIR) being proposed at that time by Professors Benston and Kaufman and their colleagues on the U.S. Shadow Financial Regulatory Committee. Early intervention and resolution were intended to curtail taxpayer obligations to insured depository institutions. In fact Section 38(a) of FDICIA states that its purpose "is to resolve the problems of insured depository institutions at the least possible long-term loss to the deposit insurance fund."

The U.S. financial sector experienced a "double whammy," being confronted with debacles first in the thrift and then in the banking industries in the 1980s and early 1990s. In the decades after World War II the banking and thrift industries had been profitable and had experienced a period of calm that bred complacency among their regulators. FDIC historical statistics show that supervisors allowed the banking industry's capital-to-total assets ratio to decline from 8.1 percent in 1960 to 5.7 percent in 1974 in order to promote competition at home and abroad and allow the industries to expand. That ratio remained low until the 1990s, rising and subsequently remaining above 8 percent only in 1995. Capital ratios in the thrift industry were lower—indeed negative when market values were used.

The thrift debacle

At same time that bank and thrift capital ratios were falling, the economic environment was changing. Inflation caused market interest rates to rise, especially after the Federal Reserve tightened monetary policy sharply in 1979 to combat price escalation. The authorities deregulated deposit rates to allow banks and thrifts to compete with mutual funds, which were not subject to interest rate regulation. Thrifts funded their long-term fixed rate mortgages with short-term deposits. After deregulation the rates they paid in their liabilities rose faster than those they received on their assets, and they incurred heavy losses. Moreover, under both generally accepted and regulatory accounting standards, thrifts did not recognize the losses they were incurring in the market value of their portfolios. In an unsuccessful attempt to avert disaster, Congress enacted laws in the 1980s to allow them to broaden their asset base beyond their traditional 30-year fixed-rate

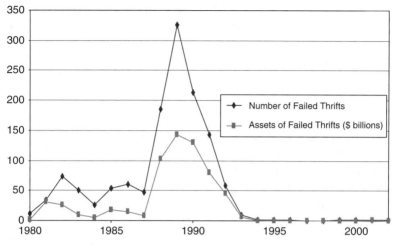

Source: The data come from the FDIC's Historical Statistics.

Figure 4.1   Number and assets of failed thrifts since 1980

mortgages and to conceal their deteriorating capital positions with regulatory accounting gimmicks.

Helped by an overgenerous and moral hazard-inducing increase in deposit insurance coverage to nine times per capita GDP in 1980, weak and insolvent thrifts continued to attract deposits. Many gambled for recovery but lost their bets and became insolvent, even under relaxed regulatory accounting standards. Figure 4.1 shows the seriousness of the situation in the late 1980s as the number of failures and the value of their assets rose sharply. The Federal Savings and Loan Insurance Fund (FSLIC) was already underfunded in the early 1980s and by the mid-1980s became unable to cope with the losses the industry was then incurring. It forbore, partly because it did not have the resources to compensate insured depositors.

Thrift trade associations played a part in concealing the extent of the scandal as it developed in the thrift industry. They focused on the role the industry played in providing American dream housing and assured supervisors, Congress, and the administration that industry was viable if granted whatever help they requested.[20] The trade associations, therefore, pressured supervisors to be lenient with the industry and give it time to "recover." Their actions explain, in part, the fact that the press was slow to comprehend the nature and extent of the thrift problem and so did not alert the public until very late in the debacle.

Congress was ineffective in its oversight of the supervisory agencies, and this served to encourage forbearance. Some congressmen and senators were indebted to the thrift industry for campaign contributions. They even interfered in the regulatory agencies, thwarted effective oversight, and encouraged forbearance. Other members of the House and the Senate wanted to promote housing and ensure low interest rates for homeowners and so ignored calls to recognize the developing debacle. GAO sent a succession of reports to Congress in the 1980s that described the nature and extent of the problems, with little effect. I characterized the report-to-Congress process as similar to "throwing a pigeon to the cats"—after an initial flurry of activity when the cats pounced on, killed, and devoured it, the bird would disappear without trace, not a feather would remain.[21]

At the same, the administration wanted to delay facing the outlays necessary to deal with failing thrifts because its economic policies had already led to a large budget deficit. It did not, therefore, encourage thrift regulators to deal promptly and firmly with the industry's problems. Arguably, it discouraged them from doing so. "Not on my watch!" became the operative policy.

Supervisors, themselves, showed marked signs of regulatory capture—putting the interests of the industry they were overseeing above those of the public at large.[22] Instead, supervisors practiced forbearance, which is widely believed to have exacerbated the losses and resulted in insolvency of the FSLIC in 1988. Moreover, the United States has different regulators for different types of depository institutions. They were accused in the 1980s of competing with one another—competing in regulatory and supervisory laxity—and thus weakening oversight and the industry they were overseeing.

It would take a change of administration, a switch in the party in power in the Senate, and a new chairman of the House Banking/Financial Services Committee to allow the authorities to confront the thrift scandal. After the Senate's series of expose? hearings in 1988, Congress and the administration could no longer ignore the crisis.[23] Consequently, when that new administration came into office in January 1989 it joined with Congress in a bipartisan effort to craft legislation to deal with the thrift industry's problems. Congress enacted the Financial Institutions Reform Recovery and Enforcement Act (FIRREA) in August, but that was not the end of the country's problems with its depository institutions.

Problems in the banking industry

Banks were also experiencing serious problems. The Latin American debt crisis in the early 1980s weakened some of the very large banks in the United States. Interest rate deregulation and tight monetary policy increased bank costs across the board. The localized structure of the U.S. banking industry placed restrictions on branching within many states and inhibited banks from crossing state borders. This made the industry geographically undiversified and exposed it to the regional problems that rolled across the states during this period—problems that ranged from farm failures in the early 1980s, which weakened agricultural banks, to industry closings, which bankrupted banks in the old industrial states, to rapid declines in oil prices, which caused bank insolvencies in oil-producing states in the middle of the decade, to busts following real estate booms, which weakened banks in the Northeast and Southwest at the end of the period.

Regulators granted forbearance to large banks whose capital had been depleted by the international debt crisis. Most recovered slowly but the FDIC was unprepared to deal with the deluge of banks that failed during the regional recessions. On comparing figures 4.2 and 4.3 we find that the FDIC was coping with a similar number of banks failures to those facing the FSLIC, but that the value of failed bank assets was lower. Although the level of reserves in the Bank Insurance Fund was higher than that of FSLIC, it was still insufficient. Congress and the administration delayed dealing with problems in the banking industry until the Bank Insurance Fund became technically, and temporarily, insolvent in 1991 and needed a loan from the Treasury in order to meet its obligations.

Fixing the blame

The need to provide funds to cover insurance obligations in both the banking and thrift industries and a fear that the banking industry would

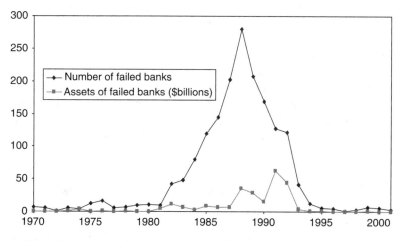

Source: The author obtained the data from the FDIC's Historical Statistics.

Figure 4.2   Number and assets of failed banks: 1970–2001

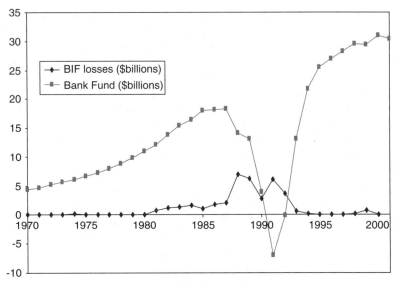

Source: The data come from the FDIC's Historical Statistics.

Figure 4.3   Bank insurance fund and losses from 1970

follow the thrifts into meltdown gave rise to a bipartisan to effort to ensure "never again!" Cleaning up the bank/ thrift mess required the administration and Congress to agree on a solution, while the need for the taxpayer to cover the deficiencies in the deposit insurance fund elicited a search for those to blame. The administration was naturally reluctant to admit its mistakes. While Congress held spectacular "Keating Five" hearings on legislative interference with the regulators, it was otherwise unwilling to acknowledge its contribution to the debacle.[24]

It was easier to blame regulatory capture and supervisory forbearance. Mandatory PCA and least cost resolution were enacted to minimize forbearance and to reveal, and so diminish, political interference in the future. At the same time funding arrangements for deposit insurance were sharply revised to considerably reduce the likelihood of a subsequent call on the taxpayer.

PCA has achieved part, but not all, of what was expected

There is evidence that markets have behaved better since the passage of the FDICIA in that creditors appear to believe that they will incur losses if banks fail and therefore have imposed market discipline (Flannery and

Sorescu 1996). By mid 2008 the efficacy of PCA was facing its first severe test as the subprime crisis began to cause bank and thrift failures. It is unclear, as yet, how effective PCA will be in protecting the taxpayer from losses at failed institutions. Even before this crisis, some supporters of PCA had expressed disappointment at its achievements.

Eisenbeis and Wall (2002), for example, have argued that "if the agencies were truly following FDICIA's prompt corrective action and early intervention provisions, then losses as a percentage of assets should be close to zero." They compared FDIC losses before and after the enactment of the FDICIA in the period 1986–2000, and instead of a sharp reduction in percentage loss rates they found no discernable difference in losses pre- and post-FDICIA—the "losses are huge in both dollar amounts and as a percentage of assets." They concluded that except in failures involving fraud either book values of capital were an unreliable guide to true asset values or the agencies were still practicing forbearance and failure minimization instead of loss minimization. Moreover, in July 2008 the FDIC estimated that it will incur a huge loss of between $4 billion and $8 billion in protecting insured depositors at IndyMac FSB.

Both of these explanations are likely to be contributing factors to Eisenbeis and Wall's observations on losses in failure resolution. Book-value capital ratios are notoriously lagging indicators of financial health, so that a number of analysts recommend additional, even alternative triggers, such as spreads on subordinated debt, to make corrective action more prompt (Evanoff and Wall 2000). And forbearance is still feasible for supervisors who are attracted to it. Knowing that an institution is in trouble but hoping that delaying punitive action will give it an opportunity to recover, the procrastinators may reason that delay will not become evident for several months until the call report data have become publicly available.

Kaufman (2004) has also been concerned that post-FDICIA loss rates have not fallen as expected. He compared FDIC losses over a longer period, 1980 through 2002, and found that "although the number of bank failures declined sharply after the implementation of FDICIA in 1993, the FDIC's loss rate increased significantly" (p. 13). He concluded that the "major objective of FDICIA of reducing losses to the FDIC from bank failures has not been fully realized to date" (p. 19), and he questioned whether the legislation was flawed. He offered a third explanation for "the large losses experienced by the FDIC in the post-FDICIA period." He attributed them to "other factors, including a change in the size distribution of failed banks and a change in the incidence of major fraud or gross mismanagement as a cause of bank failure" (p. 17). Kaufman shows that relatively more small banks failed in the post-FDICIA period and fewer large banks than in the earlier period. This shift increased the average loss rate at the

FDIC because large banks traditionally have lower percentage loss rates than small banks.

One of the reasons for the difference in loss rates is that large banks have higher percentages of uninsured deposits and nondeposit funds. The 1993 Depositor Preference Act gave the FDIC's claims over the assets of a failed bank priority as compared with the claims of nondeposit creditors, so that nondeposit creditors now incur a larger share of losses on the assets of large banks and the FDIC enjoys a smaller share. The FDIC correspondingly foots a larger share of the losses at small failed banks.

Conclusions

I would not be surprised if regulators in the EU opposed the introduction of mandatory PCA in Europe. It is indicative of opposition that the opportunity to incorporate PCA into Pillar 2 of the Basel II capital accord was not utilized. Nor is there any role for the leverage ratio in the Basel 2 capital accord or in the European system of capital regulation. Thus, the likelihood of enacting PCA in a new EU directive would seem to depend on the possibility of banking crisis is the EU—unless, that is, the EU can reform its system in advance to reduce the chances of a crisis.

In some respects the situation in Europe today is different from that in the United States in the late 1980s and early 1990s. At the time of writing, some European economies were still growing moderately, although others were facing banking problems and recession. Monetary authorities there had previously tamed inflation and were attempting to prevent its resurgence. There were few bank failures and there was little disquiet with the supervisors' performance of their duties, although this complacency might end if subprime woes were to spread widely to Europe's banks. There was, as yet, no public outrage over taxpayer outlays to cover industry losses, so there was no political consensus in favor of PCA. Instead, there appeared to be annoyance with the U.S. penchant for the leverage ratio, as was evidenced in audience participation at the LSE/ESFRC conference.

In many other respects there are parallels in the EU today with the United States two-to-three decades ago—in the period just before its banking and thrift debacles. The banking industry in Europe was (at least until the second half of 2007, when the situation began to deteriorate) quiescent, profitable, and liquidIt is undergoing consolidation, is utilizing new products, and facing competition from new institutions (e.g., hedge funds). The regulatory community is putting new Basel II capital standards into place. They could reduce capital levels significantly, especially for LCFIs, as the Quantitative Impact Studies for the United States and the EU have revealed. Analysts are concerned that there is competition in laxity between regulators and supervisors in different member states and that, while designed to promote their flagship banks, it will weaken the industry. The absence of standardized publicly available call report data places the EU into a similar information gloom that preceded the creation of the FFIEC in the United States. It is difficult to hold European supervisors accountable—either in the domestic or cross-border context—in this situation and for the public to exercise effective market discipline.

There are concerns that failures, particularly among large complex institutions that span national borders, could be mishandled—a prospect made more likely by the unclear and multiparty process of containing possible contagion (Garcia and Nieto 2007). Moral hazard exists because of high coverage in some deposit insurance systems—many of which may be underfunded. It is feared that some governments may be unable or unwilling to cover the costs of deficiencies in their supervisory and deposit insurance schemes especially where failed banks cross national borders. Even were they so willing, insured depositors' receipt of compensation would be slow and uninsured creditors would need to wait for the failed bank's assets to be sold—a situation that would have adverse repercussions on the macroeconomy. Forbearance, to be followed by open bank assistance, might well appear to be an attractive alternative, especially if an agreement were in place to share the financial burdens of such actions. The reader is invited to assess whether these similarities suggest that there is risk of a crisis developing in the not-to-distant future in the EU, or whether they trust that the greater robustness of the banking system that Huertas (2007) and Huertas and Dewar (2007) describe will be sufficient to prevent crises from developing.

Preliminary evidence from the United States suggests that implementing PCA in Europe—especially if it were accompanied by triggers that are more timely than book capital ratios—would strengthen the financial sector and reduce the likelihood of either catastrophe or bailout/open bank assistance. But that evidence also forces recognition that PCA is not a panacea—its results have been somewhat disappointing in the United States. Of course outcomes might have been worse without it and least cost resolution has been found to have enhanced market discipline. In any event, having adopted PCA in the EU could have reduced the chances that banks would fail and that a crisis would develop.

PCA would appear to be a necessary but not sufficient condition for strengthening the EU safety net and avoiding the choice between the unwanted alternatives of bailout or crisis. The EU also needs a revised system of deposit insurance and bank resolution that would require prompt closure, prompt estimate of recovery values and imposition of haircuts, immediate reopening of the recapitalized bank to facilitate the continuation of its core functions with access for depositors to their accounts (full for insured depositors and partial for uninsured depositors and other creditors) and for borrowers to their pre-existing credit lines, and prompt reprivatization of nationalized banks (Kaufman 2006; Mayes 2007). It might be easier to establish a new bank-funded system of EU-wide deposit insurance and failed bank resolution for LCFIs than to harmonize the existing disparate systems in member countries. Such a body might succeed in avoiding both of two current unwanted alternatives—bailouts that follow forbearance and failure to act that results in financial and economic crisis.

Notes

*The author thanks, for their helpful comments, Douglas Evanoff, George Kaufman, Maria Nieto, Larry Wall, and participants at the North American Economics and Finance Association meetings in Seattle on June 30, 2007, and at the European Shadow Financial Regulatory Committee's conference on Prompt Corrective Action and Cross-Border Supervisory Issues in Europe held at the London School of Economics on November 20, 2006.

1. See just a few examples, such as Boot (2007), Eisenbeis and Kaufman (2007), Garcia and Nieto (2005 and 2007), and Goodhart (2005).
2. The First and Second Banks of the United States each had 20-year charters, but this experiment ended in 1836.
3. The number of bank and thrift failures are taken from Chart 1,1–1 of the FDIC (1998).
4. Senior FDIC staff expressed these reservations at a bipartisan meeting with Senate Banking Committee staff prior to FDICIA's passage.
5. Kaufman (2004: 14–15) offers a more precise evaluation as follows: "FDICIA prohibits the FDIC from protecting any uninsured claims if doing so increases its losses," unless the systemic risk exception is invoked. Consequently "since 1992 the FDIC has protected uninsured depositors only in a very few instances at small banks, where the acquiring bank bid a premium to assume the small amount of uninsured deposits that was greater than the pro-rata loss on these deposits," thus imposing no loss on the fund.
6. They number of a bank's accounts is operationally important to the FDIC. The largest post-FDICIA failure is Superior Bank, which failed in 2001 with 90,000 deposit accounts, which makes it much smaller than the largest U.S. banks that today have over 50 million accounts.
7. Once the supervisor fears that a bank will fail, and certainly when it becomes critically undercapitalized and has 90 days to recapitalize or be closed, it works closely with the FDIC, which normally has access to the bank and its books, plans the least costly form of resolution, and estimates recovery values. The FDIC has less time when fraud causes the bank to fail suddenly.
8. Records would be changed, among other things, so that each bank would give each of its depositors an identifying number so that his/her multiple deposits

could be aggregated to determine whether the aggregate falls above of below the insurance limit. That is, whether a haircut would be appropriate or not.

9. The largest failures (Continental Illinois, First Republic, and Bank of New England) occurred before FDICIA was enacted. Each bank had less than $40 billion in assets, whereas the four largest U.S. banks today have over $300 billion in assets.

10. The regulators published a new MoU in 2008, but it too is unenforceable.

11. Switzerland (home of two large international banks but not a member of the EU) has said that it will not aid customers beyond its borders.

12. There were 76 signatories to the 2005 MoU, and the EU has added new member countries since it was signed.

13. Horvitz (1995) discusses that opposition.

14. One well-respected European regulator expressed opposition to compulsory PCA during the conference. Moreover, PCA is not practiced in many countries in the world today. Of those that have adopted it, Canada had experienced serious financial problems with its deposit insurance system, while Japan, Korea, and Mexico had undergone costly banking crises.

15. Section 38(c) of FDICIA allows the federal banking regulators, by regulation, to choose the risk-based measure "to establish any additional relevant capital measures" and to set the numerical boundaries for the ratios defining the capital groups.

16. Shibut, Critchfield, and Bohn (2003) examined the 92 banks that fell below the 2 percent leverage ratio between 1994 and the end of 2000. They found that 48 banks failed. Of the 44 that did not fail, 21 were absorbed into another institution within one year of breaching the 2 percent barrier, 18 were still operating one year later, and five "had special circumstances." It is not clear how many of the 18 were recapitalized, and the authors do not describe what happened to them after that one year.

17. Technically conservatorship is also possible, but the FDIC uses it only for thrifts, not commercial banks.

18. A loss of $25 million or 2 percent of the failed institution's assets is deemed to be material.

19. William Seidman, when chairman of the FDIC proclaimed that FDICIA "produced the greatest overload of regulatory micromanagement seen anywhere in the world" (Seidman 1993, p. 47). I observed similar opposition when I worked on the 1989 Financial Institutions Reform, Recovery, and Enforcement Act (FIRREA) and the 1991 FDIC Improvement Act (FDICIA) as a member of the chairman's staff on the Senate Banking Committee.

20. I observed this behavior in the late 1980s; for example, when I represented the Government Accountability Office (GAO) at a major thrift trade association conference in 1997. At the time GAO was trying to demonstrate that the industry's problems were urgently in need of Congressional action. The organizers treated me graciously but I knew I was "the enemy."

21. After testifying before the House Financial Services Committee on one of these reports, deputy comptroller general told me that he had never in his very long career at GAO experienced such a hostile reception.

22. Regulatory capture was facilitated by the charter of the Federal Home Loan Bank, which instructed the agency to promote home ownership.
23. Congressional staffs were busy in fall 1988 drafting legislation to be ready to introduce immediately in the new session at the beginning of 1989.
24. Senator William Proxmire, chairman of the Senate Banking Committee until he retired at the end of 1988, was an exception. He admitted his entirely honest mistakes in his *mea culpa* farewell speech to the Senate Chamber.

References

Bair, Sheila. 2007. Remarks before the Exchequer Club, Washington D.C., March 21. www.fdic.gov.

Bernanke, Ben. 1983. Nonmonetary effects of the financial crisis in the propagation of the great depression. *American Economic Review* 73: 257–76.

Bliss, Robert, and George Kaufman. 2006. A comparison of U.S. corporate and bank insolvency resolution, Federal Reserve Bank of Chicago. *Economic Perspectives* Second Quarter: 44–56.

Boot, Arnoud. 2007. Supervisory arrangements, LOLR, and crisis management in a single European banking market. In *International financial instability: Global banking and national regulation,* ed. Douglas D. Evanoff, George G. Kaufman, and John Raymond LaBrosse, 387–406. Singapore: World Scientific Co.

Carnell, Richard. 1995. Is systemic risk dead? In *Banking, financial markets, and systemic risk: Research in financial services private and public policy,* ed. George G. Kaufman and Hampton Hill, 311–15. Greenwich, CT: JAI Press.

———. 1993. The culture of ad hoc discretion. In *Assessing bank reform: FDICIA one year later,* ed. G. Kaufman and R. Litan,113–21. Washington D.C.: The Brookings Institution.

Directive 94/19/EC of the European Parliament and the Council of May 30, 1994, Deposit guarantee schemes, *Official Journal of the European Communities* L 135, May 31, 1994.

Directive 2001/24/EC of the European Parliament and the Council of April 4, 2001, The reorganization and winding-up of credit institutions, *Official Journal of the European Communities* L 125, May 5, 2001.

Eisenbeis, Robert, and George Kaufman. 2006. Cross-Border banking: Challenges for deposit insurance and financial stability in the European Union. In *Prompt corrective action & cross-border supervisory issues in Europe,* ed. Harald Benink, Charles AE Goodhart, and Rosa Maria Lastra. Financial Markets Group, Special Paper 171, 5–61.

——— and Larry Wall. 2002. The major supervisory initiatives post FDICIA: Are they based on the goals of PCA? Should they be? In *Prompt corrective action in banking: 10 years later,* ed. George G. Kaufman, 109–42. Greenwich, CT: JAI Press.

European Central Bank. 2005. Memorandum of understanding on cooperation between banking supervisors, central banks and finance ministries of the European Union in financial crisis situations, *press release,* May 18.

————. 2003. Memorandum of understanding on high-level principles of cooperation between the banking supervisors and central banks of the European Union in crisis management situations, *press release*, March 10.

European Shadow Financial Regulatory Committee. 2006. Basel II and the scope for prompt corrective action in Europe, Statement no. 25. In *prompt corrective action and cross-border supervisory issues in Europe*, ed. Harald Benink, Charles AE Goodhart, and Rosa Maria Lastra, Financial Markets Group, Special Paper 171, 150–53.

Evanoff, Douglas, and Larry Wall. 2002. Subordinated debt and prompt corrective regulatory action. Working Paper, Federal Reserve Bank of Atlanta.

Federal Deposit Insurance Corporation. 2007. *Historical statistics www.fdic.gov.*

————. 2006. Large-Bank deposit insurance determination modernization proposal, *Federal Register,* 71, Chapter III, 74857.

————. 1998. *Managing the Crisis: The FDIC and RTC Experience 1980–1994.* Washington D.C.: FDIC.

Flannery, Mark, and Sorin Sorescu. 1996. Evidence of bank market discipline in subordinated debenture yields: 1983–1991. *Journal of Finance* 51(4): 1347–75.

Fonteyne, Wim. 2007. Crisis resolution and burden sharing for systemic cross-border EU banks, Paper presented at an IMF/EU Department seminar, March 22, in Washington D.C.

Friedman, Milton, and Anna Schwartz. 1963. *A Monetary History of the United States, 1867–1960,* National Bureau of Economic Research. Princeton, NJ: Princeton University Press.

Freixas, Xavier. 2003. Crisis management in Europe. In *Financial supervision in Europe,* ed. Jeroen Kremers, Dirk Schoenmaker, and Peter Wierts, 102–19. Cheltenham: Edward Elgar.

Garcia, Gillian. 2007. The politics of prompt corrective action and the leverage ratio. In *prompt corrective action and cross-border supervisory Issues in Europe,* ed. Harald Benink, Charles AE Goodhart, and Rosa Maria Lastra, Financial Markets Group, Special Paper, 171, 136–49.

————. 2008. Sovereignty versus soundness: Crossborder/interstate banking in the European Union and in the United States: Similarities, differences, and policy issues. *Contemporary Economic Policy,* forthcoming.

————. 2000. Deposit insurance actual and good practices. Occasional Paper no. 197, International Monetary Fund, Washington, D.C.

———— and Maria Nieto. 2007. Preserving financial stability: A dilemma for the EU, *Contemporary Economic Policy* 25(3): 444–58.

———— and ———— 2005. Banking crisis management in the European union: Multiple regulators and resolution authorities. *Journal of Banking Regulation* 6(3): 206–26.

Goodhart, Charles. 2005. Multiple regulators and resolutions. In *Systemic Financial Crises: Resolving Large Bank Insolvencies,* ed. D. Evanoff and G. Kaufman, 252–73. Singapore: World Scientific.

———— and Dirk Schoenmaker. 2006. Burden sharing in a banking crisis in Europe, London School of Economics, Financial Markets Group, Special Paper no. 163, September.

———— and Stephen Smith. 1993. Stabilization. In *The economics of community public finance* (Reports and studies), *European Economy* 5: 417–56.

Horvitz, Paul. 1995. Banking regulation as a solution to financial fragility. *Journal of Financial Services Research* 9: 369–80.

Huertas, Thomas. 2007. Dealing with distress in financial conglomerates. In *Prompt corrective action and cross-border supervisory issues in Europe,* ed. Harald Benink, Charles AE Goodhart, and Rosa Maria Lastra, Financial Markets Group, Special Paper, 171, 112–35.

———— and Sally Dewar. 2007. Market-based risk is changing banking. *Financial Times' Risk Management Supplement,* May 1, 4.

Ingves, Stefan. 2007. Cross-Border banking regulation—A way forward: The European Case. In *International financial instability: Global banking and national regulation,* ed. Douglas D. Evanoff, George G. Kaufman, and John Raymond LaBrosse 3–12. World Scientific.

Kaufman, George. 2006. Using efficient bank insolvency resolution to solve the deposit insurance problem. In *Deposit insurance,* ed. A. Campbell, R. Labrosse, D. Mayes, and D.Singh. Basingstoke: Palgrave Macmillan.

————. 2004. FDIC losses in bank failures: Has FDICIA made a difference? Federal Reserve Bank of Chicago. *Economic Perspectives,* Third Quarter, 13–25.

————. and Steven Seelig. 2002. Post-Resolution treatment of depositors at failed banks: Implications for the severity of banking crises, systemic risk, and too big to fail, Federal Reserve Bank of Chicago. *Economic Perspectives,* Second Quarter, 27–41.

Lastra, Rosa, and Clas Wihlborg. 2006. Law and economics of crisis resolution in cross-border banking. In *Prompt corrective action and cross-border supervisory issues in Europe,* ed. Harald Benink, Charles AE Goodhart, and Rosa Maria Lastra, Financial Markets Group, Special Paper, 171: 89–111.

Mayes, David. 2007. Bridge banks and too big to fail: Systemic risk exemption. In *International financial instability: Global banking and national regulation,* ed. Douglas D. Evanoff, George G. Kaufman, and John Raymond LaBrosse, 331–54. New Jersey: World Scientific.

————. Maria Nieto, and Larry Wall. 2007. Multiple safety net regulators and agency problems in the EU: Is prompt corrective action partly the solution? In *Prompt corrective action and cross-border supervisory issues in Europe,* ed. Harald Benink, Charles AE Goodhart, and Rosa Maria Lastra. Financial Markets Group, Special Paper, 171: 62–88.

Nieto, Maria, and Larry Wall. 2006. Preconditions for a successful implementation of supervisors' prompt corrective action: Is there a case for a banking standard in the EU? *Journal of Banking Regulation* 7(2): 191–220.

Parker, George. 2007. Trichet kills EU plan for public rescue of failing banks. *Financial Times,* April 23: 2.

Rush Jr., Jeffrey. 2002. Statement before the Committee on Banking, Housing, and Urban Affairs, U.S. Senate, February 7.

Shibut, Lynn, Tim Critchfield, and Sarah Bohn. 2002. Differentiating among critically undercapitalized banks and thrifts. In *Prompt corrective action in banking: 10 years later,* ed. George G. Kaufman, 143–202. Greenwich, CT: JAI Press.

Schoenmaker, Dirk, and Sander Oosterloo. 2005. Financial supervision in an integrating Europe: Measuring cross-border externalities. *International Finance* 8: 1–27.

Seidman, L. William. 1993. The Banking Crisis in Perspective, in *FDICIA: An Appraisal* (Federal Reserve Bank of Chicago), 46–47.

U.S. Congress. 1991. Federal Deposit Insurance Corporation Improvement Act of 1991, Public Law 102–242, 102nd Congress, December 19.

5

Uncertainty, Transparency, and Future Monetary Policy

Marc D. Hayford and A. G. Malliaris[*]

Introduction

In 2004, Chairman Greenspan argued in his address to the American Economic Association that the Federal Reserve's experiences over the past two decades "make it clear that uncertainty is not just a pervasive feature of the monetary policy landscape; it is the defining characteristic of the landscape" (Greenspan 2004, p. 36). Further elaborating the notion of monetary policy under uncertainty, at the Fourth Conference on the International Research Forum on Monetary Policy, Federal Reserve vice chairman Donald L. Kohn (2006) discussed in detail the role of uncertainty and its influence on the formulation of monetary policy. Greenspan and Kohn use the concepts of "uncertainty" and "risk" loosely rather than formally. Economists often describe "uncertainty" to mean Knightian random events with limited or no prior occurrence and thus without known probability distributions in contrast to "risk" that measures sampling from a known pool of probable events with an empirical probability distribution calculated from repeated past occurrences.

In this chapter we discuss (1) the various sources of uncertainty that play an essential role in the formulation and conduct of monetary policy, (2) the degree of uncertainty faced by monetary policymakers and conditions that influence uncertainty about monetary policy. The discussion of these various aspects of uncertainty leads to the issue of transparency. We then (3) critically review central bank transparency abroad and in the United States citing advantages and disadvantages. Finally, (4) we assess the empirical impact of monetary policy transparency on the uncertainty about future monetary policy using T-bill rate forecast dispersions from the Survey of Professional Forecasters (SPF) as a proxy for monetary policy uncertainty.

Sources of Uncertainty

There are several sources of uncertainty that play an important role in the formation of monetary policy. Greenspan (1996, 2002, and 2004), Kohn (2006), and others identify at least five sources of uncertainty faced by central bankers in determining monetary policy:

First, uncertain economic data: economic data cycles, with the exception of financial prices, provide only lagged and incomplete information that is subject to later revisions about the current state of the economy. When central bankers meet, most often the actual state of the economy is not clearly known and even the recent past state is only partially described from data to be further revised in the future. Obviously, high-frequency financial data such as tick-by-tick stock prices, interest rates, currency exchange rates, and numerous commodity prices are known and not subject to revision, but all these are driven by future expectations and subject to sudden reversals; thus, they contribute to the uncertainty faced by the central bankers. Beyond such data uncertainty, central bankers need to consider particular variables such as risk taking, risk aversion, the formation of bubbles, current and future equity premia, and others for which no data are directly available, current or lagged.

Second, uncertain forecasts: projections by economists may vary widely, even for the current quarter, indicating uncertainty about the very near-term economic outlook. This holds even more so for forecasts a few quarters ahead. These forecasts are then further disrupted by "shocks," which of course by definition are unpredictable. Greenspan, himself a forecaster in his earlier career, has repeatedly emphasized forecasting as an indispensable tool for formulating monetary policy. Greenspan (1996) argues that "we need to be forward looking, taking actions to forestall imbalances that may not be visible for many months. There is no alternative to taking actions on forecasts." Greenspan (2004) extends his thinking to the risk management approach to monetary policy that considers various possible future scenarios about the state of the economy with associated probabilities of occurrence where a low-probability negative event with a high-potential economic loss is given by monetary policy higher attention over a higher-probability event with lower loss. This risk management approach to monetary policy has elevated forecasting to an even more prominent place in monetary policy deliberations by central bankers.

Third, there is uncertainty in model building. Both professional and academic economists develop macroeconomic models describing the behavior of the economy. Such a development requires both scientific and judgment skills. The scientific part refers to certain well-developed theories that have received empirical support, while the judgment part reflects unsettled issues that receive dissimilar emphasis by various model builders. Standard macroeconomics textbooks cover the received doctrine of dynamic post-Keynesian stochastic macroeconomic modeling, but controversial topics such as the incorporation of asset bubbles in such models remain a topic of debate. Beyond the macroeconomic model building, economists have to deal with econometric issues of estimation and an evaluation of such models in terms of their forecasting performance. It is rather discouraging that the actual record of econometric model building remains weak. John Williams (2004) reviews several of these issues and proposes possible improvements to model development, and Greenspan (2001) discusses in detail the challenges of modeling a dynamic economy. Robert Tetlow and Brian Ironside (2006) evaluate the real-time model uncertainty of the Fed model during the 1996–2003 period and conclude that model uncertainty is a substantial source of uncertainty.

Fourth, uncertain policy effects: central banks cannot predict with a high degree of confidence how, how much, or how quickly monetary policy actions will affect the economy. As summed up long ago by Milton Friedman (1960), the impact of current monetary policy on the economy is subject to "long and variable lags." Actually, the management by central bankers of expectations by market participants remains a very critical issue. But even if done carefully, Greenspan (2004) states that "perhaps the greatest irony of the past decade is the gradually unfolding success against inflation may well have contributed to the stock price bubble of the latter part of the 1990s." Put differently, policymakers incorrectly expected inflation stabilization to lead to financial market stability rather than to stock market exuberance.

Finally, global dimensions of uncertainty have become more pertinent in the conduct of monetary policy. Even under flexible exchange rates that allow the central bank to follow an independent monetary policy, events such as the Asian Crisis, the Russian Default, and the recent rise in world commodity prices enter the set of uncertainties faced by the Fed.

These five sources of uncertainty are further magnified during periods of rapid technological and structural change that may or may not result in changes in the values of key economic variables, such as the natural rate of unemployment, the output gap, the natural real interest rate, and the neutral federal funds rate (FFR). The values of all these parameters are important to know when setting monetary policy. Unfortunately none of them are directly observable and hence can only be estimated. The values of these parameters apparently drift over time and during certain episodes the confidence policymakers have in their estimated values decreases.

What does the uncertainty faced by central bankers imply about the uncertainty that financial market participants confront over future monetary policy? Certainty financial market participants tackle all the uncertainty faced by central bankers and in addition also consider the uncertainty of how central bankers will respond to current and future events. Central bankers have systematically attempted to reduce this last source of uncertainty. Beginning in 1994, U.S. monetary policymakers increased the transparency of monetary policy. Consequently, at least in recent years, various Fed officials, such as William Poole (2005) and Ben Bernanke (2007), have emphasized that the Fed has access to pretty much the same data as everyone else who follows the economy and that the Fed has no special insights beyond what economists in the private sector have about the future path of monetary policy.

Degrees of Uncertainty

In this section we discuss the economic conditions under which market participants are likely to be the most uncertain about the future path of monetary policy. For some of these conditions, faced by monetary policymakers and market participants alike, policymakers themselves may be no more certain about what they will do in the future than market participants putting together their private forecasts and economic outlooks. We can think of at least four such conditions or environments.

First, there is greater uncertainty in the face of price shocks rather than with aggregate demand shocks. The goals of price stability and maximum sustainable growth unambiguously imply that the Fed should increase the FFR in the face of a positive aggregate demand shock and decrease it in the face of a negative aggregate demand shock. However, what the Fed should do when there is an aggregate supply (price) shock depends on preferences over inflation variability versus real GDP variability. If these preferences are unknown by market participants then price shocks may lead to greater uncertainty about future monetary policy.

Second, during an episode of rapid technological innovation, the underlying structure of the economy, such as the values of natural rate of output, unemployment, and the natural real interest rate, will be even more uncertain than usual since the economy may be behaving in a way that is not consistent with historical data. A monetary policy framework that relies on estimates of unobserved variables such as NAIRU, neutral FFR, and potential GDP can generate greater uncertainty during periods when the values of these parameters are thought to be estimated with lesser precision (Meyer 2000). This makes market participants potentially more uncertain about current and future monetary response to the economy. An example of this is the 1990s when the unemployment rate was below historic estimates of NAIRU but inflation was not accelerating.

Third, market participants are likely to be more uncertain about the path of future monetary policy when the Fed itself is least certain. Fed uncertainty about future monetary policy is likely to be the greatest when the FFR is in the neutral range and there is uncertainty about whether inflation is accelerating or not or if the economy is going into a recession. If this case Fed policy becomes "data dependent" with uncertainty about future monetary policy potentially increased if the data give conflicting signals about inflation or economic growth. This happened during the fall of 2006 and spring 2007. During periods when the FFR is in the "neutral zone" and the future path of monetary policy is "data dependent," there is greater uncertainty about monetary policy than when, for example, output is below potential and the FFR is above neutral.

Finally, the degree of market participant uncertainty about monetary policy will depend of course on the degree of transparency of monetary policy. It is perhaps the goal of greater transparency of monetary policy to make market participants as certain/uncertain about future monetary policy as policymakers themselves. As the Fed articulates its assessment about the state of the economy and evaluates the relative risks in terms of inflation versus real economic growth with an acknowledgment of its own forecasting limitations, the Fed encourages market participants to take risks and present their own forecasts under alternate scenarios. Such an approach offers a larger menu of scenarios and diminishes future overreactions. Spencer Krane (2006) argues that most professional forecasters link economic activity with agents' beliefs about permanent and transitory shocks. Krane finds that forecasts of professional economists differ noticeably from forecasts of simple econometric models. Krane suggests that professional forecasters are much more heavily influenced by incoming high-frequency economic and financial data than is the average econometric model. The transparent monetary policy issue is addressed in greater detail in the next section.

Central Bank Transparency

The discussion above identified numerous factors contributing to economic uncertainty as well as conditions that influence these factors. In view of the fact that the Fed has been given enormous economic responsibilities to preserve price stability and promote economic growth, the question naturally arises as to how the Fed should exercise its responsibilities in a democratic society guided by institutions of freedom and accountability. Academic economists and policy makers agree that the Fed's accountability for its actions to preserve low inflation and promote economic growth is best expressed in its degree of transparency.

There is a wealth of literature that focuses on the concept of transparency as it relates to central banks monetary policy. But before one can debate the economic consequences of transparency, it is essential to define the concept. A widely used theoretical definition of transparency in economic literature on central banks and monetary policy describes transparency as the lack of asymmetric information between monetary policymakers and market participants. This is equivalent to saying that transparency describes the presence of symmetry of information between the two. Although it is accepted that lack of transparency leads to greater uncertainty, transparency, even in the absolute sense, does not lead to certainty but only to reduction in uncertainty.

This intuitive and theoretical approach requires that monetary policymakers and market participants have equal access to the same information and that neither have private nor valuable information that is withheld from each other. However, there are many, especially practitioners, who have reservations about this definition of transparency. Although many practitioners are in favor of more transparency, they advocate a practical rather than a theoretical approach to transparency. They argue that it is necessary to define transparency in terms of its requirements and economic consequences. Only then will it be useful in practice. After all, transparency deals with more than data availability. Central banks use the economic data as input in their economic models, which they rely on to form their respective monetary policies.

Additionally, definitions found in the academic literature have historically ignored an essential dimension of transparency, namely, communication. Since economic information is often multifaceted and complex, it has to be organized and structured through interpretive economic models. The output of such "manipulation" requires further simplification if it is to be useful to the market. That is, effective communication of this information to market participants is an essential component of transparency. As O. Issing explains, "Data are often not self-explanatory, as their information content changes depending on the way they are communicated by the sender" (Issing 2005, p. 67). B. Winkler (2000) also complains that the communication issues surrounding transparency are underestimated and that

> most of the existing academic literature casts no light on the question of how central banks should go about conveying information in a way that is

best understood by the public. It assumes that simply making more information available . . . automatically translates into greater transparency. In
other words there is no friction in the process of transmitting information.

The importance of communication to monetary policy transparency
leads Winkler (2000) to advance a different and broader definition of transparency. He defines it "as a measure of genuine understanding and successful communication." He suggests approaching transparency in terms of
openness, clarity (simplified, structured, and interpreted information), hon-
esty (using the same framework for both explaining monetary policy and for
structuring information in internal decision making), and common understanding (common mode of interpretation for policymakers and market
participants).

In a comprehensive treatment of transparency, P.M Geraats (2001) distinguishes five categories of transparency that correspond to different stages
in the policymaking process. Central banks can enhance transparency in
each of these stages. She lists political, economic, procedural, policy, and
operational transparencies. While each of these aspects is important to the
goal of achieving asymmetry of information, practitioners protest that "any
meaningful discussion on the requirement for transparency cannot ignore
the question of what this implies in practice" (Issing 2005). Others, such as
S. Carpenter (2004), argue that it is not useful to define transparency in a
theoretical setting because "transparency is a multifaceted concept that can
only be defined and evaluated in very specific contexts."

It is difficult to find people who would argue against the need for transparency in the monetary process, but there are considerable disagreements
as to the extent to which transparency can be implemented for both theoretical as well as practical reasons because at the heart of central banks
transparency debate a friction persists between theory and practice.

The most common argument for central bank transparency is the
accountability principle. The argument asserts that since central banks
are governmental institutions with high levels of independence, they
must be accountable to the public. Without transparency there is no true
accountability.

Although this argument appears to be compelling and in many ways
has directly influenced the latest trend in transparency of central banks
around the world, its economic benefits are less obvious. Initial resistance
to more transparency by central banks and Federal Reserve officials was
centered on the argument that transparency would contribute to unneces-
sary volatility and instability in the market. Furthermore, it would com-
plicate and increase the cost of implementing such policies. Although this
view has softened in the past decade, the debate over the meaning and level

of transparency has intensified. At the heart of the issue is an inconsistency between two important values: accountability of a public institution in a democracy and overall public interest. Poole (2004), president of Federal Reserve Bank of St. Louis, addressed the difficulty in determining the level of transparency that maximizes both values. Poole's argument (2004) is,

> Anything that would diminish the effectiveness of the policy process would be inconsistent with the Fed meeting its responsibilities. Accountability requires only that a central bank be open and honest about its objectives and be held accountable for achieving those objectives. Certainly, the ultimate test is whether disclosure yields better policy outcomes.

Advocates of greater transparency argue that transparency has a positive effect on the financial markets as it reduces instability and volatility by reducing uncertainty, which, in turn, reduces the risk premium in the market. The resulting net effect is positive to both the bond and equity markets. According to this argument, financial markets function more efficiently when the objectives of monetary policymakers are provided in timely matter and communicated more clearly. According to Alan Blinder (1998), greater openness allows the public to adjust their expectations of future interest rate movements in a more systematic manner and enhances market participants' ability to predict and anticipate monetary policy adjustments. When market participants can better anticipate the change in monetary policy, it has the benefit of reducing market volatility.

Another argument for transparency in monetary policy revolves around the benefits gained from an open debate over such policies. This argument, also asserted by Jim Saxton (1997, p. 5), claims that opening the debate over monetary policy to the private sector would "oblige the monetary authority to defend its policy objectives, decisions, and procedures." The consequences of such open debate would lead to better monetary policies because the Federal Reserve "would be forced to openly confront and reconcile inconsistencies in its policy" (Saxton 1997). However, others such as Poole (2004, p. 4) disagree about the value of such debate and argue that "such a practice would curtail the free and open exchange of ideas that characterize FOMC meetings."

An additional reason in favor of greater transparency claims that implementing a more transparent monetary policy enhances the credibility of central banks. Proponents of this argument advocate that an important trust relationship is built between the public and central banks if they became more transparent about their objectives, tools, and procedures. According to this argument, public awareness places pressure on central banks to meet their stated goals. Additionally, when they consistently meet their objectives using the stated tools and procedures, their credibility is enhanced. George Kahn (2007, p. 31) points out how this can happen.

> Communicating an explicit policy path may help demonstrate policymakers' commitment to achieving long-run goals. For example, if policymakers announce a commitment to lower inflation from an unacceptable high level, that commitment may be more credible if policymakers simultaneously announce the policy path they expect will be required to achieve that inflation objective. In addition, once the inflation objective and policy path are announced, reneging on either commitment may become more difficult.

But Kahn cautions that commitments like this make necessary changes in both policy and procedures more difficult and costly. This loss of flexibility often worries central bankers.

The advantages of transparency are recognized by politicians, too. Here are some offered by Congressman Saxton (1997):

1. Transparency limits the ability of policymakers to manipulate policy for political gains.
2. The more transparent the Federal Reserve is in its monetary policy, the better the relationship will be between the monetary policymakers and Congress, which is responsible for oversights of these policies.
3. Transparency is one of the theoretical conditions required for a free market to be efficient.

The case for transparency seems compelling. However, the full-fledged complexity of the issue appears when one tries to practice transparency. We have already mentioned the inherent friction between accountability of a public institution and overall public interest.

Historical Perspective on Transparency

Historically, transparent monetary policy of the Federal Reserve and central banks around the world has not been a top priority. In fact for a long time, the actions, policies, and objectives of central banks were shrouded in secrecy. Over time a movement toward greater transparency was due in part to the recognition by central bankers of the economic benefits of more transparency with respect to the design, procedures, and tools employed in carrying out the policies. Here is a summary of Poole's (2005) brief history of transparency:

The first central bank to initiate a move towards more transparent monetary policy was the Reserve Bank of New Zealand in 1990. The bank assumed the responsibility from the government for maintaining inflation within a specified range, thereby becoming transparent about its policy objectives.

Soon after, the central banks of Canada, the UK, and Sweden followed suit. These central banks became known as "inflation targeters" because they announced specific numeric inflation objectives.

Currently, 28 central banks around the world follow this new transparent approach regarding policy objectives as well as the policy instruments. Included in this group is the Bank of Canada, the Reserve Bank of Australia, the Bank of England, and the central banks of Albania, Brazil, Chile, Colombia, the Czech Republic, Georgia, Hungary, Iceland, Israel, Mexico, Norway, Peru, the Philippines, Poland, Serbia, Sierra Leone, South Africa, South Korea, Sri Lanka, Sweden, Switzerland, Tanzania, Thailand, and Turkey. All these central banks communicate with market participants any changes in the setting of their policy instrument, but differ in their practice regarding the release of forward-looking information such as forecasts for future economic developments.

The European Central Bank (ECB) also adopted a more transparent monetary policy objective but differs from the "inflation targeters" banks in its approach. The ECB does not specify numeric inflation numbers, but rather specifies an objective of keeping the inflation rate close to or below 2 percent per annum "in the medium run." The ECB doesn't disclose forecasts for the European Union or official proceedings of policy discussions but releases information regarding changes in its policy rates.

Transparency and Monetary Policymaking at the Federal Reserve

In the United States, there has been an evolution in the practice of transparency at the Federal Reserve. This evolution can be separated into two multiple dimensions. With regard to transparency concerning policy objectives, the road began with the Freedom of Information Act, which took effect in 1967. As a result of this act, Federal Open Market Committee (FOMC) began to publish the minutes of the Fed meetings. However, the minutes were divided into two documents. One was called the Memorandum of Discussion, which was released after a five-year lag. This document identified the speakers and contributors, but was not a verbatim transcript. The other was a shorter document called the Record of Policy Action, which was released with relatively little delay. This document provided a summary of the committee's deliberation and discussion but did not identify which FOMC member took which position.

In 1979, in response to a court suit challenging the legality of delay of the release of the memorandum, the FOMC discontinued its publication.

The FOMC continues to publish the Record of Policy Action but in 1993 changed its name to "Minutes of FOMC Meetings." Over time, the release lag of this document was shortened and currently is available two days after the next scheduled FOMC meeting.

Transparency of FOMC with respect to policy actions has improved considerably over the past ten years. Beginning in 1994 the Federal Reserve System went through a series of changes in the reporting of monetary policy. Prior to February 1994, financial market participants had to guess, infer, or estimate the current target of the FFR as well as the likely future path of monetary policy. A number of economists, some of whom had previously worked for the Federal Reserve System, worked as "Fed watchers" with the task of divining monetary policy. Fed watchers still exist, although the Fed has made certain aspects of their jobs easier.

Starting with the February 1994 FOMC meeting, the postmeeting press releases began to signal changes in the FFR target without explicitly stating the target. When no postmeeting statement was released this was taken to signal no change in the federal funds target.

Beginning with the July 1995 FOMC meeting, the Fed began to explicitly state the federal funds target. Starting with the May 1999 FOMC meeting, in addition to the federal funds target announcement, the postmeeting statements began to include the reasoning behind the target level as well as an indication of the expected future path of the FFR (Carlson et al. 2006).

Vector Autoregressions of Impact of Monetary Policy Transparency

This section uses structural vector autoregressions (SVAR) to characterize the dynamic impact of economic and monetary policy on the T-bill rate forecast dispersions for two sample periods: before and after the increase in monetary policy transparency. SVARs have been used extensively in the empirical monetary policy literature (see, e.g., Bernanke and Mihov 1998). As a proxy for the various sources of uncertainty about future monetary policy we use the forecast dispersions for T-bills from the SPF. The SPF is conducted by the Federal Reserve Bank of Philadelphia. The data are available on their Web site (see http://www.phil.frb.org/econ/spf/index.html). Since the T-bill rate closely tracks the FFR, it seems plausible that forecasters of the future T-bill rate are essentially attempting to forecast future monetary policy. Figure 5.1 shows the close relationship (correlation = 0.996) between the FFR and the three-month T-bill rate since 1981. Clearly movements in the T-bill rate closely track the FFR. Hence, we assume that forecasters of the future T-bill rate are influenced in large degree by what they think the Fed is going to do with future monetary policy. This suggests

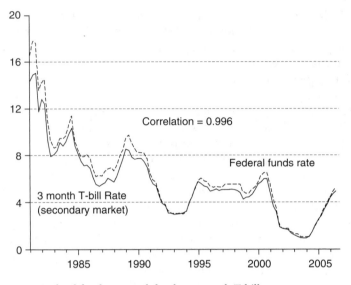

Figure 5.1   Federal funds rate and the three-month T-bill rate

that the dispersion of T-bill rate forecasts across forecasters provides a measure of uncertainty about future monetary policy.

Since the third quarter of 1981, after the release of the advance national income and product accounts (NIPA) data for previous quarter, that is, in the beginning of February, May, August, and November, the SPF has asked a group of about 30–50 people who make a living as forecasters on Wall Street or in business for their forecast of the three-month T-bill rate one to five quarters into the future. Using these forecasts from each, we proxy for uncertainty about future monetary policy as the standard deviation of these T-bill rate forecasts one to five quarters ahead (STF_{jt}) by calculating

$$STF_{jt} = \sqrt{\sum_{i=1}^{n_t} \frac{\left(TF_{jt}^i - E(TF_{jt})\right)^2}{n_t}} \qquad (1)$$

where TF_{jt}^i is the three-month T-bill forecast of forecaster i in quarter t and $E(TF_{jt})$ is the mean forecast for quarter t and for both j = 1, 2, 3, 4, 5 quarters ahead. The number of forecasters each quarter is n_t, which varies from around 30–50 people.

Figure 5.2 shows the standard deviation of T-bill rate forecasts, our measure of forecast dispersion, one to five quarters ahead from the SPF.

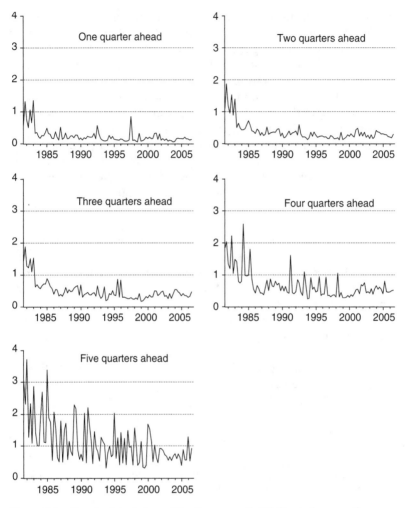

Figure 5.2   Standard deviation of the three-month T-bill rate (survey of professional forecasters)

For the aid of comparison the scale of the vertical axis of each graph is identical. Two things can be noted from figure 5.2. First, note that the standard deviation of forecasts was relatively higher in the early 1980s. Second, notice that the standard deviation of forecasts increases as the forecast horizon increases from two to five quarters ahead.

As can be seen in figure 5.2, a lot of the volatility in the forecast dispersion occurs in the early 1980s, although this is less true for the four-to five-quarters-ahead forecasts than the nearer-term forecasts. Some of the volatility in the forecast dispersion perhaps can be attributed to the transition to lower inflation following the recessions of 1980 and 1981–1982. By the end of 1983 inflation had stabilized around 4 percent, and we take this to be the end of the "first" transition to lower inflation.

Table 5.1 reports the mean of the forecast dispersions for the sample split according to the evolution of the transparency of monetary policy. The differences in the mean dispersions (tests not reported) are all statistically significantly different from the 1981:3 to 1993:4 pretransparency sample as well as from the 1984:1 to 1993:4 sample. Also the changes in the mean dispersions are quite large. As shown in the table below the decline in the mean dispersion is between 25 and 50 percent. The second row of numbers uses the sample 1984:1 to 1993:4 as the "pretransparency" period.

As discussed above, during the sample period the intention of monetary policymakers was to increasingly make monetary policy more transparent. If the Fed has gotten better at communicating its intentions, then there should be a greater consensus on the path of future monetary policy and hence lower forecast dispersions on an average. Hence, to the extent that the Fed was successful at increasing transparency, the goal of which presumably is to reduce the uncertainty about monetary policy, the forecast dispersions should decrease. This indeed seems to be the case. Figure 5.2 and table 5.1 both indicate that going from the 1980s into the 1990s and 2000s, forecast dispersion has decreased.

Table 5.1   Sample: 1981:3 to 2006:3

Sample	STF1	STF2	STF3	STF4	STF5
Mean of standard deviation of three-month T-bill survey forecast one to five-quarters ahead					
81:3 to 93:4	0.328	0.497	0.640	0.868	1.418
84:1 to 93:4	0.233	0.357	0.502	0.732	1.269
94:1 to 06:3	0.160	0.248	0.370	0.494	0.826
95:4 to 06:3	0.159	0.247	0.357	0.477	0.796
99:3 to 06:3	0.157	0.275	0.384	0.499	0.765
Percentage change in mean dispersion from 1981:3 to 1993:4 sample					
94:1 to 06:3	−51.2%	−50.1%	−42.2%	−43.1%	−41.7%
95:4 to 06:3	−51.5%	−50.3%	−44.2%	−45.0%	−43.9%
99:3 to 06:3	−52.1%	−44.7%	−40.0%	−42.5%	−46.1%
Percentage change in mean dispersion from 1984:1 to 1993:4 sample					
94:1 to 06:3	−31.3%	−30.5%	−26.3%	−32.5%	−34.9%
95:4 to 06:3	−31.8%	−30.8%	−28.9%	−34.8%	−37.3%
99:3 to 06:3	−32.6%	−23.0%	−23.5%	−31.8%	−39.7%

Table 5.2 isolates spikes in the forecast dispersions. Spikes in the forecast dispersions are identified as values of STF1, STF2, STF3, STF4, or STF5 greater than or equal to their means plus one standard deviation. Table 5.3 reports the dates and magnitudes of the spikes. For the 91 quarters from 1984:1 to 2006:3 there are 34 quarters where at least one forecast dispersion spikes. In only 2 quarters do all five spike, while in 13 quarters only one forecast dispersion spikes. With the exception of STF4, all forecast dispersions spike between 13 and 17 times. Some of these spikes can be associated with changes in the stance of monetary policy and some with financial or political events.

The SVARs are estimated using quarterly data from two samples: a "pre-transparency period" from 1981:3 to 1993:4 and the "transparency period" from 1994:1 to 2006:3. The general specification of the structural form of the models is given by

$$AX_t = B(L)X_{t-1} + \varepsilon_t \tag{2}$$

Table 5.2   Sample: 1984:1 2006:3, observations $= 91$

	STF1	STF2	STF3	STF4	STF5
Mean	0.19	0.30	0.43	0.60	1.02
Median	0.16	0.27	0.39	0.51	0.87
Maximum	0.85	0.72	0.88	2.59	3.39
Minimum	0.06	0.12	0.18	0.24	0.31
Std. Dev.	0.12	0.12	0.16	0.34	0.60
Sample autocorrelations (standard error $= 0.21$)					
Lag 1	0.11	0.54	0.40	0.24	0.13
2	0.09	0.45	0.48	0.14	0.12
3	0.10	0.36	0.35	0.16	0.12
4	-0.07	0.27	0.27	0.39	0.31
*Unit root tests**					
ADF test statistic	-8.45	-3.84	-3.52	-2.52	-1.90
(probability)	(0.00)	(0.00)	(0.01)	(0.11)	(0.33)

*Augmented Dickey Fuller test with lag length chosen using the Schwartz information criterion.

Comments on table 5.2:

1. The mean, median, and minimum and standard deviation of the forecast dispersion (standard deviation of forecasts) increases with the forecast horizon. The maximum also increases going from the two- to five-quarters-ahead forecast dispersion.

2. Unit root tests indicate that the one- to three-quarters-ahead forecast dispersions are stationary. The four- and five-quarters-ahead forecast dispersions appear to be nonstationary.

3. The sample autocorrelations indicate that the one-quarter-ahead forecast dispersions are serially uncorrelated. Lags 1 to 3 of the four- and five-quarters-ahead forecast dispersions are not serially correlated, while the fourth lag is. However this series is nonstationary. Does this make sense? The two- and three-quarters-ahead forecast dispersions are serially correlated.

Table 5.3   Sample 1984:1 to 2006:3

Date	STF1	STF2	STF3	STF4	STF5	Event
84:1		0.43	0.57		1.92	Monetary tightening (+26 bps)
84:2		0.43	0.67	2.59	2.70	Monetary tightening (+87 bps)
84:3		0.47	0.72	0.98		Monetary tightening (+87 bps)
84:4	0.36	0.58	0.73	0.96		Monetary ease (−212 bps)
85:1	0.48	0.72	0.88	0.99	3.39	Monetary ease (−79 bps)
85:2	0.32	0.59	0.79	1.80	1.89	Monetary ease (−55 bps)
85:3			0.64		1.75	No change in monetary policy
85:4			0.59			Monetary tightening (20 bps)
86:1					2.06	Monetary ease (−28 bps)
86:2	0.38	0.46				Monetary ease (−90 bps)
87:1	0.52				1.79	No change in monetary policy
87:4	0.34	0.52	0.61		1.72	Stock market crash
89:1			0.59		2.30	Monetary tightening (+97 bps)
89:2		0.45	0.64		2.17	Monetary tightening (+28 bps)
89:3		0.47	0.67			Monetary ease (−64 bps)
90:1			0.69			Monetary ease (−36 bps)
90:3					2.03	No change in monetary policy
91:1					2.20	Monetary ease (−132 bps)
91:2				1.61	1.66	Monetary ease (−56 bps)
92:1	0.32					Monetary ease (−80 bps from previous quarter)
92:3	0.57	0.59	0.66			Monetary ease (−50 bps from previous quarter)
93:2				1.09		No change in monetary policy
93:3			0.63			No change in monetary policy
95:1					2.03	Monetary tightening (+64 bps)
95:3			0.87	0.94		Monetary ease (−22 bps)
96:1			0.84			Monetary ease (−36 bps)
97:3	0.85					Asian financial crisis
98:2				1.05		No change in monetary policy
98:4	0.32					Russian LTCM crisis, −67 bps ease
00:1					1.68	Monetary tightening (+37 bps)
01:1	0.32	0.43				Monetary ease (−88 bps from previous quarter)
01:2	0.33	0.48				Monetary ease (−127 bps from previous quarter)
01:4	0.31					Post 9/11, Monetary ease (−136 bps)
04:1		0.41				No change in monetary policy
# of spikes	13	14	17	9	15	

Notes:

1. Definition of spikes is the mean plus one standard deviation which for the various measures of fore-cast dispersion works out as $STF_{1t} \geq 0.31$, $STF_{2t} \geq 0.42$, $STF_{3t} \geq 0.59$, $STF_{4t} \geq 0.94$, and $STF_{5t} \geq 1.62$.
2. Monetary tightening or ease is measured as the change in the FFR from the previous quarter.

where, X_t is an $n \times 1$ vector of endogenous variables, A is $n \times n$ parameter matrix with ones on the main diagonal and the off diagonal elements capturing the contemporaneous relationships between the variables, $B(L)$ is a polynomial matrix in the lag operator, and ε_t is an $n \times 1$ vector of structural shocks. The standard or reduced forms VAR is given by

$$X_t = D(L)X_{t-1} + \mu_t \qquad (3)$$

where $D(L) = A^{-1}B(L)$ and $\mu_t = A^{-1}\varepsilon_t$. Given estimates of the forecast errors of the standard form VAR μ_t, a necessary condition for identification of the structural shocks, ε_t can be obtained by imposing $\dfrac{n(n-1)}{2}$ restrictions on the A matrix (see Enders 1995 or Hamilton 1994). The endogenous variable vector is given by $X_t' = [INF_t, U_t, FFR_t, STF_{jt}]$. The variable INF_t is the growth rate from the same quarter of the pervious year of the consumption expenditure price excluding energy and food, U_t is the unemployment rate, and FFR_t is the effective FFR. The data for these three variables come from the Federal Reserve Bank of St. Louis: http://research.stlouisfed.org/fred2/. The structural shocks are given as $\varepsilon_t' = [\varepsilon_t^{inf}, \varepsilon_t^u, \varepsilon_t^{ffr}, \varepsilon_t^{tfj}]$. For the purposes of discussing identification and without loss of generality, rewrite equation (3) as

$$\begin{bmatrix} 1 & a_{12} & a_{13} & a_{14} \\ a_{21} & 1 & a_{23} & a_{24} \\ a_{31} & a_{32} & 1 & a_{34} \\ a_{41} & a_{42} & a_{43} & 1 \end{bmatrix} \begin{bmatrix} INF_t \\ U_t \\ FFR_t \\ STF_{jt} \end{bmatrix} = \begin{bmatrix} \varepsilon_t^{inf} \\ \varepsilon_t^u \\ \varepsilon_t^{ffr} \\ \varepsilon_t^{tfj} \end{bmatrix}$$

The necessary condition to just identify the structural shocks is to impose restrictions on six of the elements of A. The traditional VAR approach to identification is assume the Choleski decomposition, that is, the assumption that the A matrix consists of zeros above the main diagonal. We will try to justify these restrictions structurally with the following assumptions:

1. Inflation is predetermined and thus does not depend on contemporaneous values of the unemployment, the FFR, or the T-bill rate forecast dispersion. The justification for this assumption is usual sticky wage and price model. With inflation predetermined, $a_{12} = a_{13} = a_{14} = 0$.
2. The unemployment rate is assumed to respond contemporaneously to inflation shocks, but not to financial market shocks via the FFR or the T-bill rate forecast dispersion. Hence $a_{23} = a_{24} = 0$.
3. Finally, and with perhaps the least amount of justification, it is assumed that Fed in setting the FFR, is concerned solely with inflation

and unemployment shocks, so $a_{34} = 0$. This assumption is tenuous if the Fed responds to increases financial market uncertainty, that is, an increase in forecast dispersion by changing (perhaps decreasing) the FFR.

Discussion of the Impulse Response Functions

The impulse response functions for the estimated SVAR are shown in figures 5.3a through 5.3e. Each figure compares, for each sample period, the impulse response functions of the T-bill rate forecast dispersions in response to shocks to inflation (INF), unemployment (U), the federal funds rate (FFR), and the forecast dispersion itself. Three patterns emerge from these comparisons.

First, the initial response of the T-bill forecast dispersions to inflation shocks increases by a factor of 4 comparing the before transparency sample to the transparency sample. This result is somewhat surprising as it suggests that as monetary policy has become more transparent, inflation shocks have resulted in greater initial forecast dispersions. If greater monetary policy transparency implies that market participants are more certain about how monetary policy itself will respond to inflation shocks, one would expect a decrease in forecast dispersions in response to inflation shocks.

Second, with the exception of the three-quarter forecast dispersion, there is essentially no change across the two sample periods in the response of T-bill forecast dispersions in response to unemployment rate shocks. Finally, the response of T-bill forecast dispersions to shocks to the FFR is mixed. For the one-, two-, and three-quarter-ahead T-bill forecast dispersions, the initial response to a FFR shock decreases from the before transparency to the transparency period. This suggests for one-, two-, and three-quarter-ahead forecasts of monetary policy, increased transparency results in FFRs having a smaller impact, actually negative, on uncertainty about future monetary policy. However, for the four-quarter-ahead forecast dispersion, there is no change, while the five-ahead T-bill forecast dispersion increases in response to a FFR shock.

In summary, the comparison of before transparency with the transparency periods of the impulse response functions for the T-bill forecast dispersions suggests that transparency has had a mixed impact on uncertainty about future monetary policy. The SVAR results suggest that inflation shocks generate more uncertainty about future monetary policy in the transparency period while at least out to three quarters into the future, shocks to the FFR result in less uncertainty about future monetary policy.

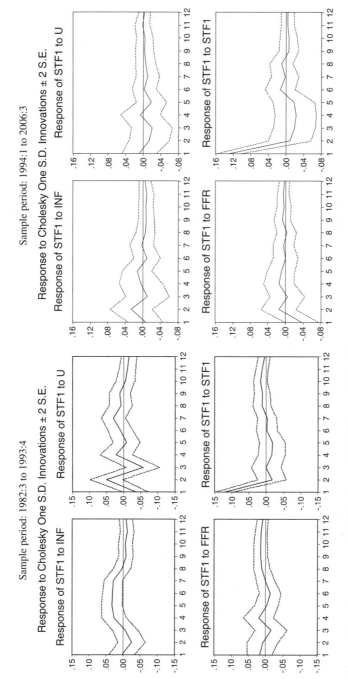

Figure 5.3a   One quarter ahead three-month T-bill forecast dispersions

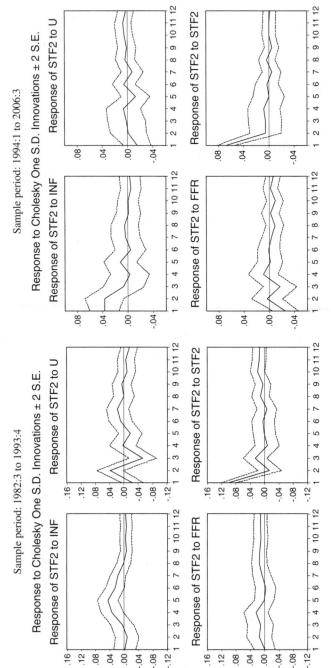

Figure 5.3b Two quarters ahead three-month T-bill forecast dispersions

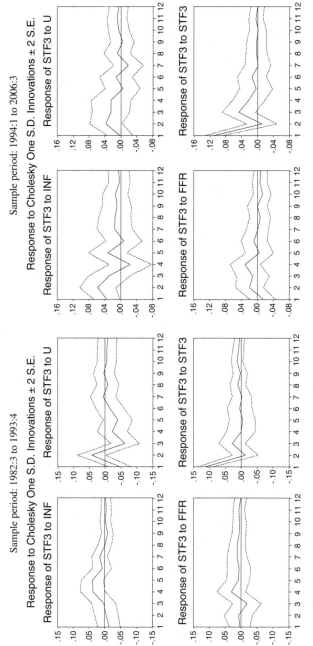

Figure 5.3c Three quarters ahead three-month T-bill forecast dispersions

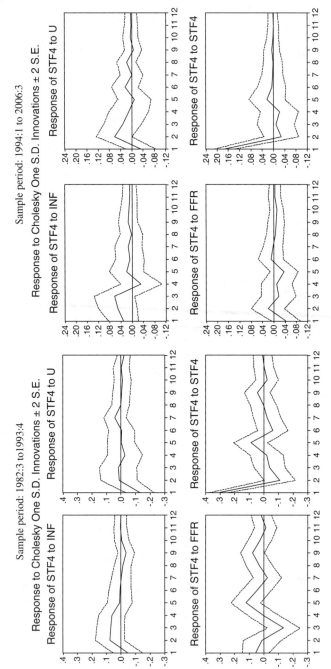

Figure 5.3d Four quarters ahead three-month T-bill forecast dispersions

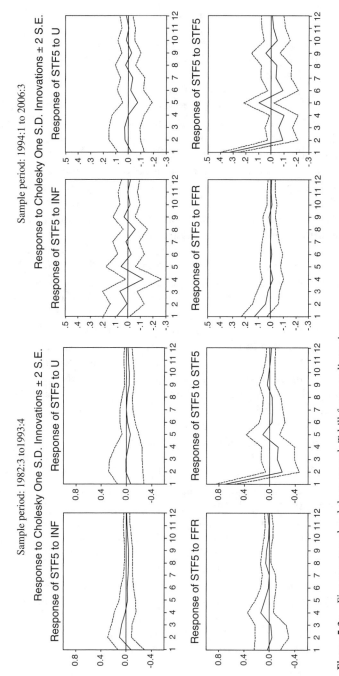

Figure 5.3e Five quarters ahead three-month T-bill forecast dispersions

Conclusions

In 1994 the Federal Reserve System moved to a more transparent reporting of monetary policy. In this chapter we first discussed the various sources of uncertainty that play an essential role in the formulation and conduct of monetary policy and evaluated the degree of uncertainty faced by monetary policymakers. Among the sources of uncertainty we identified the following: uncertain economic data, uncertain economic forecasts, uncertainty in model building, uncertainty in the transmission of monetary policy, and uncertainty due to globalization.

We also analyzed the conditions that influence uncertainty about monetary policy and gave an overview of central bank transparency abroad and Federal Reserve transparency in the United States. In view of the fact that the Fed has been given enormous economic responsibilities to preserve price stability and promote economic growth, the question naturally arises as to how the Fed should exercise its responsibilities in a democratic society guided by institutions of freedom and accountability. Academic economists and policymakers agree that the Fed's accountability for its actions to preserve low inflation and promote economic growth is best expressed in its degree of transparency.

The standard definition of transparency is the commitment to provide reliable, complete, and timely information to the widest possible audience. Transparency has multiple attributes, each of which is essential to maintain the meaning of the concept. Thus, failing to provide information, providing unreliable information, providing information in an untimely way, or providing information that is abstruse or difficult to understand violates the integrity of the concept.

If we extend the concept of transparency to monetary policy, then a transparent monetary policy is one that delivers all attributes of the concept concurrently. Transparency means the supply of information that is reliable, complete, and timely in a language that is understood by people within or outside the policy process.

Finally, we assessed the empirical impact of monetary policy transparency on the uncertainty about future monetary policy. As a proxy for the various sources of uncertainty about future monetary policy, we used the forecast dispersions for T-bills from the SPF.

Data plots and sample statistics suggest that the Fed has been successful at reducing uncertainty about future monetary policy. The broader empirical question is what else might account for the decline in forecast dispersion other than the increase in the transparency of monetary policy. Thus, it is necessary to control for that the absolute size of the changes in the federal funds and the occurrence of financial crises when estimating the impact of transparency on the forecast dispersion of T-bill.

We finally performed SVAR to characterize the dynamic impact of economic and monetary policy shocks on the T-bill rate forecast dispersion. The comparison of before transparency with the transparency periods of the impulse response functions for the T-bill forecast dispersions suggests that transparency has had a mixed impact on uncertainty about future monetary policy. However, the initial response of T-bill forecast dispersions, from one to three quarters ahead, to FFR shocks is smaller after monetary policy becomes more transparent. This is consistent with the Fed's monetary policy transparency being successful in credibly communicating its future stance. Thus, our empirical findings provide some evidence that Federal Reserve transparency has reduced the uncertainty of future monetary policy anticipated by market participants.

*The authors are both at Loyola University, Chicago. The authors are very grateful to Robert DeYoung who offered detailed comments as a discussant at the International Western Economics Association Meetings. The authors are also grateful for comments and encouragement to Doug Evanoff, Robert Bliss, George Kaufman, and Harvey Rosenblum.

References

Ang, Andrew, Gaert Bekaert, and Min Wei. 2006. Do macro variables, asset markets or surveys forecast inflation better, Staff Working Paper, 2006–15, Federal Reserve Board, February 13, 2006.

Bernanke, Ben.2007. Semiannual monetary policy report to the Congress. Testimony before the Committee on Banking, Housing, and Urban Affairs, U.S. Senate, February 14.

——— and Ilian Mihov. 1998. Measuring monetary policy. The Quarterly Journal of Economics 113: 1025–53.

Blinder, Alan. 1998. Central banking in theory and practice. Cambridge, MA: MIT Press.

Carlson, John, Ben Craig, Patrick Higgins, and William Melick. 2006. FOMC communications and the predictability of near-term policy decisions, Federal Reserve Bank of (Cleveland).

Carpenter, S .2004. Transparency and monetary policy: What does the academic literature tell policymakers? The Board of Governors of the Federal Reserve System, no. 35.

De Haan, Jakob, Sylvester Eijffinger, and Krzysztof Rybinski. 2007. Central bank transparency and Central Bank communication: editorial introduction. European Journal of Political Economy 23: 1–8.

Ehrmann, M, and M. Fratzscher. 2007. Transparency, disclosure, and the Federal Reserve. International Journal of Central Banking 3: 829–69.

Friedman, Milton. 1960. A program for monetary stability (Fordham University Press).

Geraats, P.M. 2001. Why adopt transparency? The Publication of Central Bank Forecasts, European Central Bank, Working Paper No. 41.

Geraats, P.M., 2002. Central bank transparency. The Economic Journal 112: F532–F565.

Greenspan, Alan. 1996. The challenge of central banking in a democratic society. The annual dinner and the Francis Boyer lecture of the American Enterprise Institute for Public Policy Research, December 5, in New York.

———. 2001. The challenge of measuring and modeling a dynamic economy. Speech at the Washington economic policy conference of the National Association for Business Economics, March 27, in Washington D.C.

———. 2002. Economic Volatility, Symposium sponsored by the Federal Reserve Bank of (Kansas City), August 30, 2002.

———. 2004. Risk and uncertainty in monetary policy. American Economic Review Papers and Proceedings 94: 33–48.

Issing, O. 2005. Communication, transparency, and accountability: Monetary policy in the twenty-first century. Federal Reserve Bank of St. Louis Review 65–83.

Kahn, G. 2007. Communicating a policy path: The next frontier in central bank transparency? Federal Reserve Bank of Kansas, Economic Review 25–51.

Kohn, Donald. 2006. Monetary policy and uncertainty. The fourth conference of the International Research Forum on monetary policy, December 1.

Krane, Spencer. 2006. How professional forecasters view shocks to GDP, Federal Reserve Bank of Chicago, Working Paper no. 19.

Meyer, Laurence. 2000. Structural change and monetary policy, The joint conference of the Federal Reserve Bank of San Francisco and the Stanford institute for Economic Policy Research, March 3, 2000.

Moskow, M. H., 2006. Reflection on monetary policy: flexibility, transparency, and inflation, The Federal Reserve Bank of Chicago.

Poole, William. 2004. FOMC transparency. Presentation at the Ozark Chapter of the Society of Financial Services Professionals, October 6.

———. 2005, How predictable is Fed policy? Federal Reserve Bank of St. Louis Review 87: 659–68.

Saxton, Jim. 1997. Transparency and the Federal Reserve monetary policy. Joint Economic Committee of the United States Congress.

Tetlow, Robert, and Brian Ironside. 2006. Real-time uncertainty in the United States: The Fed From 1996–2003, European Central Bank Working Paper Series no. 610.

Walsh, C. E. 2003. Accountability, transparency, and inflation targeting. Journal of Money, Credit, and Banking 35: 829–49.

Williams, John. 2004. Robust estimation and monetary policy with unobserved structural change, Federal Reserve Bank of San Francisco, Working Papers in Applied Economic Theory.

Winkler, B. 2000. Which Kind of Transparency? On the need for clarity in monetary policy-making, European Central Bank Working paper series no. 26.

6

The Trimmed Mean PCE Inflation Rate: A Better Measure of Core Inflation

Harvey Rosenblum and Nicole Y. Cote[*]

Introduction

Over the last two decades, the Federal Reserve and numerous other central banks have placed increased emphasis on low and stable inflation as a primary goal of monetary policy. Many central banks have set out explicit numerical inflation targets, often with guidance from their country's legislatures. Across the globe, central banks have been successful in their quest for low and stable inflation. The process began with the G-7 countries (the U.S., UK, Germany, France, Italy, Canada, and Japan) and was aided by the Maastricht Treaty, which pressured Western European countries to converge to low inflation rates if they wished to join the Euro-currency area (figure 6.1). More recently, several previously high-inflation countries (Mexico, Israel, Turkey, Spain, Portugal, and Greece, to name just a few) have joined the select circle of low-inflation countries.

As central banks make policy choices about whether to ease or tighten monetary policy in order to get closer to achieving their inflation objectives, it is critical that they understand accurately the trajectory of inflation. This task is more difficult than it sounds because inflation statistics often contain a good deal of "noise," which has to be separated from the underlying inflation signal.

The importance in real time of extracting the correct inflation signal from the inflation indexes cannot be overstated. If monetary policy fails to keep inflation low and stable, the higher rate of inflation will ultimately

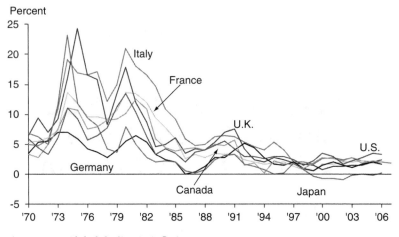

Figure 6.1   Global decline in inflation

become embedded in long-term interest rates. This can have adverse impacts on investment in long-lived assets with unfavorable repercussions on a country's overall economic performance.

Core Inflation

Beginning in the mid-1970s, food and energy prices in the United States were more volatile than many other prices that were included in the measures of inflation compiled in that era. It was believed by some that excluding food and energy price changes from the broader inflation indexes would provide a better measure of underlying inflation trends than would be obtained by leaving in such "noisy data." This ex-food and energy measure of inflation, dubbed "core inflation," has, over much of its life, done a good job of maximizing the signal-to-noise ratio[1] (Blinder and Reis 2005; Mishkin 2007).

Beginning in 2002, energy prices began to follow an upward trend, one that, for all intents and purposes, has not reversed itself in six years. More recently, food prices have also shown an upward trend. Due in part to globalization and the search for alternative fuels from biosources, particularly ethanol derived from corn and sugar, food and energy prices have become more correlated than in the past; both appear to be on a sustained upward trend owing more to surging global demand than to supply disruptions. In these circumstances, the use of a core inflation measure that excludes food and energy seems questionable because it may be removing an important signal of structural change in the global economy and leaving in the noise.[2]

Getting an inflation measure "right" involves more than just measurement accuracy. Central banks must also be concerned with their credibility in the eyes of the public they serve. If a country's citizens lack faith and confidence in their central bank, they will begin to distrust their nation's banking system and currency. So it is important that a country's citizens believe central bank statements that inflation is low and stable. In the words of Federal Reserve chairman Ben Bernanke, "Experience suggests that high and persistent inflation undermines public confidence in the economy and in the management of economic policy generally, with potentially adverse effects on risk-taking, investment, and other productive activities that are sensitive to the public's assessments of the prospects for future economic stability" (Bernanke 2007, p. 1).

Because people have to eat and drive on a daily basis, core inflation measures that routinely exclude food and energy have become a hard sell to the general public and have created some degree of animosity toward those who insist on using such inflation measures.[3]

The choice of an inflation measure for policy use encompasses factors other than accuracy and credibility—forecasting power, timeliness and the extent of data revisions, and the degree of measurement bias.

The Choice between Consumer Price Index and Personal Consumption Expenditures

In its choice for an indicator of a broad measure of inflation faced by households, the Federal Reserve has a choice between the consumer price index (CPI) and personal consumption expenditures (PCE). The CPI is the better known index and has been available for a longer period of time. Because it is used to index public expenditure programs, the federal income tax, wage contracts, and social security payments, the CPI is widely followed by politicians and the public. Unfortunately, the CPI has expenditure weights that change with sluggish frequency. Moreover, new products and services are included with a long lag. This often introduces serious measurement biases into the CPI. On the other hand, the monthly CPI data are available quickly—a couple of weeks after the end of the month being measured—and are rarely revised.

For more than a decade, the Federal Open Market Committee (FOMC) has relied heavily on the PCE inflation measure. It is also available monthly, but with a slightly longer time lag than the CPI. The PCE includes a wider range of goods and services than the CPI does. In addition, the expenditure weights on PCE components reflect both changes in consumer tastes and the substitution effects stemming from changes in relative prices each month. Unfortunately the PCE data are subject to annual revisions, which, from time to time, can be sizeable. These revisions can lead to erroneous judgments about the efficacy of past monetary policy decisions that were made on the basis of "real-time data," which tend to disappear from databases that typically include only the latest revised data.[4] While the FOMC makes reference to both the CPI and PCE, it has tended to put the majority of its emphasis on core PCE in recent years. In recognition of the public's growing dissatisfaction with measures of inflation that exclude movements in food and energy prices, the FOMC has begun to publish FOMC members' projections for both PCE and core PCE as part of its new and enhanced procedures to better communicate with the public.[5]

The Trimmed Mean Alternative

Even when movements in food and energy prices were transitory in nature, the public has tended to be skeptical of inflation measures that routinely excluded important items that are consumed frequently. Many people seem less concerned about inflation measures that exclude, for example, computers or TVs, which are purchased once in every several years. The responses of informal focus groups appear to indicate that an inflation measure that excludes food and energy angers many people and makes the Federal Reserve seem "out of touch." There seems to be an important need to trim out inflation noise in a more politically palatable manner while, at the same time, satisfying policymakers' and statisticians' needs to better predict underlying trend inflation. One inflation measure that satisfies these diverse criteria is the Dallas Fed Trimmed Mean PCE (Dolmas 2005).

Before explaining how it works, let me illustrate how statisticians often deal with the problem of finding a representative average of a series of numbers. This example is taken from the skating competition at the Winter Olympic Games. A few years ago, some of the judges showed political bias in scoring the various skaters. It was decided that in the next Olympic Games the high and low marks would be excluded and the mean of the remainder of the scores would be computed, that is, trim out the extremes and average the rest. The same methodology can be applied to monthly price measurements.

Here's how it works. The Dallas Fed Trimmed Mean PCE measure excludes the biggest price changes—whether increases or declines—regardless of whether it is food, energy, housing, consumer electronics, et cetera. The index is designed to provide the best fit to the trend of overall PCE inflation. It trims off the top 25% of expenditure weights of price increases and 19% of the expenditure weights of prices that declined or rose the least. It then takes the average of the 56% of the expenditure weights in the middle. It is much like using the interquartile range and excluding the top and bottom quartiles. Inflation has been in a downward drift over the 1979–2002 sample period; the use of this asymmetric trimming avoids introducing a bias into the trimmed mean. While the trimmed mean PCE does not routinely trim out the food and energy components of monthly price changes, it does almost always trim out consumer electronics from the index. Consumer electronic prices have been in a steep, secular downward trend for the last decade. Thus the trimmed mean PCE routinely trims out one of the disinflationary benefits that globalization brings to the U. S. economy.

The Dallas Fed Trimmed Mean PCE is designed to provide an approximation of the trend in overall PCE inflation. To illustrate, figure 6.2 shows overall, or headline, PCE inflation going back to 1977 and its 36-month moving average trend. Shown in figure 6.3 is the same 36-month moving average, as well as core PCE and trimmed mean PCE. While it is not readily apparent in figure 6.3, the trimmed mean does come much closer to approximating "trend inflation" than does the ex-food and energy measure. This holds true for both the root mean squared error (RMSE) and the Absolute Error, with the gain in accuracy varying between one-quarter and three-quarters of a percentage point.

The trimmed mean does a better job of forecasting *overall* PCE inflation over a six-to-twelve-month time horizon than does the core PCE. This is critically important since price stability is one-half of the Federal Reserve's dual mandate, or primary goals, for monetary policy. It should be noted, however, that forecasting is not the primary purpose for which the trimmed

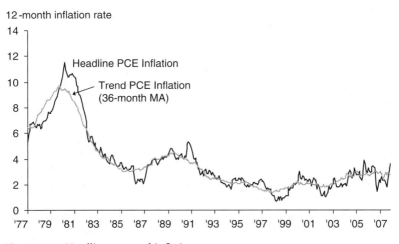

Figure 6.2   Headline vs. trend inflation

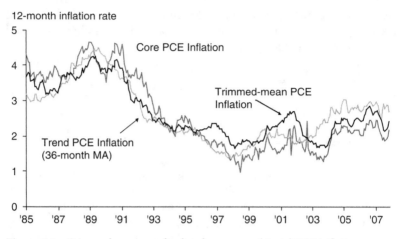

Figure 6.3   Trimmed mean, ex-food and energy, and trend PCE inflation

mean was designed. Its forecasting record is an ancillary benefit of the trimmed mean PCE. If one wants to forecast future inflation, a multivariate forecasting equation would generally do better.

Recent History: Core versus Trimmed Mean PCE

Since 2000, the trimmed mean PCE has, for the most part, been higher than the core PCE (figure 6.4). This does not happen by design. Each series has a distinctly different trend. This can happen only if food and energy prices, excluded from the traditional core measure, tend to be rising consistently faster than other price changes. The opposite occurred in the first half of the 1990s (figure 6.3).

The differences between the two inflation measures have important monetary policy implications for the Federal Reserve. The trimmed mean PCE suggests that trend inflation is outside and above the so-called comfort zone of 1%–2% mentioned in past speeches by many FOMC members. The core PCE, on the other hand, has, on several occasions, since 2004, touched down to the 2% "upper bound of the comfort zone," from above, only to rise again. Nonetheless, the persistently higher level of the trimmed mean PCE raises important policy dilemmas. The first policy dilemma is that, by following the core PCE inflation measure, the FOMC may have an inadvertently easier monetary policy than it intends. That is to say, the true trend of overall consumer inflation may be higher than that suggested by PCE inflation excluding food and energy if food and energy prices are in a secular uptrend that is higher, on a sustained basis, than overall inflation.

12-month changes, percent annualized

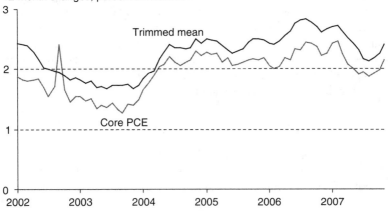

Figure 6.4   Recent history on core inflation: Trimmed mean PCE vs. ex-food and energy

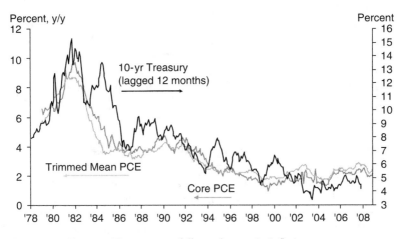

Figure 6.5   Ten-year Treasury rate follows changes in inflation

The second, and related, policy dilemma and the one that is quite important for financial markets revolves around the tendency for the level of long-term interest rates to reflect, or embed, changes in inflation and inflation expectations, with a lag (figure 6.5). The ten-year U.S. Treasury rate is highly correlated with the core PCE and the trimmed mean PCE, with a correlation coefficient of 0.87–0.90 depending on the chosen lag. Over the 1978–2007 period, the highest correlation of 0.899 occurs between the ten-year Treasury rate and core PCE with a lag of 12 months, while the highest correlation of 0.873 for the ten-year Treasury rate and trimmed mean PCE occurs with a lag of 48 months. In any event, if the FOMC is misleading itself by focusing too heavily on PCE ex-food and energy, it could wake up to an uncomfortable surprise in the future if financial markets begin to embed the resulting higher inflation into inflation expectations and the term structure of interest rates. Clearly, there is a lot at stake to getting the inflation measurement "right."

Key Takeaways

The trimmed mean PCE inflation measure has several advantages over other available inflation indicators. First, it tracks well with the trend in overall inflation. Second, it maximizes the signal relative to the noise. Third, it is a politically palatable measure to the general public because it does not routinely eliminate food and energy, which must always be purchased. Because of this last point, a fourth advantage of the trimmed mean PCE is that it is about the most credible inflation measure available.

The trimmed mean PCE is not perfect, however. It does have two disadvantages. First, it is elegant, but not simple. The underlying calculations and assumptions are not easy to explain to the general public. Second, the trimmed mean provides additional and conflicting information, which adds to the ambiguity of policy decisions and discussions and may add dissonance to the understanding of inflation trends by the general public.

Conclusion

Despite a few shortcomings, the trimmed mean PCE is the inflation measure that best meets the broad set of criteria for use in determining monetary policy in the United States. Because it is not easy to understand by the general public and because it often, though not routinely, excludes items that households purchase regularly, the trimmed mean PCE might not be the best inflation measure to be used for explicit inflation targeting, should the FOMC ever go in this direction. The public cares about the impact of overall, or headline, inflation; thus policy goals should be stated in terms of such broad inflation measures. For the making of policy decisions—to tighten, ease, or leave the stance of policy unchanged—the trimmed mean is clearly superior to the core PCE.

Notes

*The authors are, respectively, executive vice president and director of research and economic analyst at the Federal Reserve Bank of Dallas. The views expressed in this chapter are those of the authors and should not be attributed to the Federal Reserve Bank of Dallas or the Federal Reserve System. The authors would like to thank Jessica Renier for research assistance.

1. Blinder and Reis (2005), pp. 46–50, suggest that during the Greenspan era, changes in food and energy prices tended to be transitory rather than permanent. In this respect, they suggest that Chairman Greenspan was "luckier" than his predecessor, Paul A. Volcker.
2. The rising importance of China and India in the global economy since the beginning of the twenty-first century has added some 3 billion consumers to the demand for higher caloric and protein intake and to improved transportation, both of which have increased the demand for energy.
3. See Hagenbaugh (2007). This article is representative of a flurry of articles that appeared beginning in the summer of 2007 that questioned and criticized the Federal Reserve's use of ex-food and energy inflation measures.
4. For more detail on this, see Kliesen and Schmid (2004) and Fisher (2006).
5. See Federal Open Market Committee (2007), especially pp. 9–16.

References

Bernanke, Ben. 2007. Inflation expectations and inflation forecasting. Speech delivered at the Monetary Economics Workshop of the National Bureau of Economic Research Summer Institute, July 10, Cambridge, MA.

Blinder, Alan, and Ricardo Reis. 2005. Understanding the Greenspan standard, Federal Reserve Bank of Kansas City Symposium, August 25–27. *The Greenspan Era: Lessons for the Future*, 11–96.

Dolmas, Jim. 2005. A fitter, trimmer core inflation measure. Federal Reserve Bank of (Dallas), *Southwest Economy*, May/June, 1, 4–9.

Federal Open Market Committee. 2007. Minutes of the Federal Open Market Committee, October 30–31.

Fisher, Richard. 2006. Confessions of a data dependent. Remarks before the New York Association for Business Economics, November 2.

Hagenbaugh, Barbara. 2007. Food, energy costs' exclusion debated. *USA Today*, June 14, B-3.

Kliesen, Kevin, and Frank Schmid. 2004. Monetary policy actions, macroeconomic data releases, and inflation expectations. Federal Reserve Bank of St. Louis *Review*, May/June, 9–22.

Mishkin, Frederic. 2007. Headline versus core inflation in the conduct of monetary policy. Speech at the Business Cycles, International Transmission and Macroeconomic Policies Conference, October 20, in Montreal, Canada.

7

Payday Lending and Payments Services: A Historical and Modern Analysis

*Robert DeYoung and Ronnie J. Phillips**

Introduction

Payday lending—the business of buying postdated personal checks from consumers at a discount—is a booming business. Despite carrying annual percentage rates (APRs) of 300%, 400%, and higher, payday loans have quickly become a very popular means of consumer credit. The number of payday loan "stores" in the United States increased from only about 300 in 1994 to over 21,000 by 2004, and over 10 million U.S. households take out at least one payday loan each year.[1] The rapid growth of payday lenders has come at the expense of pawn shops, which have lost considerable market share over the past decade. Apparently, consumers find payday loans to be a superior alternative to other, more traditional "fringe finance" products.

When compared with any other consumer lending, payday lending rates seem exorbitant. For example, when compared with the rates on credit cards of 18%–24%, which themselves are viewed as excessive by many consumer advocates, the question that immediately arises is whether the users of payday lending services are being grossly exploited. In contrast, when payday loan fees are compared with nonsufficient funds (NSF) fees or overdraft fees charged by many banks, thrifts, and credit unions—typically $30 per item or higher—payday lending rates can seem much less excessive.

According to Bill Carter, a payday loan owner-operator in Colorado, "Our customers are cost-conscious. They count every penny." But why do supposedly cost-conscious people use expensive payday lending services?

For Carter the answer is simple: it is "cheaper than bouncing a check" (Accola 2006). These comments succinctly express the thesis that we present and investigate in this chapter—that under many reasonable circumstances, taking out a payday loan with an APR of 300% or 400% can indeed be a financially prudent course of action for consumers. We argue that consumers view payday loans as a hybrid financial service—part credit product and part payments service—and that high payday loan APRs are an implicit two-part price that pays for both services.

We benchmark our pricing analysis using payday loan pricing data collected by state regulators in Colorado. The average payday loan in Colorado between 2000 and 2005 was $293 for a term of just 17 days, and carried a $52 fixed charge. That is, the typical payday borrower postdated a $293 personal check by 17 days and gave it to a payday lender in exchange for $241 in cash. After the 17 days passed, (a) the borrower retired the loan by giving the payday lender $293 in cash, (b) the payday lender deposited the check and (hopefully) the check cleared for $293, or (c) the borrower refinanced the loan with a second 17-day transaction, using the proceeds of the second loan to pay the $52 fixed fee on the first loan. Assuming that the borrower refinanced the loan every 17 days for an entire year, the repeated $52 fees would amount to an annual interest rate of roughly 382%.[2]

How can a 382% interest rate be "cheaper than bouncing a check"? Indeed, it is *not always* cheaper than bouncing a check. But we will show that under very reasonable circumstances—for instance, when a consumer has a large and important bill to pay, has too little money in her bank account to pay that bill, and has an account with a bank that charges nontrivial checking account overdraft fees—it can indeed be cheaper. The key to our analysis is understanding that a payday loan, under circumstances such as these, is not just an extension of credit, but is also a substitute for the (expensive) payments services provided by the consumer's bank.

Charging fees for payments services has a very long tradition in the United States, going back to the early eighteenth century. The practice of "exchange charges," in which banking customers had to pay explicit up-front fees to send checks through the payments system, has deep roots in U.S. banking history (Jessup 1967). We argue that payday lending, as a hybrid credit/payments product, fits squarely into this tradition. Although we are not the first to recognize the dual nature of payday lending (e.g., see Caskey 2005), we take the analysis an important step further: using the Colorado data and a simple theoretical argument, we empirically extract an implicit price for the payments services embedded in the price of the typical payday loan. And we find that the implicit price for payments services comprises, conservatively, at least one-quarter to one-third of the total price paid for payday loans.

It is important to note that recognizing the hybrid nature of payday loans—part credit product and part payments service—does not in itself justify the high fees charged by payday lenders. Indeed, as will be seen below in the discussion on the history of payments systems, high perceived exchange fees for interbank clearances were a policy concern in the United States for more than 150 years. Exchange charges were viewed by some proponents of a uniform currency system as a negative social cost for the payments system. Because of this, the Federal Reserve made attempts to impose par clearance in the check clearing system. Thus, while we argue here that the high prices paid for payday loans are not necessarily exorbitant prices, we do not rule out the possibility that government intervention (e.g., to bring in more informational transparency) could improve the efficiency of payday lending markets.

The remainder of our chapter unfolds as follows. In the next section we show how technological change during the late nineteenth and early twentieth centuries resulted in the incidence of payments costs shifting from the consumer to the merchant, and we argue that payday lending is a modern example of how another technological change has, in some circumstances, shifted the cost of payments services back to the consumer. Then, we discuss the practice and regulation of payday lending in Colorado since 2000 and present some summary statistics on the prices charged for payday loans between 2000 and 2005. Next, we present a simple method for separating payday loan prices into payments and credit components and apply the method to the averages from the Colorado data. Finally, we summarize briefly and make some observations on the implications of our arguments for public policy.

Payments Systems

Modern consumers are accustomed to making purchases "for free," using a payments system that is (effectively) costless to them at the margin. For most purchases, the banks and the merchants absorb the costs of moving money from the bank account of the consumer (the payer) to the bank account of the merchant (the payee). This has not always been the case. For example, during the late nineteenth and early twentieth centuries, it was customary for consumers making purchases from distant merchants to purchase a draft from their bank, which they then mailed to the merchant in exchange for the purchased goods. The price that consumers paid for the bank draft was called an "exchange fee," which was typically $1\%–1^1/_2\%$ of the value of the draft. We argue here that the high price of payday loans contains an implicit exchange fee and that, as such, payday lending is a

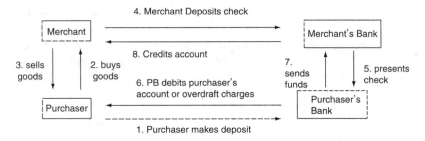

Figure 7.1   The clearing of a check

modern example of how, in certain circumstances, the costs of making payments can once again fall upon the consumer.

To illustrate our argument we turn to the economics of transactional paper pioneered by Willaim Baxter (1983)., which is the standard framework for analyzing payment systems (Rochet and Tirole 2003). A transaction paid for with a check is shown in figure 7.1.[3] There are four parties to this transaction: the purchaser of a good (P), a merchant who supplies that good (M), the purchaser's bank (P-bank), and the merchant's bank (M-bank). M and P have a demand for transactional services, while M-bank and P-bank jointly supply those services. While the exact details of the figure correspond to payment by check, a depiction of transactions that use other methods of payment would have a similar structure.

The production of payments services consumes real resources, and these expenses must be borne by some combination of the four parties or provided as a public good by society. A distinction is made between the level of prices and the structure of prices. The "price level" is the sum of the prices paid by the respective parties to the transaction, while the "price structure" is the ratio of the price paid by one group involved in the transaction to the price paid by the other group(s) involved in the transaction, that is, the incidence of the payments costs. For an equilibrium to exist in such markets, there must be a price level *and* a price structure that induces the transaction to occur. When competing payments systems exist, the system that prevails need not be the one with the lowest price, but may depend instead on the manner in which the price is split between merchants and consumers along with these parties' relative willingness to pay for the transaction. Equilibriums can occur with "highly asymmetric pricing in which one group is served at a price close to or even below marginal cost, and most or all of the gross margin is earned by serving the other group" (Evans and Schmalensee 2005, p. 79).

Though it may at first appear from this analysis that payments services are private goods, this need not be the case: the aggregate demand for them cannot be found by horizontally summing the individual consumer and merchant demands. Though P's marginal valuation of the additional unit of transactional services may differ from M's, the valuations cannot be independent of each other— because for every payer, there must be a payee. Hence, the marginal valuation of a transaction service by one party is contingent on the acceptability of this form of payment to the other party. This suggests that, in some cases, public subsidies or direct provision' of payments services may be socially efficient.

The nature and pricing of payments services has evolved over time with advances in technology and changes in legal and regulatory institutions. William Baxter (1983) points out that the distribution of transactions costs among the four parties has varied over time as the characteristics of the U.S. banking and payments systems have changed. For example, the creation of the National Banking System in 1864, in which the costs of exchange were absorbed as a public good among nationally chartered banks, led the state-chartered banks to replace bank-issued currency with a system of check clearing. As time passed, improvements in technology (e.g., train travel) reduced the overall costs of the check clearinghouse system, and as a result checks became a predominant means of exchange.

As consumers switched from bank drafts to checks for making payments to distant merchants, they avoided having to pay the exchange fee. With checks, the incidence of payments costs is distributed across the four parties as follows. M-bank and P-bank incur the costs of clearing the checks and the costs associated with bounced or returned checks. M pays the cost of float, pays any returned check fees charged by M-bank should the check bounce, and if warranted, pays a fee to a collection agency. P pays an NSF fee for bouncing a check as well as nonmonetary relationship costs with the merchant.[4]

During the 1990s, there occurred two (related) changes that set the stage for payday lending. First, increased competition in the banking industry altered the value proposition for many banks. As interest-based earnings from lending operations declined, many banks attempted to replace those lost earnings by increasing the fees they charged on inelastically demanded depositor services; one of those fee-based services was depositor overdraft protection. From the standpoint of a bank depositor, an overdraft protection fee is a composite price of two financial services: a credit product extended by the bank at a time when the depositor has a zero balance in her account and a payments product that allowed her to continue to use checks to make transactions. Thus, for banking customers who overdraft their deposit accounts, the increase in overdraft protection fees partially shifted the incidence of payments costs away from the bank and back to the consumer.

Second, the expansion of databases at credit bureaus, combined with the introduction of faster and less expensive ways to access those data, transformed the fringe finance industry. Payday lenders (which make loans secured only by a future paycheck) emerged as a viable and popular alternative to traditional pawn shops (which make loans secured by physical goods). Importantly, the entry of payday lending on the supply side occurred at about the same time as consumers on the demand side were seeking to avoid paying increased overdraft fees.

Our analysis of payday lending is depicted in figure 7.2, which follows the description of the payday lending transaction provided in the introduction above. Note that the figure is now occupied by the purchaser (the payday customer), the payday lender, and their respective banks. The merchant and the merchant's bank are included in the diagram merely for convenience, to remind us that the cash proceeds of the payday advance are used in the short run to pay for real goods and services. Note that the payday borrower may use the proceeds of a single payday advance to make purchases from multiple merchants, which will reduce the per transaction cost.

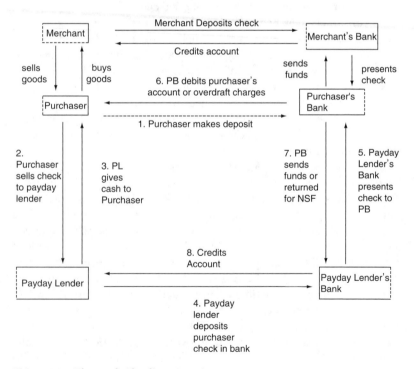

Figure 7.2   The payday lending operation

While the cost of the payday transaction is borne largely by the payday borrower, portions of the cost are also borne by the other three parties. The customer pays an explicit—and, as noted above, relatively large—fee to the payday lender.[5] Should the check ultimately bounce, then the payday lender pays an NSF fee to her bank. As with payment by check, the administrative costs of clearing the check (if this becomes necessary) are borne by the two banks. Compared with payment by check, the payday lender is absorbing the uncertainty that would have been shared by M (float, returned check fee), M-bank (administrative expenses), and P (merchant relationship costs).

Payday Lending in Colorado

As in the case of insurance products and services, there is no federal regulation of payday lending. This type of lending is regulated at the state level, and it is legal in some form in approximately three-quarters of U.S. states. It has been legal in Colorado since April 18, 2000, when the then Colorado governor Bill Owens signed the Deferred Deposit Loan Act (DDLA). This law modified the Colorado Uniform Consumer Credit Code (credit code) to regulate activities commonly known as payday loans or "postdated checks." This law was enacted following an interpretation by the credit code administrator that transactions in which a check casher advances money to a consumer in exchange for receiving a consumer's personal check to be cashed for a fee at a later date are an advance of credit and therefore governed by the credit code.

Under the DDLA, a "deferred deposit loan" is a consumer loan in which the lender advances money to the borrower and in return accepts from the consumer an "instrument" such as a check in the amount of the advance plus a fee, which is not to be cashed by the lender for a specified term of the loan. The loan principal is limited to $500 for a term not to exceed 40 days. The maximum finance charge is 20% of loan principal up to $300 and 7.5% of the loan principal that exceeds $300. The act allows the loan to be "renewed" just once (i.e., for a maximum of another 40 days, under the same pricing restrictions), but in practice this is a formality because the act does not prevent loans from being "rolled over" (i.e., a new loan is written to pay off the old loan).

The DDLA also explicitly regulates the detail and manner in which information about the terms and conditions of the loan is communicated to payday loan customers:

- Each deferred deposit loan transaction and renewal shall be documented by a written agreement signed both by the lender and by the consumer. The written agreement shall contain the name of the consumer; the transaction date; the amount of the instrument; the annual percentage rate charged; a statement of the total amount of finance charges charged, expressed both as a dollar amount and an annual percentage rate; and the name, address, and telephone number of any agent or arranger involved in the transaction.

- A lender shall provide the following notice in a prominent place on each loan agreement in at least 10-point type: "A DEFERRED DEPOSIT LOAN IS NOT INTENDED TO MEET LONG-TERM FINANCIAL NEEDS. A DEFERRED DEPOSIT LOAN SHOULD BE USED ONLY TO MEET SHORT-TERM CASH NEEDS. RENEWING THE DEFERRED DEPOSIT LOAN RATHER THAN PAYING THE DEBT IN FULL WILL REQUIRE ADDITIONAL FINANCE CHARGES."
- Any lender offering a deferred deposit loan shall post, at any place of business where deferred deposit loans are made, a notice of the finance charges imposed for such deferred deposit loans (Colorado Revised Statutes Title 5 Consumer Credit Code Art. 3.1. Deferred Deposit Loan Act, 5–3.1–101 to 5–3.1–123).

The DDLA also mandates that the credit code administrator (i.e., the Attorney General's Office) periodically examine, at intervals the administrator deems appropriate, the loans, business records, and practices of every licensed payday lender to investigate for compliance with the law. As part of these compliance examinations, the administrator collects information about the 30 most recent loan transactions preceding the compliance examination. These loan-level data include the terms of the loan (e.g., the loan principal, the finance charge, and the length of the loan) and the payday history of the borrower (e.g., whether the loan was a new loan or a rollover loan and what were the number of loans over the previous 12 months). The examiners also collect demographic data (although these data are not necessarily from the same loans as the data on loan terms), including the consumer's age, gender, martial status, monthly income, job classification, and length of time at current employment. These data indicate that the "average" Colorado borrower is a 36-year-old single woman, making $2,370 per month, employed as a laborer or office worker for about three years and six months.

DeYoung and Phillips (2007) analyzed the data collected by the Office of the Attorney General in Colorado between 2000 and 2005. The analysis generated three sets of findings. First, the authors found that the characteristics of payday loans in Colorado are similar to those of payday loans made in other states (see table 7.1). The typical payday loan in Colorado

Table 7.1   Means and standard deviations for selected characteristics of 24,792 payday loans made in Colorado between 2000 and 2005

Loan terms	Mean	Standard deviation
Loan amount	$293.25	124.22
Loan fee	$52.29	17.80
Loan characteristics		
Amount of the loan (dollars)	293.25	124.22
Loan charge (dollars)	52.29	17.80
Length of loan (days)	16.86	6.76
Annual percentage rate (APR) on loan	459.26	187.11
% of loans priced at legal ceiling	89.87	30.17
Customer borrowing patterns		
Number of payday loans during the previous 12 months	9.39	7.61
% of loans for which borrowers had continuous payday debt over the past six months	10.80	31.03
% of loans that were used to pay off a previous payday loan.	55.17	49.73
Lender market demographics		
% white population in payday lender zip code area	87.97	11.71
% black population in payday lender zip code area	1.65	4.82
% Hispanic population in payday lender zip code area	13.88	15.55
Income per household in payday lender zip code area (thousands of dollars)	43.04	14.95

Source: DeYoung and Phillips (2007).

during this period carried a fee of $52 for a $293 loan for 17 days. This amounted to an APR of 459%. Approximately 89% of these loans were priced at the legal ceiling allowed by Colorado law as described above. The typical payday loan customer took out nine payday loans per year, and 11% of payday loan customers had payday loans outstanding continuously during the previous six months. About 55% of payday loans were used to pay off or roll over a previous payday loan. The average household income in local markets that contained a payday lender (defined by the payday lenders' zip codes) was about $43,000. About 14% of the population in these local markets was Hispanic and about 2% was black.

Second, the authors identified a number of local market (again, defined by the payday lenders' zip codes) demographic characteristics that tended to attract payday lenders. In Colorado, payday lenders have been more likely to locate in heavily populated urban markets with lower-than-average household incomes but higher-than-average business and banking activity.

They found no evidence that payday lenders were more likely to locate in markets with high concentrations of minority residents.

Third, the authors found strong associations between payday loan fees and the characteristics of loan contract terms, borrower habits, and local market demographics. Among other results, payday lenders charged higher loan fees for short-term loans; higher loan fees to frequent borrowers; and slightly higher loan fees in minority neighborhoods (although the authors are careful to stress that this effect was economically small, was unlikely to be due to discrimination, and was more likely due to unobservable differences in the demand for payday loans). One of the main findings was that payday loan prices increased systematically during the six years for which data were available: only about 67% of payday loans made in 2000 carried the maximum legal loan fee, but over 95% of payday loans made in 2005 carried the maximum legal fee. According to the authors, this pattern suggests that payday lenders in Colorado used the legislated price ceiling as a "focal point" for pricing their loans and thus reducing price competition among rival lenders.

A Simple Method for Extracting a "Payments Fee" from a Payday Loan Price

We have theorized above that a payday loan is really a combination of two separate financial services: a credit product and a payments product. If this is so, then the fee charged to payday borrowers is really a joint price that covers the costs of providing both financial services. This could provide an explanation for the high prices paid for payday loans and a starting place for better assessing the extent to which the *loan* portion of payday loans is really as exorbitantly priced as it appears from simple calculations of APRs.

To assess this possibility, one needs to separate the fee (or alternatively, the APR) charged by payday lenders into two parts: an implicit interest rate paid in exchange for credit and an implicit fee paid in exchange for transactions services. In this section we devise a simple method for separating the APR calculated on a payday loan into an implicit two-part price. We stress that our method is a crude first approximation. We do not generate a scalar fraction that can be applied uniformly to the APRs of all payday loans or even to the APRs of payday loans written by a particular payday lender; rather, our approach generates a different answer for each payday borrower, depending on the idiosyncratic financial conditions and payments options facing that borrower. Moreover, our approach does not account for the possibility of synergies, which might result in a joint price for the hybrid financial service being less than the sum of the two financial services produced separately. Despite these shortcomings, to our knowledge this is the first formal attempt to separate payday loan charges into a credit component and a payments component.

Our method is based on the simple realization that the payday borrower (a) uses the loan proceeds to pay an important bill for which she currently lacks the funds and (b) does so in order to avoid using some alternative, more expensive payments mechanism. Our approach allows for the fact that the consumer has a number of potential ways to pay this important bill that may be less costly than taking out a payday loan. For instance, the consumer could use a credit card to pay the bill, which likely entails an 18%–24% annual interest rate—cheaper than a payday loan, for sure, and hence superior to a payday loan. However, there are plausible circumstances under which the credit card option will be unavailable—the creditor may not accept credit cards or the consumer may have used up her credit limit—and the consumer will have to turn to a more expensive option. Rather than taking out a payday loan, the consumer might pay the important bill by writing a check that overdrafts her checking account, which triggers a substantial fee from her bank. Because this bank overdraft fee is the opportunity cost of taking out a payday loan, we can use this fee to identify the implicit portion of the payday loan charge that is a payments fee.

The logic of this is displayed in the decision tree in figure 7.3. We begin with a consumer who has a bank account, one or more bills to pay, and a

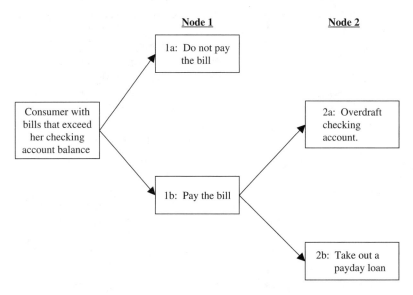

Figure 7.3   Consumer decision tree

bank balance too small to cover the bill payments. At decision node 1 the consumer has two choices: pay the bills or do not pay the bills. If one of the bills is an important one (e.g., her rent, her auto repair bill), choosing to not pay the bills imposes a high cost on the consumer (e.g., eviction from her apartment, losing her ability to get to work), so she will choose to pay the bills if possible.

At decision node 2 also, the consumer has two choices: pay the bills by overdrafting her checking account or raise the cash necessary to pay the bills by taking a payday loan. If the overall cost of overdrafting is higher than the payday lending fee, she will take out the payday loan. Note that the cost of overdrafting is not just the fee charged by the bank for writing one or more checks in amounts that exceed her bank balance—it also includes the possibility that her bank will close her account should she be unable to bring her account back into positive territory, which results in the nontrivial real cost of losing her access to the payment system.

Of course, paying the bill is not the end of the story, in either case. If the consumer uses a payday loan, she must eventually repay the loan; moreover, the consumer may have to roll over the payday loan multiple times—incurring a separate payday loan charge each time the loan is rolled over—before she finds the cash necessary to retire the loan. As so many payday loans are "rollover loans" (as seen in table 7.1, rollovers accounted for 55% of payday loans in Colorado between 2000 and 2005), they justify the use of the APR concept to represent the price of a payday loan.

It is important to realize, however, that similar, repeated charges will apply if the consumer decides to pay her bills by overdrafting her checking account. Assume, for example, that the overdrafting consumer receives pay every two weeks, but her important bills occur only at the end of each month. In this plausible scenario, the consumer will likely be able to raise her bank balance above zero sometime during the month (i.e., when her midmonth paycheck gets deposited) and thus will avoid having her account shut down. However, her bank balance will likely drift back into negative territory when she has to pay the next set of end-of-the-month loans, and this will generate another round of overdraft charges. So these repeated, monthly bank account overdraft charges justify the use of the APR concept to represent the price of bank overdrafts too.

The calculations shown in table 7.2. are based on this logic. We assume that the monthly overdraft protection provided by the bank is a payments service, and we convert a variety of prices (expressed in dollars) that banks might charge for this service into APRs. We then compare these "payments prices" to the APR on a typical Colorado payday loan. On the basis of our assumption that the prices charged for payday loans are joint prices, this comparison also reveals the "credit price" for a typical Colorado payday loan.

Table 7.2 Hypothetical portions of payday loan APRs attributable to a fee for payments services

APR on payday loan (1)	Various $ charges for overdrafting a check (2)	APR for overdrafting a check (3)	Portion of payday loan APR attributable to a fee for payment services (4)
382%	$1	4%	1%
382%	$2.50	10%	3%
382%	$5	21%	5%
382%	$10	42%	11%
382%	$15	63%	16%
382%	$20	84%	22%
382%	$25	105%	27%
382%	$30	126%	33%
382%	$35	146%	38%
382%	$40	167%	44%

Note: Column 1 displays an APR on payday loans calculated on the basis of 2000–2005 Colorado averages of a $293 payday loan with a 17-day loan term and a $52 loan fee. Column 2 displays a range of hypothetical fixed-payment fees charged by a financial institution to process a single-payment transaction, for example, covering rather than bouncing an overdrafted check. Column 3 displays the APRs to pay a reoccurring monthly bill of $293 (the size of the average payday loan made in Colorado between 2000 and 2005) on the basis of the fixed fee in column 2. Column 4 displays the ratio of column 3 to column 1, that is, the portion of the payday loan APR that, under these circumstances, could be interpreted as a fee for payments services.

Every row in column 1 displays the same payday loan APR. We calculate this joint price on the basis of averages reported in the 2000–2005 Colorado payday loan data in table 7.1. A payday loan with a $293 loan principle, a 17-day term, and a $52 charge carries an APR of 382%.[6]

Column 2 displays a range of hypothetical overdraft protection prices. Overdraft fees charged at U.S. commercial banks and thrifts range widely, from $0 in certain circumstances for established customers in good standing who accidentally overdraft their accounts to much higher prices per check of $25–$40 at some banks. Moreover, the policies governing the application of these fees also differ across banks. Some banks charge a one-time, fixed fee when the deposit balance falls below zero and then cover all checks up to a certain dollar amount (say, $500). In contrast, other banks apply a fixed fee repeatedly for each overdrafted check. For the purposes of these simple calculations, we assume that the overdrafting customer writes only a single check, so that the overdraft fee is charged only once.

In column 3, the various dollar overdraft fees are converted into APRs, assuming that the account is overdrafted by $293 (the same amount as the payday loan) but the overdraft fee is paid only once each month (roughly half as frequently as the payday loan rolls over). For example, in the third row, a single overdraft of $293 that reoccurs monthly at a bank that charges $5 per overdraft has an APR of 21%.

Column 4 simply divides the overdraft APR from column 3 (the isolated payments price) by the payday loan APR from column 1 (the joint price). The result is a crude estimation of the portion of the payday loan APR that is attributable to payments services. By construction, this "payments percentage" (PP) increases with the opportunity payments cost (in this case, the fee charged by the bank for overdraft protection) and quickly reaches nontrivial levels. For example, for a payday loan customer who faces a relatively reasonable overdraft fee of $25, PP equals 105% divided by 382%, or 0.27. For this customer in this situation, the implicit payment services fee embedded in the payday loan charge accounts for 27% of the payday loan APR.

We stress that extracting the implicit payments fee is idiosyncratic to every payday borrower, and for other customers in other situations our estimate can vary substantially. Recall that we constructed table 7.2 on the basis of the assumption that the borrower is using the payday loan to cover a single $293 bill payment. However, if the borrower is using the payday loan to cover *two* smaller bill payments that sum to $293 and if that borrower's bank charges a per check overdraft fee—just as reasonable a scenario as the assumptions underlying table 7.2—then the PPs displayed in column 4 of table 7.2 would understate *by half* the implicit payments services fee associated with the payday loan. In terms of our example above, payments services would then account for 54% of the payday loan APR.

Conclusion

In recent years, payday lending has become a substantially more important financial resource for many American households. As more and more consumers have turned to payday lenders, these firms have been increasingly criticized by consumer advocacy groups and politicians for charging high prices to financially unsophisticated and vulnerable consumers—prices that range well over 300% when calculated as APRs. Missing from this debate is the realization that a payday loan is not just an extension of credit, but is also a form of payments service. Before we can judge whether payday loan prices are indeed "exorbitant" or "predatory," we must first understand the dual nature of payday loans and the way in which the high prices of payday loans have embedded in them the implicit prices of these two separate financial services.

This chapter is a first attempt to do so. We begin by remembering that during the nineteenth century the cost of making payments was often borne directly by American consumers and that as the decades have passed the incidence of payments costs has shifted between consumers, merchants, and their banks. Thus, there is historical precedent for consumers not only paying for the goods they consume but also shouldering the costs of paying for those goods. Second, we point out that recent changes in retail banking practices—namely, high fees for overdraft protection—have once again imposed payments costs directly on consumers. We characterize overdraft protection fees as an opportunity cost of taking out a payday loan, and on the basis of this characterization we develop a simple framework for extracting implicit payments prices from Colorado payday loan prices. Considering one set of relatively conservative assumptions about the banking and payments conditions facing payday borrowers, we demonstrate that the price of payments services could easily comprise one-third to one-half of the high price of payday loans.

These calculations are driven by our working assumption that consumers turn to payday loans to clear their bills because alternative ways— for instance, by overdrafting their checking accounts—are even more expensive, not just in terms of the dollar charges imposed by their banks, but also in terms of the possible loss of access to the payments system and damage to their credit ratings should their banks close their accounts. While this working assumption is theoretically plausible, the degree to which it accurately represents the options and incentives facing payday borrowers is a matter for future empirical investigation. Nevertheless, it reminds us that the increase in the volume of payday lending may be attributable to demand-side forces—that is, the high cost of existing payments mechanisms for illiquid households—and that any public policy aimed at reforming the payday loan industry or curbing the use of this financial service must be grounded in a full understanding of this dynamic.

We stress that consumers use payday loans for reasons other than the high cost of alternative payments mechanisms and that public policy toward payday lending should take these into account as well. The reason most often advanced by consumer advocates (as well as by some federal banking regulators) is that payday borrowers are either unaware of or do not fully comprehend the terms of payday loans and their abilities to pay off these loans. These concerns—which are undoubtedly accurate for many payday borrowers—are most appropriately addressed by better education of potential payday borrowers and by regulations that prevent payday lenders from willfully misleading borrowers, for example, by making clear to consumers not just the terms of the payday loan but also the financial consequences of repeatedly rolling over that loan. Full information is necessary for any market to work efficiently and fairly.

The implications of our findings here are more subtle and are independent of concerns about insufficient information or misinformation.

Because payday loan prices have embedded in themselves both an interest rate and a nontrivial payments price, it is misleading to simply compare high payday loan APRs with interest rates on other forms of credit. This may help explain why banks have not been able to profitably provide low-cost credit alternatives to payday loans and why public policy mandates that banks do so may be misguided.

Notes

*The authors are at University of Kansas and Colorado State University, respectively.

1. Data from Flannery and Samolyk (2005).
2. The formula for the annual percentage rate, or APR, is ($52/$293)*(17 days/365 days) = 3.82 or 382%. Note that the lender's "break-even" period for this loan is ($293/$52)*(17 days) = 95 days, or just a little more than three months.
3. This analysis follows closely Baxter's (1983) seminal analysis of two-sided market platforms.
4. Though the replacement of drafts by checks as a primary means of payment changed the cost sharing, it did not end the issue of whether exchange fees should be abolished. As late as the 1940s, there was a disagreement between the board of governors of the Federal Reserve (Fed) and the Federal Deposit Insurance Corporation (FDIC). The Fed took the position that exchange fees were a payment of interest and therefore prohibited on the basis of Section 19 of the Federal Reserve Act and the board's Regulation Q, while the FDIC argued that there was an "absence of facts or circumstances establishing that [exchange charges had ever been] resorted to as a device for payment of interest" (Jessup 1967, pp. 16–17).
5. Economists have traditionally called this a discount fee, because in effect the payday lender is discounting the customer's check by paying her only a portion of its face amount.
6. This 382% APR is different from the 459% average APR displayed in table 7.1. The former is calculated using the average loan amounts ($293), loan charges ($52), and loan terms (17 days) from the observed loans, while the latter is the average APR for the observed loans.

References

Accola, John. 2006. Lenders cash in. *Rocky Mountain News*, January 11. http://www.rockymountainnews.com/drmn/other_business/article/0,2777,DR MN_23916_4379383,00.html

Baxter, William. 1983. Bank interchange of transactional paper: Legal and economic perspectives. *Journal of Law and Economics* 26: 541–588.

Caskey, John. 2005. Fringe banking and the rise of payday lending. In *Credit markets for the poor*, ed. Patrick Bolton and Howard Rosenthal, 17–45. Russell Sage Foundation.

DeYoung, Robert, and Ronnie Phillips. 2007. Strategic pricing of payday loans: Evidence from Colorado 2000–2005. Proceedings from the Federal Reserve Bank of Chicago Conference on Bank Structure and Competition, May 16–18, in Chicago, IL.

Evans, David, and Richard Schmalensee. 2005. The economics of interchange fees and their regulation: An overview, Interchange Fees in Credit and Debit Card Industries, Federal Reserve Bank of Kansas City.

Flannery, Mark, and Katherine Samolyk. 2005. Payday lending: Do the costs justify the price? FDIC Center for Financial Research, Working Paper, no. 2005–09.

Jessup, Paul. 1967. *The theory and practice of nonpar banking.* Evanston, IL: Northwestern University Press.

Rochet, Jean-Charles, and Jean Tirole. 2003. Platform competition in two-sided markets. *Journal of the European Economics Association* 1: 990–1009.

8

Insider Trading and Large Chapter 11 Bankruptcies: 1995–2006

*Tareque Nasser and Benton E. Gup**

Introduction

Several large firms that have filed for bankruptcy in recent years had been engaged in unscrupulous accounting and business practices, including, but not limited to, insider trading. For instance, several executives of WorldCom were either convicted or confessed to fraud and illegal insider trading. Bernard Ebbers, WorldCom's chief executive, was sentenced to 25 years in prison for orchestrating his $11 billion fraud of the bankrupted telecommunication giant.[1] Similarly, some Enron executives confessed to fraud and illegal insider trading and were convicted for their crimes. As a result of WorldCom and Enron debacles, lawmakers passed the Sarbanes-Oxley Act (SOX) that focused on corporate governance. Insider trading is one aspect of corporate governance that needs to be examined. In this chapter we explore insider trading in large U.S. publicly traded firms with assets of $1 billion or more that filed for Chapter 11 bankruptcy protection.

The Securities and Exchange Commission (SEC) as well as academic researchers usually refer to a firm's chairman, directors, officers, and principal shareholders with 10% or more of any equity class of securities, as the insiders.[2] The term "insider trading" includes both legal and illegal conduct. The SEC considers insider trading as legal when corporate insiders buy and sell stock in their own companies without violating any rules laid out to protect the general investors' interest. Similarly, the SEC characterizes illegal "insider trading" as buying or selling of securities by any insider, in breach of a fiduciary duty or other relationship of trust and confidence, while in possession of material, nonpublic information about the security. Insider trading violations may also include "tipping" such information, securities trading by the person "tipped," and securities trading by those who misappropriate such information. However, these tip-initiated trades are not documented as insider trading and filed with the SEC. The phrase insider trading in finance literature is often used both in the general sense and as the illegal use of private information for personal gain. In most cases it is the latter. It is generally assumed that readers can distinguish between the two from the context of the discussion.

When there are no prohibitive insider trading rules, insiders may have ample incentive to take advantage of their private information. So, the actual magnitude and pervasiveness of insider trading depends on the trade-off between the benefits and the costs that insiders observe and perceive. The Securities Exchange Act of 1934 (hereafter, the 1934 act) was enacted to insure a "fair and honest" market. The abusive use of private information by insiders is dealt with in mainly three ways in the 1934 act (Bettis, Duncan, and Harmon 1998).

First, insiders are obligated to disgorge any profit from buying and subsequent selling of securities within a six-month period, even if the trade is not on the basis of private information. This is known as the short-swing rule.

Second, there are numerous reporting requirements by insiders such that any trading undertaken by insiders is transparent. Insiders of the publicly traded companies need to report their trades and changes in ownership to the SEC using three different forms.[3] These are Forms 3, 4, and 5. Form 3 is the initial statement of beneficial ownership for all officers, whereas Form 4 reports change in an insider's ownership position. Form 5 is the annual statement of change in beneficial ownership. In addition to the above three forms, Form 144, the insider's declaration of their intention to sell restricted stock, is also filed with the SEC.

Third, it is unlawful to use any private nonpublic information to make profit through trading. In fact, the Insider Trading Sanction Act of 1984 (ITSA) and Insider Trading and Securities Fraud Enforcement Act of 1988 (ITSFEA) have allowed more severe civil and criminal penalty for insider trading. For instance, ISTA stipulates that the amount of the penalty that may be imposed on the person who committed such violation is determined by the court in light of the facts and circumstances, but should not exceed three times the profit gained or loss avoided as a result of such unlawful purchase, sale, or communication. The ITSFEA allows criminal fines up to $1,000,000 from individuals and maximum jail up to ten years. How effective the SEC has been with discouraging insider trading is a question explored in many studies with mixed evidence (Seyhun 1992; Bettis et al. 1998; Bris 2005). Here, we attempt to add to the literature concerning the state of insider trading in large U.S. corporate firms facing bankruptcy.

In this chapter we examine a sample of 129 large firms that filed for bankruptcy during the period 1995–2006. The appendix lists out the names of these firms, their bankruptcy filing date, and their asset size prior to bankruptcy. All these firms had assets over $1 billion two years prior to their bankruptcy filing. Although a total of 137 firms met the criteria of our sample selection, we had to drop 8 firms because of data limitations.

Table 8.1 shows some characteristics related to bankruptcy for all 129 sample firms that study. In this table "fraud" implies bankruptcies caused principally by fraud claims (includes securities fraud claims) against the company. These cases often began with financial difficulties from other causes, which were concealed from the investors until they were severe enough to cause the bankruptcy. "Disposition" is the outcome of the bankruptcy case. "Confirmed" means that the court confirmed a plan of reorganization. The term "§ 363 sale" means that the debtor sold all or substantially all of its assets during the Chapter 11 case.[4] "Pending" means that the case remains pending in the bankruptcy court. "Emerged" means the company has either emerged as it was before the bankruptcy or in some other form (i.e., taken over or merged with some other firms), but did not die out.

As shown in table 8.1, out of 129 sample firms, 123 firms had their Chapter 11 bankruptcy case filed by the debtor, 5 by the creditors, and 1 by

Table 8.1 Characteristics of 129 sample firms filing for Chapter 11 during 1995–2006

	Filing parties:	
Creditor	Debtor	Both
5	123	1

	Cause of bankruptcy:	
Fraud	Other than fraud
10	119

	Disposition:		
Confirmed		§ 363 sale	Pending
92		16	21

Emerged	Did not emerge
67	25

Source: WebBRD.

both debtor and creditors. Note that for 10 out of 129 firms shown in table 8.1 the cause of bankruptcy is fraud.[5] Out of these 10 firms, 8 firms emerged from bankruptcy. One firm did not survive, and another firm's case is still pending.

The bankruptcy courts have confirmed reorganization plans for 92 firms and have 21 cases pending. The remaining 16 firms of the 129 firms went though "§ 363 sale." Out of 92 firms whose reorganization/liquidation plans have been confirmed by the bankruptcy court, 67 emerged as either the same firms as before or emerged in some other forms and 25 firms did not survive.

Interestingly, none of the firms whose insiders were charged with fraud went through a "§ 363 sale." This implies that at least some of the insiders of 50 firms were at risk of losing their jobs because of either fraud or dissolution.[6] On the other hand, it is usually the firms that file for the Chapter 11 bankruptcy—not the creditor. The following facts suggest why insiders are unlikely to do trading on the basis of inside information. First, illegal insider trading is punishable by incarceration. Second, losing their job because they did illegal insider trading may impair their future employability. Third, the Chapter 11 bankruptcy process may enable managers to save their job at the time of financial distress.

In this chapter, we compare the level of insider trading of large firms filing for bankruptcy with a set of control firms. We find that insiders of firms filing for bankruptcy do not significantly sell more or buy less than the control firms in similar industries. Insider trading is measured by both number of trading insiders and the dollar volume of trading in each quarter for eight quarters before the bankruptcy filing date.

The remainder of this chapter is structured in the following way. In the next section we discuss the relevant literature for our study. Then, we cover the data and methodological issues measuring insider trading. We describe our own study and its results next and then provide the conclusion.

Review of the Literature

Insider trading in the event of bankruptcy

Although not focused on illegal insider trading, numerous academic studies report that insiders earn abnormal returns.[7] Alternatively, many studies document the presence or absence of insider trading around various corporate events or public announcements. For instance, John Elliot, Dale Morse, and Gordon Richardson (1984) tested whether insiders trade profitably before the public release of earnings, dividends, bond ratings, mergers, and bankruptcies. They found that most insiders' trading was not related to these events. Stephen Penman (1982), on the other hand, found that insiders do time their trade according to the annual earning forecast disclosure date and earn abnormal returns. Jonathan Karpoff and Daniel Lee (1991) found that insiders sell shares prior to new equity issues, while W. Van Harlow and John Howe (1993) found that insiders accumulate shares abnormally prior to management buyout.

Similarly, the question of whether insiders take advantage of material nonpublic information of the impending bankruptcy has yielded mixed results. Claudio Loderer and Dennis Sheehan (1989) did not find insiders "bailing out" of the firm. In contrast, Thomas Gosnell, Arthur Keown, and John Pinkerton (1992) found that insider selling increases significantly as the bankruptcy announcement approaches—particularly for over-the-counter (OTC) traded firms. H. Nejat Seyhun and Michael Bradley (1997) found that insiders systematically sell and buy stocks around the bankruptcy event to make abnormal profits. Yulong Ma (2001), however, found that there is not much selling by insiders before bankruptcy. But there is the significant lack of purchases by the insiders before the bankruptcy. Zahid Iqbal and Shekar Shetty (2002) looked at the problem a little differently. They found that there is significant insider trading around the month when the market anticipates the bankruptcy and not around the month when the bankruptcy filing is announced.

Motivations for insider trading

The extent of insider trading depends on the expected benefits, costs, whether they can foresee the future bankruptcy. In an experimental study using college students, Joseph Beams, Robert Brown, and Larry Killough (2003) found that subjects are more likely to trade on the basis of insider information to avoid loss than to achieve abnormal gain. Although it is often difficult to pinpoint whether a particular trade is motivated by selfish personal gains, or if it is carried out to implement the implicit compensation contract for the insiders, recent notorious bankruptcy cases are examples where insiders resorted to illegal measures for personal gains at the expense of the shareholders.

It is often not clear whether insider trading (in a general sense) is a result of an agency problem or whether it reduces agency problems. It can be argued both ways. Denis Carlton and Daniel Fischel (1983) argue that the ability of an agent to exploit his/her informational advantage can be part of implicit or explicit contract between the shareholder and the agent. In fact, trading allows an agent to renegotiate the contracts when underlying conditions change (Dye 1984). However, Fischer (1992) argues that when there is an agency problem, trading by the agents may in turn aggravate the agency problem. Fischer, echoing Frank Easterbrook (1981), argues that the uncertain compensation through trading results in suboptimal risk sharing. Also, the agents may have added incentive to cook the books and take actions that may create profitable trading opportunity for agents at the expense of shareholders.

When a firm goes bankrupt, there is high probability that the insiders can lose their jobs and any other associated quasi rents. This may prompt them to take actions consistent with what Fischer (1992) argues—particularly in the absence of a significant legal deterrence mechanism. Moreover, if the insiders bail out by selling their stock, the subsequent restructuring process may not be in the best interest of the other shareholders. Stockholders' gains are directly related to the insiders' holding because the insiders' wealth is at stake (Betker 1995).

Chapter 11 bankruptcy and insider trading

Under U.S. bankruptcy laws, firms filing for bankruptcy have a choice between Chapter 7 and Chapter 11 where they go through liquidation and reorganization processes, respectively. Under Chapter 7, a firm ceases its business immediately and goes through the liquidation process by an appointed trustee to pay off its debts. Whereas under Chapter 11, the incumbent managers still remain in control as the firm continues to operate for the duration of the reorganization process. At the same time, a reorganization plan is adopted through which all prebankruptcy claims are settled or renegotiated. However, managers with strong bargaining power can pressure the creditors to accept their terms (White 1989), and managers bargaining power is the greatest when the firm is close to solvency (Betker 1995). It is also interesting to note that during the Chapter 11 bankruptcy process the only way the stockholder's interest is represented is by the management.[8] Brian Betker (1995) reports that courts have held that shareholders cannot hold a meeting to replace the directors of insolvent firms. All these facts indicate that invoking the Chapter 11 bankruptcy process offers a wonderful opportunity for the managers to save their jobs and at the same time retain significant bargaining power when the firm is at the borderline of solvency.

Bradley and Michael Rosenzweig (1992) state that "Chapter 11 does not require that a debtor be insolvent in order to qualify for reorganization, and it includes a strong presumption favoring retention of management throughout the reorganization process. Thus, in the ordinary case, a Chapter 11 filing transforms a corporate debtor into the 'debtor-in-possession' and leaves existing management in control of the firm's resources." If the management is relatively sure that the bankruptcy restructuring process is just a temporary adjustment to solidify their grip on the reign of the firm, we can expect that there would be no insider trading. This is even more pertinent to big firms as it is often believed that they are "too-big-to-fail."

Impediments to insider trading

Many public companies have policies governing the trading of their securities by officers, directors, and employees, with the goal of preventing trades at times when insiders may be in possession of material nonpublic information (Bettis, Coles, and Lemmon 2000). Such policies are designed to ensure compliance with securities trading prohibitions, and they generally contain periodic "window periods" or "blackout periods" tied to the company's announcements of financial results or other corporate developments. During window and blackout periods, trades by insiders are conditionally permitted or prohibited, respectively. J. Carr Bettis et al. (2000) report that although firms are not required by the law to implement periodic insider trade restricting policies, the absence of such policies may be deemed as a reckless conduct by the firms from the regulator's point of view. Insider trading policies also often require insiders to obtain advance trade clearance with a designated member of the management. Public companies normally include trading windows or trading blackout periods in insider trading policies to prevent insiders from trading at or around the time of earnings announcements or the dissemination of other sensitive corporate information.

In the event of job loss, due to bankruptcy, managers want to preserve their future employment opportunities. Lynn LoPucki and William Whitford (1993) argue that managers cannot breach their fiduciary duty at the expense of the firm because they may be stigmatized and adversely affect their marketability. However, LoPucki and Whitford do not discount the possibility that there could be some unscrupulous insiders who resort to illegal means for immediate gain at the expense of shareholders and their own future human capital loss.

To a certain extent, the incidence of informed insider trading also depends on the corporate governance system in place. For instance, Marco Becht, Patrick Bolton, and Alisa Roell (2003) assert that executive stock options (ESO) "are at best an inefficient financial incentive and at worst create new incentive or conflict-of-interest problems of their own." They also criticize other mechanisms of corporate governance for their inability to exert corporate control. Bengt Holmstrom and Steven Kaplan (2003), however, respond to this contention stating that this is an exaggeration. They argue that although there are instances of stock price manipulation because of ESO carried out by firms like WorldCom, these are by no means representative. Holmstrom and Kaplan contend that that the U.S. corporate governance system with the recent regulatory overhauling through measures such as SOX is "likely to make a good U.S. system [a] better one." Bettis et al. (2000), investigating the corporate policies restricting insider trading, report that by November 1996, 92% of their sample firms had instituted policies to restrict and manage insiders' trading and 80% of the sample firms had explicit blackout period prohibiting insider trading. Thus, the extent to which the corporate control mechanisms deter insider trading is an empirical question.

Laws and insider trading

The deterrence of informed insider trading requires both good corporate control and effective enforcement of insider trading regulations. Effective enforcement does not necessarily imply a total prohibition on inside trading. For instance, Shin (1996), modeling optimal regulation of insider trading, concludes that in the presence of research-informed market professionals, some insider trading is better than a total ban on insider trading to help decrease the loss of liquidity traders. Similarly, DeMarzo, Fishman, and Hagerty (1998) recognize that effective insider trading regulation requires monitoring and enforcement in a market setting. However, in doing so, regulators must use market data that are very noisy and costly to decipher. On the basis of their model, they conclude that it is optimal for the regulators to investigate if and only if trading volume exceeds some threshold—where the threshold depends on the information released concerning share value. DeMarzo et al. also propose that it is optimal that if the insider is caught trading more than a critical level, then he/she must pay the maximum feasible penalty, otherwise pays no penalty.

A study by Arturo Bris (2005), using data from 52 countries, found that the incidence and profitability of insider trading increases with the enforcement of insider trading laws. He measured the insider trading before the tender offer announcement and found that after some enforcement of insider trading laws, insiders appropriate a larger portion of the takeover gains. However, he concluded that harsher laws work better in reducing insider trading. Bris found that the United States, among all 52 countries, has the toughest insider trading regulation and the lowest profit for the insiders. Most academic studies on insider trading deterrence conclude that harsher penalties discourage insider trading. It seems that the U.S. legal system is going toward a harsher penalty over major insider trading and frauds as evidenced at the beginning of this chapter.

Anup Agrawal and Jeffrey Jaffe (1995) report that even though short-swing trades may not be actively prosecuted by the SEC, they are generally challenged by lawyers if they perceive the prosecution is profitable. Agrawal and Jaffe explain that all these lawyers have to do is to buy a share of the company where they find any violations of the short-swing rule and file the suit as a shareholder. When successfully prosecuted, they receive the legal fees from the trading profits that the insider returns to the firm.

On the basis of previously cited studies, we infer that the two most likely types of illegal insider trading involve (1) small trades that fall into the category of short-swing trades and those that the regulatory authority may overlook and (2) large trades that are the result of gross breach of fiduciary duties. Insider trades of intermediate size are not worth the risk of getting caught at the expense of future economic and human capital loss.

Methods and Data

In this section, we provide a brief overview of the methodologies and data used.

Measuring insider trading

Use of purchases and sales information to measure insider trading
One of the earliest measurements of insider trading, conducted by Lorie and Niederhoffer (1968), is based on identifying an intensive selling month or buying month and then measuring the market price movement in the six months subsequent to the event. They define an intensive selling (buying) month as a month with at least two more sellers (buyers) than buyers (sellers) among the insiders of a company. Lorie and Niederhoffer do not measure the presence of insider trading around any particular corporate event or information released but rather simply attempt to establish its existence.

Jaffe (1974) uses a modified method to measure the insider trading. He computes the number of net buyers[9] and sellers for each firm during a randomly picked month. He then defines a month as a "month of net purchasers" if the number of net buyers is more than number of net sellers and similarly defines "month of net sellers." He regards these months as information-based trading events. Jaffe then employs a technique similar to the event study methodology developed earlier by Ball and Brown (1968) and Fama, Fisher, Jensen, and Roll (1969) to measure the abnormal return.

Using CAR to assess insider trading

The use of abnormal returns and cumulative abnormal returns (CAR) is widely recognized in academic studies. Seyhun and Bradley (1997) base their whole insider trading argument using event study methodology in several ways. One obvious way they use the event study method is to measure abnormal return and CAR. However, Seyhun and Bradley alter the standard event study method to take account of some unique features of the data in the event of bankruptcy. For example, it is quite normal that before bankruptcy is announced, several firms either cease trading of their shares temporarily or they are delisted altogether. Also, when the prices fall to single digit, standard CAR estimate may grossly misrepresent the true abnormal return over the period. For these reasons Seyhun and Bradley, instead of using a standard market model, use a bootstrapping method to calculate the mean abnormal holding period return over different periods.[10] Another way they use the event study method is to compute abnormal insider trading, where, instead of return, they measure insider trading in trading volume.

Setting the benchmark level of insider trading

While measuring insider trading, it is crucial to establish a normal insider trading level that accounts for portfolio rebalancing, liquidity needs, or any other reasons except private information-based trading. Most of the "abnormal" insider trading is typically evidenced by documenting any significant excess trading or the lack of trading or a deviation from the normal level in the direction indicated by the nature of the information. Therefore, how the researchers account for the normal level of trading is reflected in the methods they implement. In many cases, the normal level of trading is established using a set of control firms. Typically, it involves matching with the subject firms' two-digit SIC code and controlling for size in terms of either asset size (e.g., Loderer and Sheehan 1989) or market capitalization (e.g., Gosnell et al. 1992; Ma 2001). The matching is generally done on the basis of data related to above, that is, two to five years prior to the event.

Seyhun and Bradley (1997) criticize this method stating the following. First, picking a set of control firms from the same industry may produce firms with similar problems (e.g., financial distress). Second, in cases such as bankruptcy, the subject firms may shrink in size over the period creating a size disparity between the subject and the control firms. However, Seyhun and Bradley (1997), with their modified use of event study to measure the abnormal insider trading, did not bypass the use of control firms. In their study, Seyhun and Bradley "center" the time series of the insider trading data on the event date and then measure the average trading per firm for each month over the event window. Here, they code sales as a negative number and purchase as a positive number. They measure the abnormal insider trading (both in number of shares traded and in dollars) for each period (in months) as the difference between actual trading activity for a given firm and amount of insider trading activity of a "control portfolio" of similar sized firms over the same period. They construct these control portfolios by, first, calculating the mean annual equity value of all firms reporting any insider trading activity over their study period. Then they rank these firms, excluding the subject sample firms, according to market capitalization and categorize them in deciles. Using this method they create the "expected" insider trading data for portfolios of firms of each size decile and insider category for each month over the study period. We, however, believe that judiciously choosing the time of matching (i.e., not too far away from the event time) may alleviate the size disparity problem significantly and would not require similar methods as adopted by Seyhun and Bradley. Furthermore, Agrawal and Jaffe (1995) argue that matching on the basis of two-digit SIC classification is broad enough to have little or no effect of the event on the control firm.

Bypassing the control firms to assess insider trading
Many researchers forgo the use of control firms altogether and try to establish the normal level of insider trading by using time series data. Karpoff and Lee (1991) developed such a technique and others have used it (e.g., Harlow and Howe 1993; Iqbal and Shetty 2002; and Irani 2003). Karpoff and Lee (1991) derived the mean abnormal and the cumulative number of net sellers and associated statistics to assess the abnormal number of net sellers in the event of new issues of common stock. Harlow and Howe (1993), on the other hand, used the same method to find the abnormal number of net buyers for leverage buyout announcements.

When researchers do not use control firms, they use other approaches. One general approach used by Joseph Finnerty (1976), Penman (1985), John and Lang (1991), and Josef Lakonishok and Inmoo Lee (2001) involves developing indices or ratios. The typical way of constructing these would be computing ratios as $(P-S)(P+S)$ or $P[(P+S)/2]$ or some other complicatedvariations. Here P may represent the number of insiders purchasing stock, the number of purchasing transactions, the number of shares purchased, the dollar value of transactions, or any other construct that researchers feel would convey information related to the study. Similarly, S would represent any of the above corresponding constructs related to sales. These ratios were used in different regression equations to explain returns or abnormal returns and thereby evaluate insider trading.

Method used in our study

Many researchers believe in the efficacy of control firms for benchmarking purpose and hence use them. Of course, the form of analysis may differ considerably. For instance, Agrawal and Jaffe (1995), while assessing the insider purchases around merger announcement, use matched control firms in addition to time series controls. They use matched-pair t-statistic for measuring the cross-sectional difference between the means of the target and control firms. However, Ma (2001) argues that insider trading activity is quite infrequent, nonnormal, and highly skewed in magnitude thus calling for statistical analysis that does not require distributional assumptions. He claims that nonparametric method is suitable for this purpose. Hence, he uses Wilcoxon signed-rank test, a nonparametric technique, to compare insider trading measures of bankruptcy firms with those of the control firms. We used this method in our study along with other descriptive statistics.

The next obvious issue is the appropriate measures of insider trading. Agrawal and Jaffe (1995) use several measures for insider trading. These are the number of insiders who buy in a given period, shares purchased in a period, dollar value of purchase, and percentage of equity bought. In contrast, Ma (2001) uses the number of transactions, number of insiders, and dollar amount of trade. Other measures such as percentage of outstanding equity purchased, percentage of total share purchase volume, percentage of total dollar purchase volume are also used in the literature.

Against this background, we concentrate on two constructs: (1) the number of insiders buying or selling each quarter and (2) the purchases or sales in dollars (trading volume) for each quarter. The number of insiders helps to explain how widespread the inside information utilization is in the firm. Generally, we do not expect many insiders trading at the same time, unless there is some motivating reason such as many of them are aware of price changing information. Hence, if we see that the number of insiders who are trading in a particular period is significantly higher, it may be because of inside information. For instance, if we find the number of insiders who are selling in a particular quarter for the firm filing for bankruptcy is abnormally high, then it is evidence of insider trading.

Finally, trading volume captures the magnitude of use of insider information. We will use these two constructs at the same time. If only one of them is significant while the other is not, it is not a strong case of insider trading. However, if both are significant at the same time, it is strong evidence of insider trading.

Justification of the method used in our study

Although there is no clear cut evidence that any one method described above is superior to others, we selected the method used in our study for several reasons. First, we were after a simple proven test to measure the extent of insider trading. The method that we adopt meets this criterion.

Second, we avoid the usual criticism of the use of control firms to set normal insider trading level. Then we show that the criticism of Seyhun and Bradley (1997), using control firms from the same industry may produce firms with similar problems, such as financial distress, is absent in the control sample. Moreover, Seyhun and Bradley's other objection in using control firms that the subject firms may shrink in size over the period creating a size disparity between the subject and the control firms is avoided by using a shorter time period (i.e., using two years prior data instead of five years prior data for the matching process).

Third, insider trading activity is infrequent, nonnormal, and highly skewed in magnitude. Hence, using a nonparametric technique such as Wilcoxon signed-rank test we can do away with the distributional assumption that is needed for other statistical techniques.

Data

Sources of sample firms
Professor Lynn M. LoPucki's Bankruptcy Research Database (WebBRD)[11] provides an extensive listing of firms that filed for bankruptcy in the U.S. bankruptcy courts. It also has a data query web interface where researchers can get lists of bankruptcy filing firms with a variety of specifications. We used this web query to get a list of firms that had asset size greater than or equal to $1 billion prior to filing for bankruptcy during the 1995–2006 period. The asset size of the firms filing for bankruptcy in the WebBRD is recorded in current dollars. However, we also screened these firms further on the basis of criterion that firms should have asset size, as reported in the Compustat, over $1 billion two years prior to filing for bankruptcy. This criterion was imposed to ensure that there is no mistake in the asset size reported in the WebBRD[12] and also because we had decided to use matched control firm on the basis of asset size and industry for our analysis.[13] It yielded 137 firms. Unfortunately, we were not able to get the insider trading data for 8 firms. Hence, our final sample includes 129 firms that had assets of more than $1 billion prior to filing for bankruptcy during 1995–2006.

Getting the insider trading data
Most of the previous studies of insider trading used data from the Ownership Reporting System (ORS) or the Official Summary of Securities Transactions and Holding published by SEC. Currently, Thomson Financial provides the same information though TFN Insider Filling Data (TFN Insiders). We used TFN Insiders to get the insider trading data. Note that it is possible that some insiders buy and sell their securities without

reporting their trade to the SEC (Meulbroek 1992). However, we have no information on either accepting or refuting such activity. Hence, the data that we are using is based on only the reported trades.

To extract the appropriate data, we needed each firm's corresponding CUSIP Issuer Code (CUSIP6) and the date when it filed for bankruptcy. The WebBRD only provides the bankruptcy filing year, not the exact filing date. Therefore, we obtained the bankruptcy filing date by searching 10-K Wizard SEC filings. When these were not available in the 10-K Wizard, we obtained the Chapter 11 filing dates using web search of different news sources and "BankruptyData.com." The CUSIP6 was derived from matching each firm's name within Compustat and CRSP.

We obtained insider trading data for the 129 firms in our sample covering a two-year period prior to the bankruptcy from TFN Insiders. We only use the open market purchases or sales data in TFN Insiders and exclude purchases related to options exercises. Insider trading activity equals zero for any firm that has a registered insider documented by TFN Insiders but has no open market trades reported by TFN Insiders during the sample period. We exclude trades that buy or sell fewer than 100 shares or with a total value exceeding $100. Trades lacking transaction prices in TFN Insiders are excluded from our sample.

We use trading data for two years prior to the filing for bankruptcy. Although we believe that insiders cannot foresee the actual bankruptcy as far as two years down the road, we still use the two-year time span since is this the shortest period used in the previous literature.

Constructing the set of control firms

Like some previous studies, we used a set of control firms to assess the prevalence of insider trading. Given the choice between matching control firms on the basis of market capitalization and asset size we opted for the latter for two reasons. First and the obvious reason is that we picked our sample firms on the basis of asset size. Second, rapidly growing firms can have market capitalization that is equal to or greater than that of some mature firms that are growing slowly or shrinking (Gup and Agrrawal 1996). Thus, market capitalization, per se, can be misleading when comparing across the two samples. Consequently we matched asset sizes for two years prior to the bankruptcy using Compustat Industrial Annual and a two-digit SIC code to get the control firms.

Although we could obtain a match for most of the firms, if the firm's asset size was missing in the two years prior to bankruptcy, we used one-year prior data. Also, if the closest match was an ADR of some foreign firm or another bankruptcy filing firm or a firm not in the TFN Insiders, then we found the next closest match in asset size.

Table 8.2   Comparison between the bankrupt firms and their matched control firms

Panel A: Summary statistics of asset size (in million dollars)

	Bankrupt firms	Asset matched firms	Difference
N	129	129	129
Mean	6,614	6,375	554
t-test		1.2363	
Median	2,579	2,399	79
Wilcoxon sign-rank test		0.858	
Std. Dev.	12,167	12,018	2,131

Panel B: Number of firms with zero trading

	Bankrupt firms	Matched Firms
Purchase	29	31
Sales	28	21
Both	16	13

The symbols *, **, and *** denote statistical significance at the 0.10, 0.05, and 0.01 levels, respectively, using a 2-tail test.

The descriptive statistics of the sample bankrupt firms and their control counterparts are shown in Panel A of table 8.2. The mean and the median of the bankruptcy sample firms' asset size are $6,614 and $2,579 million, respectively. For their matched control firms, they are $6,375 and $2,399 million, respectively. The standard deviation of the asset size for the subject firms is $12,167 million and for the control firms is $12,018 million. The t-test for the mean difference and the Wilcoxon sign-rank test for the median difference are not statistically significant in any of the commonly used significant level. Hence, the asset size distributions of both the samples are similar.

As shown in Panel B of table 8.2, 16 firms had no insider trades for two years prior to their bankruptcy. For the matched firms, 13 firms had no insider trading during the same period. From Panel B of table 8.2 we find that 41 (=29 + 28 – 16) of the bankrupt firms have no insider purchase or sales or both during the period under examination. The corresponding number for the matched control firms is 39 (=31 + 21 – 13). This implies that more than 30% of the bankrupt firms and their corresponding control firms had no insider trades for the two years prior to the filing date. Stated otherwise, insider trading is an infrequent activity.

Results and Analysis

We cannot talk about the existence of insider trading before we look into the abnormal returns. It is obvious that significant negative abnormal returns prior to bankruptcy filing provide the motive for insider trading. Panel A of table 8.3 shows average cumulative abnormal returns (CAAR) of the bankrupt firms over different periods.[14] These are calculated on the basis of the OLS market model using CRSP Equally Weighted Index. For the 58 trading days, the period starting 60 days before date the firm filed for bankruptcy and ending 2 days before the filing date relative to the filing date ($-60, -2$), the average CAAR is -38.18%. The Patell Z value is -12.201 and is significant a 0.1% level. Similarly, for the period ($-30, -2$) and ($-1, 0$) the average CAAR is -39.86% and -20.35%, respectively, and both are significant at 0.1% level. This test determines whether the abnormal stock return equals zero, assuming cross-sectional independence. From this we can conclude that there is ample loss of returns at stake, and this creates a strong motivation for insider trading.

Panel B of table 8.3 shows the average CAAR of the control firms over the same period used for their matching bankrupt firms. We are interested in the average CAAR values to establish that the control firms are not going through similar financial distress or some other events that will cause abnormal returns. We find that for the three time period ($-60, -2$ days), ($-30, -2$ days) and the average CAARs are -2.80%, -1.70% and -1.24% respectively and only the period ($-1, 0$ days) CAAR is significant at 5% level of significance. Figure 8.1 shows the CAAR over the 60 days prior to the filing date for both the samples. The matched control firms' CAAR does not show any significant movement compared with that of the bankrupt firms. This dispels the possibility raised by Seyhun and Bradley (1997) that using control firms from the same industry may produce firms with similar problems like financial distress.

As previously mentioned, we compared the bankrupt firms to matched control firms in order to evaluate the extent of insider trading. Table 8.4

Table 8.3   CAAR of bankrupt firms and their matched control firms

Days	N	CAAR	Patell Z
Panel A: Bankrupt firms			
($-60, -2$)	45	-38.18%	-12.201***
($-30, -2$)	45	-39.86%	-14.613***
($-1,0$)	43	-20.35%	-23.317***
Panel B: Matched control firms		($-60, -2$)	94
-2.80%	-0.997		
($-30, -2$)	94	-1.70%	-1.075
($-1,0$)	94	-1.24%	-2.143*

The Patell z-test examines whether abnormal stock return equals zero assuming cross-sectional independence. The symbols $, *, **, and *** denote statistical significance at the 0.10, 0.05, 0.01 and 0.001 levels, respectively, using a 1-tail test.

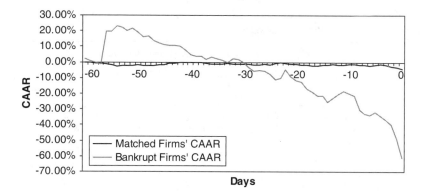

Figure 8.1   Bankrupt firms' and their matched control firms' CAAR for a period of two months prior to filing for bankruptcy

provides the descriptive statistics on trading volume in millions of dollars. We categorize firms into three categories: positive net purchase (i.e., firms purchased more dollars worth of shares than they have sold), negative net purchase, and zero net purchase (essentially, these are firms with no trading activity). Data on Panel A are based on two years of insider trading data of both the bankruptcy and control firms. The two-year time span starts from two years prior to date of the bankruptcy, and the same time span is used for the corresponding control firm. Similarly, data on Panel B and Panel C come from quarter and monthly data, respectively, prior to the bankruptcy. If the insiders use their private information about future bankruptcy, they would sell more than they would purchase, and we would expect more firms categorized as the negative net purchase firms. However, in Panel A we observe that in the bankruptcy sample, only 58 out of 129 firms have negative net purchase firms, which is roughly equal to the number of positive net purchase firms. In the control sample, negative net purchase firms are almost thrice in number compared with the positive net purchase firms. Over a shorter period of time, as shown Panels B and C, the number of firms with negative net purchase declined sharply.

A closer inspection two samples reveal that all statistics in negative net purchase category are larger in size for the control firms. Similar results were found for the positive net purchase firm. Hence the statistics reported in table 8.4 suggest that the insiders of the bankrupt firms as a whole do not sell or buy more than those of other firms. Also, insiders of a larger number of bankrupt firms stopped trading as the period approaches the date for filing for bankruptcy.

One may argue that some insiders of the bankrupt firms do sell more shares, but the dollar value is lower because of lower stock prices. However,

Table 8.4   Descriptive statistics of trading volume over different time horizons prior to the filing date for bankruptcy

Panel A: Net purchases of firms for two years prior to bankruptcy filing date

(In million dollars)		Positive net purchase			Negative net purchase			Zero
		Mean	*Median*	*SD*	*Mean*	*Median*	*SD*	
Bankrupt	Purchase	8.81	1.21	20.69	2.34	0.18	7.33	
Firms	Sale	1.73	0.09	6.31	77.99	8.12	188.86	
	Net purchase	7.08	0.95	16.51	−75.65	−6.47	189.21	
	N		55			58		16
Matched	Purchase	31.78	2.88	106.99	3.89	0.20	27.83	
Firms	Sale	4.39	0.18	12.08	80.51	11.67	224.76	
	Net purchase	27.39	1.95	96.59	−76.62	−11.09	215.06	
	N		33			83		13

Panel B: Net purchases of firms for one quarter prior to bankruptcy filing date

(In million dollars)		Positive net purchase			Negative net purchase			Zero
		Mean	*Median*	*SD*	*Mean*	*Median*	*SD*	
Bankrupt	Purchase	2.32	0.11	4.42	0.05	0.00	0.22	
Firms	Sale	0.97	0.00	2.84	1.72	0.23	3.34	
	Net purchase	1.35	0.11	2.41	−1.67	−0.23	3.33	
	N		15			24		90
Matched	Purchase	1.77	0.16	3.81	0.01	0.00	0.03	
Firms	Sale	0.05	0.00	0.16	15.93	1.45	63.34	
	Net purchase	1.72	0.15	3.69	−15.92	−1.45	63.34	
	N		22			51		56

Panel C: Net purchases of firms for one month prior to bankruptcy filing date

(In million dollars)		Positive net purchase			Negative net purchase			Zero
		Mean	*Median*	*SD*	*Mean*	*Median*	*SD*	
Bankrupt	Purchase	1.06	0.56	1.57	0.00	0.00	0.00	
Firms	Sale	0.05	0.00	0.13	1.32	0.13	3.13	
	Net purchase	1.01	0.43	1.57	−1.32	−0.13	3.13	
	N		6			10		113
Matched	Purchase	0.48	0.06	0.78	0.01	0.00	0.02	
Firms	Sale	0.00	0.00	0.01	5.34	0.76	12.50	
	Net purchase	0.48	0.05	0.79	−5.33	−0.76	12.50	
	N		10			29		90

the use of private information would imply that insiders should have sold the shares before the price declined. For instance, the CEO of Warnaco Group Inc., one of the bankrupt firms in our sample, sold approximately 1 million shares for $12.4 million, 18 months before the filing date, and bought back these shares for $3 million 12 months later (6 months before bankruptcy), netting $9.4 million. The real reason of these trades is not known to us, but it raises questions about the use of private information.

> We performed the Wilcoxon signed-rank test as well as t-test on two insider trading measures—trading volume in dollars and the number of insiders. The results are presented in tables 8.5 and 8.6. Each of the insider trading measures is documented for purchases (Panel A), sales (Panel B) and net purchases (Panel C) for the eight quarters prior to the bankruptcy. If we are to find profitable or loss avoiding insider trading by the bankrupt firm, the test statistics should have negative sign for purchases and net purchases, and positive sign for sales for both the insider trading measures.[15] However, only few statistics show the sign consistent with insider trading, and they are not even significant at any accepted level. On the contrary, any significant statistics that the table presents points to no insider trading. Note that for both insider trading measures (i.e., tables 8.5 and 8.6), insider sales (i.e., Panel B) z-statistics are significant and negative for the quarters -4 to -1. This implies insiders of control firms are significantly selling more than that of the bankrupt firms. Similarly, z-statistics reported in Panel C of table 8.5 and 8.6 confirm that insiders of control firms are either selling more or buying less than that of bankrupt firms.

Table 8.5 shows that in the quarter prior to bankruptcy, less than 25% (15%) of the bankrupt firms have insider selling (purchasing). Similarly, Table 8.6 shows that in the same quarter less that 7% of the bankrupt firms have more than two insiders selling; whereas for the corresponding control forms this figure is more that 25%. Hence, contrary to the popular belief, insiders of large public firms do not engage in trading on the basis of private information for private gain or loss avoidance. It does not mean that there is no insider trading, but insider trading is more of an exception than the rule.

Since insider trading activity is very infrequent, we used quarterly data for the previous analysis. For a robustness check, we report test statistics in table 8.7 with similar results on the basis of monthly data. In fact, we conducted a battery of robustness checks. For instance, we increased the sample size by lowering the asset size cutoff point, as well as using an alternative control group that matched firms on the basis of market capitalization. In all cases were essentially the same. We also checked for insider trading in subgroups. For example, we examined for any discernible differences between the 50 firms that "either filed for bankruptcy because of fraud or did not survive the bankruptcy process" and the remaining 79 firms. However, we did no find any difference in the insider trading behavior between these two groups.

Our results are similar to those of Loderer and Sheehan (1989). Seyhun and Bradley (1997) criticize Loderer and Sheehan's (1989) sample size and

Table 8.5   Trading volume

This table presents the summary statistics of the trading volume along with t-test for mean equality and Wilcoxon signed-rank test for the equality of the median. If the test statistics take a negative value it implies that the bankrupt firms' trading volume is lower than that of their matched control. The last two columns present the percentage of banks that have zero insiders trading (in Panel A only purchase, and in Panel B only sales). Note that since the median data are always zero, they are not presented here.

Panel A: Purchase volume (in million dollars)

	Bankrupt firms		Matched samples		Statistics		% of zeros	
Quarter	Mean	S.D.	Mean	S.D.	t-test	Wilcoxon Z	Target	Matched
−1	0.28	1.64	0.31	1.68	−0.127	−2.025**	86.05	75.19
−2	0.64	4.98	0.66	4.20	−0.030	−1.135	79.84	70.54
−3	0.95	6.20	0.91	6.19	0.057	1.489	69.77	76.74
−4	0.34	1.65	0.26	1.42	0.390	0.227	68.99	72.87
−5	0.80	5.23	0.89	5.34	−0.143	0.267	65.89	70.54
−6	1.09	5.73	6.87	58.40	−1.119	−0.273	70.54	69.77
−7	0.54	2.95	0.60	3.02	−0.151	1.211	53.49	68.99
−8	0.17	0.54	0.13	0.62	0.488	0.614	68.22	68.22

Panel B: Sales volume (in million dollars)

	Bankrupt firms		Matched samples		Statistics		% of zeros	
Quarter	Mean	S.D.	Mean	S.D.	t-test	Wilcoxon Z	Target	Matched
−1	0.43	1.83	6.31	40.40	−1.651*	−3.563***	76.74	57.36
−2	1.04	5.23	6.16	32.70	−1.752*	−3.484***	80.62	62.02
−3	2.42	14.90	10.90	86.60	−1.093	−3.668***	81.4	59.69
−4	1.79	10.80	13.10	83.90	−1.512	−3.703***	72.09	51.94
−5	3.65	17.20	4.22	16.10	−0.288	−1.485	72.87	62.02
−6	3.19	14.60	3.69	19.00	−0.414	−2.240**	72.09	58.91
−7	14.00	86.90	2.99	9.59	1.431	−0.780	63.57	60.47
−8	9.34	46.70	5.59	30.80	0.783	−0.467	62.79	55.81

Panel C: Net purchase volume (in million dollars)

	Bankrupt firms		Matched samples		Statistics		% of zeros	
Quarter	Mean	S.D.	Mean	S.D.	t-test	Wilcoxon Z	Target	Matched
−1	−0.15	1.83	−6.00	40.40	1.641	2.520**	69.77	43.41
−2	−0.40	7.28	−5.51	33.10	1.710*	2.592***	64.34	44.19
−3	−1.46	14.80	−9.99	86.90	1.095	3.562***	58.91	45.74
−4	−1.45	10.90	−12.80	83.90	1.522	3.365***	50.39	41.86
−5	−2.85	18.10	−3.33	17.20	0.230	1.310	50.39	44.19
−6	−2.10	15.80	3.18	57.90	−1.054	1.703*	52.71	41.86
−7	−13.40	87.00	−2.39	10.10	−1.436	1.162	37.21	40.31
−8	−9.17	46.70	−5.45	30.80	−0.776	0.859	41.86	40.31

The symbols *, **, and *** denote statistical significance at the 0.10, 0.05, and 0.01 levels, respectively, using a 2-tail test.

Table 8.6   Number of insiders buying or selling

This table presents the summary statistics of the number of insiders buying or selling along with t-test for mean equality and Wilcoxon signed-rank test of the equality for the median. If the test statistics take a negative value it implies that the bankrupt firms' number of insiders is lower than that of their matched control. The last two columns present the percentage of banks that have more than one insiders trading (in Panel A only purchase, and in Panel B only sales). Note that since the median data are always zero, they are not presented here.

Panel A: Number of insiders buying

Quarter	Bankrupt firms		Matched samples		Statistics		% of > 2 insiders	
	Mean	S.D.	Mean	S.D.	t-test	Wilcoxon Z	Target	Matched
−1	0.32	1.04	0.60	1.61	−1.718*	−2.125**	6.20	11.63
−2	0.40	1.11	0.70	2.28	−1.556	−1.820*	6.20	10.85
−3	0.70	1.39	0.78	3.33	−0.240	1.172	16.28	12.40
−4	0.81	1.57	0.67	3.25	0.410	1.127	19.38	9.30
−5	0.95	1.92	0.69	1.51	1.163	1.017	18.60	16.28
−6	0.72	1.52	0.64	1.54	0.409	0.734	16.28	10.85
−7	1.08	1.71	0.71	1.44	1.920*	2.363**	22.48	16.28
−8	0.98	2.01	0.66	1.66	1.464	1.035	20.93	13.95

Panel B: Number of insiders selling

Quarter	Bankrupt firms		Matched samples		Statistics		% of > 2 insiders	
	Mean	S.D.	Mean	S.D.	t-test	Wilcoxon Z	Target	Matched
−1	0.33	0.70	1.14	1.88	−4.632***	−3.976***	6.98	27.13
−2	0.38	1.09	0.92	1.60	−3.339***	−3.561***	6.98	20.16
−3	0.35	1.24	1.36	2.71	−4.001***	−4.691***	5.43	27.13
−4	0.53	1.36	1.22	1.98	−3.032***	−3.397***	10.08	24.03
−5	0.71	1.76	1.03	2.11	−1.269	−1.344	14.73	20.93
−6	0.71	1.58	1.25	2.14	−2.591**	−2.484***	14.73	27.13
−7	1.01	2.44	1.07	2.35	−0.209	−0.361	16.28	21.71
−8	1.30	2.99	1.15	1.90	0.526	−0.583	19.38	24.81

Panel C: Net number of insiders buying

Quarter	Bankrupt firms		Matched samples		Statistics		% of > 2 insiders	
	Mean	S.D.	Mean	S.D.	t-test	Wilcoxon Z	Target	Matched
−1	−0.02	1.12	−0.54	2.60	2.052**	2.109**	11.63	37.21
−2	0.02	1.56	−0.22	2.89	0.938	1.281	12.40	29.46
−3	0.35	1.85	−0.59	3.93	2.412**	4.208***	20.93	35.66
−4	0.27	2.09	−0.54	3.51	2.217**	3.986***	27.13	31.78
−5	0.23	2.66	−0.34	2.61	1.724*	2.305**	31.01	34.11
−6	0.02	2.27	−0.60	2.50	2.195**	2.371**	28.68	34.88
−7	0.07	3.10	−0.36	2.85	1.181	1.956*	35.66	35.66
−8	−0.32	3.74	−0.49	2.54	0.458	1.485	36.43	33.33

The symbols *, **, and *** denote statistical significance at the 0.10, 0.05, and 0.01 levels, respectively, using a 2-tail test.

Table 8.7   Wilcoxon signed-rank test on the basis of monthly data

This table presents statistics for Wilcoxon signed-rank test of the equality for the median. If the test statistics take a negative value it implies that the bankrupt firms' trading volume or number of insiders, whichever is appropriate, is lower than that of their matched control.

	Z-statistics for trading volume in dollars			Z-statistics for number of insiders		
Month	Purchase	Sale	Net purchase	Purchase	Sale	Net purchase
−1	−1.417	−3.391***	2.489**	−1.411	−3.478***	2.353**
−2	−1.297	−2.695***	1.679*	−1.232	−2.553**	1.152
−3	−0.469	−2.730***	2.502**	−0.793	−2.634***	2.060**
−4	−0.704	−2.350**	1.538	−1.240	−1.896*	0.510
−5	0.451	−2.695***	2.793*	0.225	−2.636***	2.374**
−6	−0.695	−2.738***	1.537	−1.008	−2.329**	1.092
−7	0.487	−1.496	1.448	0.725	−1.627	1.570
−8	1.739	−2.479**	2.568**	1.323	−2.802***	3.159***
−9	1.136	−3.995***	3.612***	1.076	−4.035***	3.558***
−10	−0.177	−2.715***	1.807*	0.305	−2.827***	2.933***
−11	0.709	−2.560**	2.601***	1.041	−2.471**	2.696***
−12	1.206	−2.895***	3.288**	1.361	−2.647***	3.191***

The symbols *, **, and *** denote statistical significance at the 0.10, 0.05, and 0.01 levels, respectively, using a 2-tail test.

data arguing that they were unable to capture all insiders trading. Seyhun and Bradley (1997) argue that Loderer and Sheehan (1989) used proxy statements to collect the insider trading data, and this data selection technique yields a sample of mostly large exchange listed firms. We, however, intentionally picked large firms in our sample to observe behavior of the insiders during the last 12 years as there are many cases of large firms filing for bankruptcy amid a torrent of bad corporate governance practice allegations.

Ma's (2001) results are similar to ours. He finds that there is significantly less insider purchase especially prior to the bankruptcy but no significant insider selling. Ma uses a relatively small sample of 89 during the period 1982–1990 for firms that filed for Chapter 11 bankruptcy.

The obvious question is whether the results presented in tables 8.5 and 8.6 are expected or not. We address this issue in two different ways. One of the arguments stems from Chapter 11 bankruptcy process favoring insiders and the other from a good corporate governance and legal system. We realize that the majority of the Chapter 11 filings are self-initiated (i.e. debtor initiated). Also, filing for Chapter 11 helps managers to restructure their firm and at the same time keep their job. Therefore, insiders may perceive that either saving their job or future employability outweighs any potential benefit from insider trading. Although there is considerable controversy about the state of the corporate governance in the United States, Holmstrom and Kaplan (2003) provide evidence that U.S. corporate governance is in much better shape than that of the rest of the world. Also, as evidenced by Bettis et al. (2000), most U.S. firms have instituted mechanism restricting insider trading. Moreover, current development toward more transparent and speedy reporting instituted by SOX and harsher penalty imposed by the legal system on corporate fraud and insider trading severely deter any large insider trading.

Conclusion

In this chapter we examined the extent of insider trading for 129 large Chapter 11 bankruptcy filings firms for the period 1995–2006. Although, these firms suffered significant reduction of stock price over the period as documented by significant negative CAAR, the insiders of these firms are found not to engage in trading that is significantly different from insiders of firms of similar size and of similar industry in most cases.

In some cases where the trading is significantly different, it shows that insiders of similar nonbankrupt firms are either selling more or buying less than the insiders in the bankrupt firms. There are, however, incidences of insider trading as reported in the media; these are exceptions rather than common practice. There are several possible explanations as to why this is so. One reason is that managers of these large firms find it profitable to file for Chapter 11 bankruptcy to save their jobs. Any insider trading activity would put their current job or future jobs at risk. Another reason is that there is a good corporate governance and legal system in place that actively deters insider trading.

Appendix: List of 129 sample bankrupt firms

The asset size in millions of dollars as reported in the Compustat two years prior to the bankruptcy filing year.

Name	Bankruptcy filing date	Asset size (In million dollars)
WORLDCOM INC.*	July 21, 2002	98,903
CONSECO INC.	December 18, 2002	58,589
REFCO FINANCE INC.	October 17, 2005	48,765
ENRON CORP.*	December 2, 2001	33,381
GLOBAL CROSSING LTD.*	January 28, 2002	30,185
PACIFIC GAS & ELECTRIC CO.	April 6, 2001	29,715
CALPINE CORP.	December 20, 2005	27,304
DELTA AIR LINES INC.	September 14, 2005	26,356
UAL CORPORATION (UNITED AIRLINES)	December 9, 2002	24,355
MIRANT CORP.	July 14, 2003	22,754
ADELPHIA COMMUNICATIONS CORP.*	June 25, 2002	21,499
DELPHI CORPORATION	October 8, 2005	20,904
KMART CORP.	January 22, 2002	14,630
RELIANCE GROUP HOLDINGS INC.	June 12, 2001	14,616
NORTHWEST AIRLINES CORPORATION	September 14, 2005	14,154
FINOVA GROUP INC.$^\wedge$	March 7, 2001	14,050
NTL INC.	May 8, 2002	13,026
NRG ENERGY INC.	May 14, 2003	12,895
PG&E NATIONAL ENERGY GROUP$^\wedge$	July 8, 2003	10,329
FEDERAL-MOGUL CORPORATION	October 1, 2001	9,945
US AIRWAYS, INC.	August 11, 2002	9,127
AT HOME CORP$^\wedge$	September 28, 2001	9,104
XO COMMUNICATIONS INC.	June 17, 2002	9,085
DANA CORPORATION	March 3, 2006	9,019
COMDISCO INC.$^\wedge$	July 16, 2001	7,807
HOME HOLDINGS INC.	January 15, 1998	7,593
MCLEODUSA INC.	January 30, 2002	7,366
ARM FINANCIAL GROUP INC.$^\wedge$	December 20, 1999	7,138
ANC RENTAL CORP$^\wedge$	November 13, 2001	6,350
BETHLEHEM STEEL CORP$^\wedge$	October 15, 2001	5,536
INTEGRATED HEALTH SERVICES INC.$^\wedge$	February 2, 2000	5,393
LTV CORP.$^\wedge$	December 29, 2000	5,324
OWENS CORNING	October 5, 2000	5,101
TRENWICK GROUP LTD.	August 20, 2003	4,929
GENUITY INC.$^\wedge$	November 27, 2002	4,899
BUDGET GROUP INC.$^\wedge$	July 29, 2002	4,520
PSINET$^\wedge$	May 31, 2001	4,492
LORAL SPACE & COMMUNICATIONS LTD.	July 15, 2003	4,390
ARMSTRONG WORLD INDUSTRIES, INC.	December 6, 2000	4,273
GLOBAL TELESYSTEMS INC.$^\wedge$	November 14, 2001	4,002

(*Continued*)

Name	Bankruptcy filing date	Asset size (In million dollars)
AMERCO^	June 20, 2003	3,773
FLEMING COMPANIES INC.	April 1, 2003	3,655
IRIDIUM LLC^	August 13, 1999	3,646
ASIA GLOBAL CROSSING LTD.^	November 18, 2002	3,633
CHS ELECTRONICS INC.^	April 4, 2000	3,572
SOLUTIA INC.	December 17, 2003	3,408
KAISER ALUMINUM CORP.	February 12, 2002	3,343
COVANTA ENERGY CORP.	April 1, 2002	3,295
COLLINS & AIKMAN	May 17, 2005	3,191
FLAG TELECOM HOLDINGS LTD	April 12, 2002	3,079
WINSTAR COMMUNICATIONS INC.^	April 18, 2001	3,065
TOUCH AMERICA HOLDINGS INC^	June 19, 2003	3,059
SPECTRASITE HOLDINGS INC.	November 15, 2002	3,054
MARINER POST-ACUTE NETWORK INC.	January 18, 2000	3,037
TOWER AUTOMOTIVE INC.	February 2, 2005	2,846
PHILIP SERVICES CORP.*	June 25, 1999	2,823
WINN-DIXIE STORES INC.	February 21, 2005	2,790
HAYES LEMMERZ INTERNATIONAL INC.	December 5, 2001	2,777
USG CORP.	June 25, 2001	2,773
WARNACO GROUP INC.	June 11, 2001	2,763
VIATEL INC.	May 2, 2001	2,704
ENCOMPASS SERVICES CORPORATION	November 19, 2002	2,700
NORTHWESTERN CORP.	September 14, 2003	2,617
CHIQUITA BRANDS INTERNATIONAL INC.	November 28, 2001	2,596
SUN HEALTHCARE GROUP INC.	October 14, 1999	2,579
NATIONAL STEEL CORP.^	March 6, 2002	2,565
W.R. GRACE & COMPANY	April 2, 2001	2,493
FRUIT OF THE LOOM INC.	December 29, 1999	2,483
LEAP WIRELESS INTERNATIONAL INC.	April 13, 2003	2,451
CONTIFINANCIAL CORP.^	May 17, 2000	2,355
EXIDE TECHNOLOGIES	April 14, 2002	2,299
TRUMP HOTELS & CASINO RESORTS INC.	November 21, 2004	2,196
TRANS WORLD AIRLINES INC.^	January 10, 2001	2,137
PEGASUS SATELLITE COMMUNICATIONS INC.^	June 2, 2004	2,111
POLAROID CORP^	October 12, 2001	2,040
PEREGRINE SYSTEMS INC.*	September 22, 2002	2,004
HIGHLANDS INSURANCE GROUP INC.^	October 31, 2002	2,001
RCN CORPORATION	May 27, 2004	1,990
AMES DEPARTMENT STORES INC.	August 20, 2001	1,975
SERVICE MERCHANDISE COMPANY INC.^	March 27, 1999	1,951
HEILIG-MEYERS COMPANY	August 16, 2000	1,948
LOEWS CINEPLEX ENTERTAINMENT CORP	February 15, 2001	1,907
SPIEGEL INC.	March 17, 2003	1,890
ADELPHIA BUSINESS SOLUTIONS INC.*	March 27, 2002	1,889
BURLINGTON INDUSTRIES INC.*^	November 15, 2001	1,876

(Continued)

Name	Bankruptcy filing date	Asset size (In million dollars)
AMF BOWLING INC.	July 3, 2001	1,827
RSL COMMUNICATIONS LTD.^	March 19, 2001	1,803
ALLEGIANCE TELECOM INC.^	May 14, 2003	1,775
EXODUS COMMUNICATIONS INC.^	September 26, 2001	1,743
AURORA FOODS INC.*^	December 8, 2003	1,723
UNICAPITAL CORPORATION^	December 11, 2000	1,670
HECHINGER COMPANY^	June 11, 1999	1,668
VIASYSTEMS GROUP INC.	March 11, 2003	1,667
PILLOWTEX CORP. (2000)	November 14, 2000	1,654
INTERSTATE BAKERIES CORPORATION	September 22, 2004	1,646
WORLD ACCESS INC.^	April 24, 2001	1,630
ICG COMMUNICATIONS INC.	November 14, 2000	1,625
MAGELLAN HEALTH SERVICES INC.	October 1, 2002	1,611
PAGING NETWORK INC.	July 24, 2000	1,581
PENN TRAFFIC CO	March 1, 1999	1,564
NATIONSRENT INC.	December 17, 2001	1,559
BOSTON CHICKEN INC.*	October 5, 1998	1,544
POLYMER GROUP INC.	May 11, 2002	1,508
DVI INC.^	August 25, 2003	1,478
PINNACLE HOLDINGS INC.	May 21, 2002	1,470
LODGIAN INC.	December 20, 2001	1,424
ATLAS AIR WORLDWIDE HOLDINGS INC.	January 30, 2004	1,401
WESTPOINT STEVENS INC.	June 1, 2003	1,369
CRIIMI MAE INC.	October 5, 1998	1,367
GENTEK INC.	October 11, 2002	1,351
PAYLESS CASHWAYS INC.	July 21, 1997	1,344
UNITED COMPANIES FINANCIAL CORPORATION^	March 1, 1999	1,337
IT GROUP INC.^	January 16, 2002	1,323
IMPERIAL SUGAR COMPANY	January 16, 2001	1,281
MORRISON KNUDSEN CORP.	June 25, 1996	1,273
ANCHOR GLASS CONTAINER CORP.	September 13, 1996	1,264
APW LTD.	May 16, 2002	1,214
WASHINGTON GROUP INTERNATIONAL INC. *	May 14, 2001	1,196
AMERICAN BUSINESS FINANCIAL SERVICES INC.	January 21, 2005	1,159
GST TELECOMMUNICATIONS INC.^	May 17, 2000	1,151
OAKWOOD HOMES CORP.^	November 15, 2002	1,149
COVAD COMMUNICATIONS	August 15, 2001	1,148
MOBILEMEDIA COMMUNICATIONS INC.^	January 30, 1997	1,143
TELIGENT INC	May 21, 2001	1,132
INACOM CORP.^	June 16, 2000	1,104
GRAND UNION COMPANY	June 24, 1998	1,061
METALS USA INC.	November 14, 2001	1,049
SUNTERRA CORP	May 31, 2000	1,021
CALDOR CORPORATION^	September 18, 1995	1,006

The symbols * and ^ represent firms filing for bankruptcy because of fraud and firms that did not survive the bankruptcy process, respectively.

Notes

*Both authors are at the University of Alabama.

1. Dionne Searcey, Shawn Young, and Kara Scannell, "Ebbers Is Sentenced to 25 Years For $11 Billion WorldCom Fraud," *Wall Street Journal (Eastern edition)* (2005): A.1.

2. The legal definition of a corporate insider is any person who is obligated to report his/her securities trading and file with the SEC a statement of ownership regarding those securities. They include a company's officers and directors and any beneficial owners of more than 10% of a class of the company's equity securities registered under Section 12 of the Securities Exchange Act of 1934.

3. Previously insiders were to report any changes in their holding by the tenth day of the following month. However, after the Sarbanes-Oxley Act of 2002 insiders are required to report their trade within two business day after the trade has occurred.

4. Usually, if a Chapter 11 debtor wanted to sell all or substantially all of its assets, it would do so through a plan of reorganization or a plan of liquidation. Lately, however, Bankruptcy Courts have permitted such a sale based on Section 363 of the Bankruptcy Code prior to the plan solicitation and confirmation process so long as certain requirements are satisfied. This is commonly known as "§ 363 sale."

5. The 10 firms that filed for Chapter 11 because of fraud are indicated in the appendix A with the symbol*.
   Source: WebBRD.

6. $(50 = 10 + 25 + 16 - 1)$.
   Number of bankruptcy filing caused by fraud = 10; number of firms whose reorganization/liquidation plan was confirmed but did not survive = 28; number of firms that went through 363 sale = 15; and number of firms that bankruptcy filing caused by fraud and did not survive = 2.

7. See, for instance, Jaffe (1974), Seyhun (1986), Rozeff and Zaman (1988), Lin and Howe (1990), Meulbroek (1992), and Lakonishok and Lee (2001).

8. This obviously involves deviations from absolute priority in Chapter 11 bankruptcy.

9. A net buyer here is if an insider buys more days than sell in that month. Net seller is defined analogously.

10. Seyhun and Bradley (1997) measure the abnormal returns, the difference between the return of the investing portfolio of firms that filed for bankruptcy, and the average return of the bootstrap distribution of the set of control firms of the bankrupt portfolio of firms.

11. Researchers who want know more about WebBRD's data sources and quality may browse (http://lopucki.law.ucla.edu/frequently_asked_questions.htm).

12. We found some discrepancies between asset size reported in WebBRD and Compustat, after accounting for current dollars conversion.

13. As it will be explained later in this chapter, we matched asset sizes for two years prior to the bankruptcy using Compustat Industrial Annual and a two-digit SIC code to get the control firms.

14. Note that the number of firms used in estimating the CAR is smaller than 129 sample bankrupt firms. This is because many firms stopped trading their shares some time prior to the bankruptcy filing, and hence lack data to calculate the CAR.
15. The test statistics are computed as (Bankruptcy firms quarter$_i$ – control firms quarter$_i$, where $i = -8, -7, \ldots, -1$).

References

Agrawal, Anup, and Jeffrey Jaffe. 1995. Does Section 16b deter insider trading by target mangers? *Journal of Financial Economics* 39: 295–319.

Ball, Ray, and Phillip Brown. 1968. An empirical evaluation of accounting income numbers. *Journal of Accounting Research* 6: 159–78.

Beams, Joseph, Robert Brown, and Larry. Killoug. 2003. An experiment testing the determinants of non-compliance with insider trading laws. *Journal of Business Ethics* 45: 309–23.

Becht, Marco, Patrick Bolton, and Alisa Roell. 2003. Corporate governance and control. In *Handbook of economics of finance,* ed. George Constantinides, Milton Harris, and Rene Stulz, 1–109. Boston, MA: Elsevier.

Betker, Brian. 1995. Management's incentives, equity's bargaining power, and deviation from absolute priority in Chapter 11 bankruptcies. *Journal of Business* 68: 161–83.

Bettis, J. Carr, Jeffrey Coles, and Michael Lemmon. 2000. Corporate policies restricting trading by insiders. *Journal of Financial Economics* 57: 191–220.

Bettis, J.C., W. A. Duncan, and W. K. Harmon. 1998. The effectiveness of insider trading regulations. *Journal of Applied Business Research* 14: 53–70.

Bradley, Michael and Michael Rosenzweig. 1992. The untenable case for Chapter 11. *Yale Law Journal* 101: 1043–95.

Bris, Arturo. 2005. Do insider trading laws work? *European Financial Management* 11: 267–312.

Carlton, Denis, and Daniel Fischel. 1983. The regulation of insider trading. *Stanford Law Review* 35: 857–95.

DeMarzo, Peter, Michael Fishman, and Kathleen Hagerty. 1998. The optimal enforcement of insider trading regulations. *Journal of Political Economy* 106: 602–32.

Dye, Ronald. 1984. Insider trading and incentives. *Journal of Business* 57: 295–313.

Easterbrook, Frank. 1981. Insider trading, secret agents, evidentiary privileges, and the production of information. *Supreme Court Review* 309–65.

Elliot, John, Dale Morse, and Gordon Richardson. 1984. The association between insider trading and information announcements. *Rand Journal of Economics* 15: 521–36.

Fama, Eugene, Lawrence Fisher, Michael Jensen, and Richard Roll. 1969. The adjustment of stock prices of new information. *International Economic Review* 10: 1–21.

Finnerty, Joseph. 1976. Insiders' activity and inside information: A multivariate analysis. *Journal of Financial and Quantitative Analysis* 11: 205–15.

Fischer, Paul. 1992. Optimal contracting and insider trading restrictions. *Journal of Finance* 47: 673–94.

Gosnell, Thomas, Arthur Keown, and John Pinkerton. 1992. Bankruptcy and insider trading: Differences between exchange-listed and OTC firms. *Journal of Finance* 47: 349–62.

Gup, Benton, and Pankaj Agrrawal. 1996. The product life cycle: A paradigm for understanding financial management. *Financial Practice and Education* 6: 41–48.

Harlow, W. Van, and John Howe. 1993. Leverage buyouts and insider nontrading. *Financial Management* 22: 109–18.

Holmstrom, Bengt, and Steven Kaplan. 2003. The state of U.S. corporate governance: What's right and what's wrong? Working Paper, National Bureau of Economic Research.

Iqbal, Zahid, and Shekar Shetty, 2002, Insider trading and stock market perception of bankruptcy. *Journal of Economics and Business* 54: 525–35.

Irani, Afshad. 2003. Management earning forecast bias and insider trading: Comparison of distressed and non-distressed firms. *Journal of Business & Economic Studies* 9: 12–25.

Jaffe, Jeffrey. 1974, Special information and insider trading. *Journal of Business* 47: 410–28.

Karpoff, Jonathan, and Daniel Lee. 1991. Insider trading before new issue announcements. *Financial Management* 20: 18–26.

Lakonishok, Josef and Inmoo Lee, 2001. Are insider trades informative? *Review of Financial Studies* 14: 79–111.

Lin, Ji-Chai., and John Howe. 1990. Insider trading in the OTC market. *Journal of Finance* 45: 1273–84.

Loderer, Claudio, and Dennis Sheehan. 1989. Corporate bankruptcy and manager's self-serving behavior. *Journal of Finance* 44: 1059–75.

LoPucki, Lynn, and William Whitford. 1993. Corporate governance in the bankruptcy reorganization of large, publicly held companies. *University of Pennsylvania Law Review* 141: 669–800.

Lorie, James, and Victor Niederhoffer. 1968. Predictive and statistical properties of insider trading. *Journal of Law and Economics* 11: 35–51.

Ma, Yulong. 2001. Insider trading behavior prior to Chapter 11 bankruptcy announcements. *Journal of Business Research* 54: 63–70.

Penman, Stephen. 1982. Insider trading and the dissemination of firm's forecast information. *Journal of Business* 55: 479–503.

———. 1985. A comparison of the information content of insider trading and management earning forecasts. *Journal of Financial and Quantitative Analysis* 20: 1–17.

Rozeff, M. S., and M. A. Zaman. 1988. Marker efficiency and insider trading: New evidence. *Journal of Business* 61: 25–44.

Seyhun, H. Nejat. 1986. Insider's profits, costs of trading, and market efficiency. *Journal of Financial Economics* 16: 189–212.

———. 1992. The effectiveness of insider trading sanctions. *Journal of Law and Economics* 35: 149–82.

———. and Michael Bradley. 1997. Corporate bankruptcy and insider trading. *Journal of Business* 70: 189–216.

Shin, Jhinyoun. 1996. The optimal regulation of insider trading. *Journal of Financial Intermediation* 5: 49–73.

WebBRD. 2006. Lynn M. LoPucki's Bankruptcy Research Database, http://lopucki. law.ucla.edu/index.htm (accessed November 1, 2006).

White, Michelle. 1989. The corporate bankruptcy decision. *Journal of Economic Perspective* 3: 129–51.